11th January 1995.

To Dad on his 7

Love - Jim

x x x x

To Dad on his 70th birthday,
Love Jim, Jen.

THE WRECK OF THE *DEUTSCHLAND*

THE WRECK OF
THE DEUTSCHLAND

Sean Street

SOUVENIR PRESS

First published 1992 by Souvenir Press Ltd,
43 Great Russell Street, London WC1B 3PA
and simultaneously in Canada

ISBN 0 285 63051 2

Printed in Great Britain by
Mackays of Chatham Ltd, Chatham, Kent

Photoset by Rowland Phototypesetting Ltd
Bury St Edmunds, Suffolk

For Joanne, Jemma and Zoë

Contents

List of Illustrations

The modern Sunk light-vessel in Harwich harbour
The lifeboat house, Harwich, built in 1876
Gerard Manley Hopkins, aged 19
Number 87, The Grove, Stratford, where Gerard Manley Hopkins
   was born
St Beuno's College, Clwyd, west front

Acknowledgements

This book has been fifteen years in the making. In 1975, I listened to a reading by Paul Scofield of Gerard Manley Hopkins' poem 'The Wreck of the Deutschland', broadcast to mark the centenary of the event. I was intrigued by the work's dedication: 'To the happy memory of five Franciscan Nuns, exiles by the Falk Laws, drowned between midnight and morning of Dec. 7th, 1875'. I wanted to know who these nuns were, what their background was, what the 'Falk Laws' were, and so on.

I started to research, and my curiosity grew. After a year or so I was in possession of a sheaf of notes, which I showed to the poet, Charles Tomlinson. He encouraged me to pursue the quest, and Peter Dent of Interim Press published a twenty-page pamphlet on the wreck and its historical context. The BBC producer, John Knight, read it, and invited me to make a Radio 4 feature on the subject, which was broadcast in 1989 to mark the centenary of Hopkins' death. Tessa Harrow of Souvenir Press heard the broadcast, and invited me to write the present work.

To all these people, who have enabled me to delve progressively deeper into this remarkable incident, and who have encouraged me at every step, I am very grateful. But without the patience, help and interest of Sister Aristilde Flake in Salzkotten, Sister Bernadette Kirn in Wheaton, Illinois, and Father Justin McLoughlin OFM of The Friary in Stratford, East London, very little would have been achieved. They have been unstinting in their generosity, helping with both text and photographs; and I acknowledge with thanks permission to use pictures and written material from the archives of Salzkotten, Stratford and Wheaton. My thanks also go to Paul Edwards of St Beuno's Spiritual Exercises Centre, for help and pictures; to Sister Frances Agnes OSC of the Convent of Poor Clares at Woodchester, for her help and for

permission to use the picture of Mary Broadway; and to Sister
M. Carola Thomann, General Secretary of the Franciscan Sisters
in Rome. I acknowledge with gratitude permission to quote from
the works of Gerard Manley Hopkins, given by the Oxford University Press on behalf of the Society of Jesus, as well as for a
photograph of the young Hopkins.

My thanks are also due to Sue and Tim Mitchell, and Helga
Hopkins, for their invaluable translating skills, and to Roger Hopkins for photographic reproductions. As always, librarians and
archivists have been wonderful; the staff of the Public Record
Office and the British Library Newspaper Library must have felt
at times that I had taken up residence. I acknowledge permission
to publish illustrations of the *Deutschland* from copies of the *Illustrated London News* in the archives of the Library; in particular, I
thank Geoff Smith, for advice along the way. Frank Sainsbury,
Howard Bloch and Jill Davies of West Ham Central Library have
been unstinting in their help, providing me with information and
also checking facts. For the picture of Father Francis Verhagen I
am grateful to Burns & Oates and to the London Borough of
Newham Local Studies Library, who also provided the picture of
Gerard Manley Hopkins' birthplace. A. M. Jackson, principal
archivist with Strathclyde Regional Archives, guided me to
accounts of the building of the *Deutschland*, and Liza Verity of the
National Maritime Museum, Greenwich, was exceptionally help-
ful. David Williamson, Head of History and Politics at Hopkins' old
school, Highgate, kindly read, and made valuable suggestions on
the sections in the book dealing with Bismarck's policies.

In Germany, I am grateful to Arnold Kludas of the German
National Maritime Museum in Bremerhaven for much infor-
mation, and for permission to publish a rare photograph of the
Deutschland in dry dock; to Mr Jurgensen of Bremerhaven Town
Archive and the editor of *Nordsee Zeitung*; to the staff of the
Aachen tourist office; and to Mr A. Pauels, Senior Inspector of
Archives in Aachen and Dr Adam C. Oellers, Director of the
Aachen Town Museum.

As for the east-coast part of the story, Robert Malster made my
quest his own, and gave me invaluable assistance throughout. I
am grateful to John Leather for his help, and for permission to
use the photograph of his great-grandfather, Thomas Barnard of
Rowhedge, and to Leonard Weaver of Harwich for some valuable

pictures. Barry Cox, Librarian of the Royal National Lifeboat Institution, provided me with some fascinating pictures and information about lifeboats in Harwich, and I acknowledge permission from the Grahame Farr Archives, RNLI, to publish illustrations of lifeboats past and present, as well as the picture of Harwich lifeboat-house. I am also grateful to the anonymous boatman who steered me round Harwich harbour on a glorious autumn day—he will never know how valuable his services were.

Joanne and Jemma Street helped with maps and line drawings —as well as with support, for which I cannot ever repay them adequately. In addition I would like to thank Father Anthony Bischoff, SJ, Paul Burns of Burns & Oates, Brigitte Fassbaender and the Fassbaender family in Aachen, Felicity Goodall, and Norman H. MacKenzie, whose Oxford University Press edition of the poems is indispensable to any study of Hopkins and who gave his advice so generously. I have endeavoured to trace and to acknowledge all sources of information and illustration; for any omissions I apologise.

Sean Street

1 Salzkotten: Promise of a New Beginning

St Patrick's Cemetery forms a large grey and white pattern of crosses over a considerable part of the London borough of Leytonstone. It stands, with the Underground railway-line—at this point still overground—skirting its north-west side, and with terraces of Victorian houses against one perimeter contrasting sharply with the high-rise modernity of the Cathall Road Estate against another. On the fourth side is Langthorne Road, from which you enter the cemetery. You pass an impressive mortuary chapel by the entrance gate, before you are plunged into a veritable sea of crosses, angels and simple stones, together with an assortment of mausoleums, the exact identities of which are not always easy to establish.

St Patrick's is the Roman Catholic graveyard for this part of Essex, and one look at its vast expanse will tell the visitor that it has served this office for many years (technically it has reached capacity, as the sign by the main gate tells you). It is a place where families have come to tend the last resting places of their loved ones for generations. Yet in doing so, most people pass by one particular grave, which, although in itself not unusual, represents the last act of a most remarkable story. The memorial stands in an area that in the past has clearly been designated for burials of an ecclesiastical nature. There is one plot whose stone exhorts us to 'Pray for the souls of the Sisters of Jesus and Mary, Chigwell'. Another mentions nuns from Bow, and another, the Sisters of Mercy of Walthamstow. Six plots away is the one marked for the Ursuline Sisters of Upton. Beside all these, the stone on plot A.13, grave number 373, looks younger than its years, and if you inquire at the cemetery superintendent's office, they will tell you that this is because in 1966 the inscription was recut.

Nevertheless, modern pollution is already beginning to do its work, for while the stone is clean, the lettering is beginning to fade back into the shining whiteness of the memorial, and on a bright day the reader needs to be attentive in order to decipher every word. It reads as follows:

Pray for the repose of the souls of
Barbara Hultenschmidt
Henrica Fassbender
Norberta Reinkober
Aurea Badziura
Brigitta Damhorst
Franciscan Sisters from Germany, who lost their lives
near Harwich in the shipwreck of the 'Deutschland', December 7th,
1875. Four were buried here, December 13th. R.I.P.

At some point between the original inscription and its renovation two words have been added by the name of Henrica Fassbender: —'not found'. On the front kerbstone of the grave is another addition, made during the 1970s: 'Franciscan Sisters, Daughters of the Sacred Hearts of Jesus and Mary, Salzkotten, Germany'. And lying on the grave itself is an engraved stone placed here in 1983 by nuns from a province in France, bearing the simple words: 'Soeurs naufragées, victimes de charité, dans votre éternité bienheureuse intercédez pour vos soeurs auprès de Dieu.'

The inscriptions are deceptive in their simplicity, holding, as they do, so many unanswered questions in a few lines. Who were these sisters? Why were they travelling over perilous seas so far from home? Where were they going? There are five names on the stone, yet the inscription says that only 'four were buried here' —what happened to the fifth . . . the sister who was 'not found'? Above all, why should nuns from Germany, wrecked off the east coast of England, come to be buried in Leytonstone? What happened on the *Deutschland* on 7th December 1875?

The basic facts of the story are quickly told. The *Deutschland*, one of the largest and best appointed of the North German Lloyd line's Atlantic fleet, sailed from the German port of Bremen on 5th December 1875 in fine weather. On board were 113 passengers, including five nuns from the little town of Salzkotten near Paderborn between Hanover and Dortmund, bound for a new life in the United States. Less than a day out, the weather changed for the worse, with blinding snow and storm-force winds. Before dawn on 6th December, the vessel struck a sandbank near the mouth of the Thames estuary, a notorious hazard called the Kentish Knock. Here the *Deutschland* languished, her propeller broken. Distress rockets were fired, but no help came. Some forty-two people lost their lives before the tug *Liverpool* managed to reach the ship and take off the survivors. The event took the form of a classic nine-days wonder, and the national press carried extensive reports. One in *The Times* of 11th December, stated: 'Five nuns . . . clasped hands and were drowned together, the chief sister, a gaunt woman, six feet high, calling out loudly and often "O Christ come quickly", until the end came.'

Away on the other side of Britain, at St Beuno's College, North Wales, the poet Gerard Manley Hopkins read the reports and was much moved. He was studying to become a Jesuit priest and had given up writing poetry, as unfitting to his new vocation. However, these reports, and the blessing of his Superior at the college, changed his mind, and he was to write one of the great religious allegories in English literature. He dedicated 'The Wreck of the Deutschland',

To the
happy memory of five Franciscan Nuns
exiles by the Falk Laws
drowned between midnight and morning of
Dec. 7th, 1875

Yet the reader who wishes to learn more of the historical background to the wreck will learn little of narrative value from Hopkins' poem. It was not his purpose to tell the story, but, rather, to use the incident and the figure of the 'tall, gaunt nun' and her dying cry as a jumping-off point for his own magnificent, complex meditation. Hopkins would have had little more than the *Times* reports to go on, anyway, and would undoubtedly have noted with curiosity that the nuns' final resting place was at Leytonstone, for Leytonstone is adjacent to Stratford, Essex, where Hopkins was born.

Such is the story of the loss of the *Deutschland*, and its poetic sequel which gave five unknown German nuns a form of literary immortality. Their story is very much one of innocents caught up in the dynastic pretensions of great powers. To understand, therefore, the motivating events behind it is, of necessity, to understand the policies of the 1870s that were building Bismarck's unified Germany.

The little Westphalian town of Olpe lies some forty kilometres south of Dortmund, in a part of Germany known as the Sauerland. It was here on 30th October 1860, with a constitution approved by Conrad Martin, Bishop of Paderborn, that Mother Clara Pfaender was to found a religious community, whose intent was to live according to the Rule of St Francis, under the name Sisters of St Francis, Daughters of the Sacred Hearts of Jesus and Mary.

Mother Clara was born Anna Theresia Pfaender, daughter of the town mayor, on 6th December 1827 in Hallenberg, Westphalia. Her moral strength and single-mindedness—qualities which were to mark her as a strong leader later in life—were to develop at an early age. Indeed, they had need to. Her mother, and then her stepmother, both died while she was quite young, leaving her father with eight children; and the third marriage of Mayor Henry Pfaender was to produce a further six children. On 4th November 1850 the young Anna Theresia, who throughout her formative years had felt a growing commitment to Catholicism, was received into the congregation of the Sisters of Christian Charity by Bishop Franz Drepper of Paderborn. From this point onwards, Anna Theresia was known as Sister Clara. Here she stayed, under the guidance of a much loved Superior, Mother Pauline von Mallinckrodt, until she was thirty-one.

The outward facts of her life thus far had not been exceptional; the daughters of large families, for whom subsistence was becoming a problem, not infrequently turned to the convents for their vocation. For many young ladies and their parents, it provided a happy and convenient answer to the problem of finding a decent place in the world. And it is really from this point in her life that we see in sharp focus, the metal that Sister Clara was made of. She had had a strong and ever-growing conviction that she must found her own congregation, and in September 1859 she wrote to Bishop Martin:

Having spent nine contented years in the community of the Sisters of Christian Charity, and having joyfully expended strength of body and soul in the service of the blind and especially in the education of young people, I have felt for several years the call to a stricter and a more perfect life for the greater honour of God and the salvation of souls.

As a result, after incessant prayer and mature consideration I have several times asked my superiors for permission to leave this congregation, so dear to me, and after much deliberation on their part, I have received this permission from them. It is now my sincerest desire to follow the manifest call of God; to lead a religious life united with several pious, like-minded young women; to aid by zealous prayer our holy Catholic Church; and to care for poor, neglected orphans.

Conrad Martin's permission, although provisional upon official archiepiscopal approval, was immediate: 'With regard to your petition . . . allow me to say that from my point of view there is no objection to be raised against the plan that you have made known to me.—' He was to remain until his death a supporter and advocate of everything Sister Clara did.

In the first instance, the purpose was 'to lead a community life according to evangelical counsels, a life borne in the spirit of love, of prayer, and of penance', and Sister Clara was installed as the Superior. From the very start, it was to be a congregation open to every need and devoted equally to God and to people. In her founding constitutional document, true to her original letter to Bishop Martin, Mother Clara stated:

Following the example of our divine Saviour and his holy Mother Mary, the congregation of the Sisters of St Francis, Daughters of the Sacred Hearts of Jesus and Mary, endeavours to integrate the contemplative and active life so that the latter is nourished and strengthened and supported through the former, and thus becomes itself rich in blessings.'

With Mother Clara came two other senior sisters: Aline Bonzel, who became invested with the name Sister M. Theresia, and Regina Loeser, who took the name Sister M. Antonia. Sister M. Antonia died shortly afterwards, but five novices also took temporary vows. It was enough; Mother Clara's new congregation had been born.

Yet there were problems; in Olpe there already existed a congregation of the Vincentian Sisters of Paderborn, whose main function was caring for the sick—one of the main aims of Mother Clara's sisters. It was felt that a little town such as Olpe could not justify two such congregations, and therefore the Franciscan motherhouse must move. Thus it was that Mother Clara began to look elsewhere for her still infant congregation, and after a number of possibilities had been examined and rejected her choice fell upon the town of Salzkotten. Although largely undistinguished, it was close to Paderborn, the seat of the bishopric, and it was on a main railway-line. Also—an important point—it had as yet no religious congregation established there.

On 15th November 1862, Mother Clara acquired a large house with a barn and garden in Hellweg Street at the eastern end of the town, which had belonged to a family called Grundhoff. Overjoyed, she wrote to Bishop Martin, who replied: 'I have high hopes of blessing and success for your congregation resulting from this transfer, since when I visited there recently I learned that the people are in general pleased with your coming. You may get in touch with me as soon as the transfer is complete and I will then give you practical suggestions.'

The move was accomplished the following spring; fourteen sisters, fifteen postulants and four orphans set out severally for Salzkotten, by way of Werl, itself long a place of pilgrimage, where the sisters prayed to the Virgin for a blessing on their new venture and their new home. It was on the feast day of St Joseph, 19th March 1863, that the Grundhoff house was named 'The Motherhouse of the Franciscan Sisters, Daughters of the Sacred Hearts of Jesus and Mary'. The event is noted in the town records of Salzkotten as follows: 'Philanthropical and charitable activity: on 1st April 1863, the seat of the motherhouse of the Poor Franciscan Sisters, who take care of the sick and concern themselves with the education of orphans, was transferred from Olpe to Salzkotten.' The discrepancy between the dates is probably due to the fact that, although the actual move and occupancy took place during March, it was not registered in the Salzkotten archives until the 1st of the month following.

The Salzkotten motherhouse quickly acquired its first daughter-house, in the town of Much in the Rhineland. This house had been established from Olpe, but Bishop Martin, in permitting both the Olpe and the Salzkotten houses to exist independently, ordered that Much should remain connected with the new congregation. There had, in fact, been a certain amount of acrimony in the move: some of the Olpe sisters and citizens had felt that the new congregation should have left everything in their former home, as most of what they had was the property of the Olpe orphanage. There were also serious differences of opinion between Mother Clara and Sister Theresia, herself a native of Olpe. Thus, right from the start, the new congregation found itself battling against controversy and internal dissension. The one consolation was that a new home meant that they could make a new start, and put the trials and uncertainties of the past behind them. For the thirty-six-year-old Mother Clara a major goal had been achieved, and her strength of will and determination had played a great and necessary part in that success. But in many ways, these early struggles were to form a pattern for the rest of her life.

The sisters found themselves far from comfortable in their new motherhouse. Conditions were cramped, and they had virtually nothing by way of possessions which would make life easier. Before long, the barn that had been acquired in the purchase of the Grundhoff house was converted into a makeshift chapel, as the chapel within the house had not been built to accommodate the numbers that now came to it for worship, both from within the congregation and from amongst the population of Salzkotten itself. Here in this chapel, connected to the motherhouse by a newly constructed passageway, the sisters maintained a round of perpetual adoration. Given their relatively small numbers, this put a strain on them. But Mother Clara was not a woman to compromise. Singing had to be well prepared, and fatigue was not to be an excuse for lacklustre worship:

Our prayer before the Lord should not be a song of woe from dejected voices, but rather a song of exultation arising from souls jubilant with the love of God and united with the angels' songs of praise . . . In highest heaven the angelic hosts sing 'Glory to the Lord', and on earth mankind, forming the Church's choir, follows this example by singing the same hymn of praise. In heaven the seraphim proclaim the hymn, 'Holy, Holy, Holy', while on earth this same hymn resounds from the community assembled in festive celebration.

Soon the congregation began to grow, thereby easing the pressures on the original group of sisters. In October 1863, the parish church of Salzkotten saw fifteen postulants receive the habit and six sisters receive their first vows. Added to this, there were almost daily applications from young girls from near and far to join the community. The congregation began to flourish, at least in terms of numbers. Financially, however, the situation was different. Although the local people had welcomed the sisters and collected for them generously, money for food was in short supply and the nuns' diet was poor and lacked variation. Potatoes and other vegetables were the main source of nutrition, with black coffee and dry bread. Marmalade was a luxury reserved only for Sundays. This, combined with long hours and extremely hard work, soon began to take its toll; many sisters became ill, some even dying as a result of the poor food, the cramped conditions and sheer exhaustion.

Through it all, however, no one could say that their leader did not play her part: Mother Clara worked with almost fanatical zeal and seemingly superhuman strength. What she demanded of her sisters, she also asked of herself. She was Superior-General, Superior of the motherhouse, and novice mistress, and she placed herself in overall charge of the postulants, a growing band, as well as of the orphans under the care of the Congregation Community. This in itself created problems, due once again to the lack of space in the motherhouse. The sisters were very much a nursing order, and cared for all the walking sick they could. But the orphanage itself could not be contained within the motherhouse, and so nearby premises had to be rented, thereby further draining the already slender financial resources of the congregation. In addition, Mother Clara was, of course, the chief administrator of the congregation—a complex task that was becoming more difficult by the day. And it was her job to maintain the status quo through correspondence with both the secular and the church authorities.

Certainly the aims of the congregation—continual prayer for the Catholic Church 'in her struggles and persecutions', care for the sick and the education of youth—put a heavy burden on the sisters joining the community. Mother Clara's exacting requirements, may be seen in this extract from her original statement of intent regarding education:

The sisters shall impart a complete elementary education to all children admitted to their home, shall train the girls in needlework, and shall give them practice in the performance of domestic duties. Their charges may not be dismissed until they have received sufficient elementary education, made their first Holy Communion, and are in a position to earn their own livelihood. When the sisters release their charges, they will endeavour to procure for them an occupation which will be favourable to the children's moral welfare in the world. They will keep them in mind as their children and support them at all times with counsel and help.

In order to carry out their vocations of nursing and teaching, the Sisters had themselves to receive training. In nursing, this was given by a local man, one Doctor Damm MD. Their newly acquired medical skills were soon to be in great demand. During the Austro-Prussian War of 1866 fifteen sisters, including Mother Clara, went to the front line in Bohemia; and during the Franco-Prussian War between 1870 and 1871, the Salzkotten congregation sent out sixty nursing sisters for first-aid care. After the wars, there were serious cholera, dysentery, smallpox and typhoid epidemics throughout Germany, and the sisters travelled far from their native motherhouse to care for the victims. As a result of this, the fame of the Franciscan sisters from the little Westphalian town spread, and after the crisis had passed a number of mission houses were established in places where the sisters had been working. As well as being familiar figures throughout the land, they were also recognised by the state, when in March 1867, after the Austro-Prussian War, Queen Augusta of Prussia wrote to Mother Clara to thank her and the sisters for their selfless service.

Meanwhile, the Salzkotten house acquired in 1862 had been hopelessly outgrown, and another crisis of space was approaching. With the help of the Paderborn ecclesiastical authorities, Mother Clara managed to purchase a meadow and some garden lands adjacent to the old Grundhoff house. Here in 1870 the cornerstone was laid for what was to be the sisters' new and permanent home in Salzkotten. For two years the Franciscans watched as the new building went up, until on 28th October 1872 Bishop Conrad Martin consecrated the new motherhouse chapel and blessed the convent. It should have been the beginning of a new era of strength and consolidation. But there were storm clouds gathering which were to threaten the congregation's very existence.

2 'O Deutschland, double a desperate name!'

Germany, in the sense of a unified political state, did not exist at the time that Mother Clara was establishing her congregation. It was only in 1871 that unification came into being, and it was to have far-reaching consequences for all she had so far achieved. The man responsible for this upheaval of the status quo was born on his family estate of Schoenhausen, some sixty miles from Berlin, on 1st April 1815, the year of Waterloo. While it is not the purpose of this book to give an analysis of Bismarck's policies, it is necessary to pause and consider the temperament and extraordinary career of the man whose ideas and character were to have such an impact on Europe from the 1860s onwards. His importance may be gauged by the thousands of books that have been written about him; and latterly some historians have asked whether his work sowed the seeds of the bitter harvest that was to be reaped under Hitler.

Otto von Bismarck was the son of a Prussian Junker, Ferdinand von Bismarck. There is no straightforward English translation of the word *Junker*, but broadly speaking it refers to a landowning class of nobility, revealed here by the presence of 'von' in the name—a preposition to which all descendants could lay claim. Generally the Junker class has been portrayed as dull and unimaginative, devoted to the military and the Prussian state. In this, Ferdinand seems to have been typical: he was once described as 'moderately wealthy and rather stupid'. The contrast between him and his wife was considerable. Otto's mother, Louise Wilhelmine, was a strong woman from a Hamburg merchant family. She possessed a powerful intellect and an equally powerful determination that her offspring were to benefit from the finest education available. Indeed, she seems to have been somewhat obsessional on this point, so that the man who was to become known as the Iron Chancellor received little in the way of motherly love. Otto hated her, and claimed later that her decision to send him to a tough Prussian school in Berlin was 'an attempt to break my autocratic spirit'. He did not do well at school.

Otto went on to university, first at Göttingen, where he arrived in 1832 to study law, then later in Berlin. His university years were marked by a rebellious irresponsibility which paid little heed to lectures, but rather more to drinking, romantic affairs, and quarrels with his peers. (While at university he fought no less than twenty-five duels.) A contemporary picture of him during these years has him 'strutting down the street, wearing the usual beer-cap of crimson and gold, a dressing-gown, enormously wide trousers and boots with iron spurs and heels. He carried an oak cudgel and wore a leather belt round his waist supporting two large pistols and a heavy duelling sword.'

Bismarck graduated from Berlin in May 1835, and then passed (narrowly) the entrance examination for the Prussian civil service. He trained for a few weeks at Potsdam, and then, at the age of twenty-one, was posted to Aachen. This spa town had only been acquired by Prussia in 1815, and Prussian administrators, of whom Bismarck was a very junior example, were strongly disliked by the largely Roman Catholic population. As far as Bismarck, a Lutheran, was concerned, the feeling was entirely mutual. This was demonstrated in dramatic fashion on one occasion when a religious procession moved through the town. As the host passed, everyone in the crowd knelt—everyone, that is, except Bismarck, who would not even doff his hat. Incensed, someone behind him knocked his hat off, and Bismarck struck the man in the face with his stick. A snarling crowd quickly surrounded him, and he escaped by dashing into the procession and placing himself in the midst of the Prussian Guard, a detachment of which was following. A riot might have developed, but the crowd thought better of taking on the military, and Otto got away.

In Aachen, Bismarck spent most of his time as he had during his university days—pursuing young Englishwomen who were making 'the Grand Tour', and even going so far as to become temporarily engaged to one of them. He also gambled and drank too much. Little wonder that in his early years, he gained the name of *der tolle Bismarck* ('the wild Bismarck'). Rather more practically, he also used his time there to develop diplomatic connections.

Prussians who had had a secondary education were required to serve a year of national service, and although he tried to evade it, Bismarck found himself back in Potsdam in 1838, serving at the garrison there. This too he disliked, and after a tedious year he was released, only to resign at once from the civil service. He saw himself as a leader, or nothing: 'I will play music the way I like, or not at all' is the oft-quoted remark so crucial to an understanding of his character, his political attitudes, and his subsequent development. At twenty-four, in 1839, he still had no real direction in life, and his mother died in that year with her hopes for him unfulfilled. Bismarck returned to work on the decaying family estates with his elder brother, but returned to the civil service in 1844—only to resign again after two weeks. He was approaching thirty, and by all accounts he was a failure in life.

It was in 1847 while still at this crossroads that he found a wife, Johanna von Puttkamer, a young, pious Lutheran.

I think I am entitled to count myself among the adherents of the Christian religion. Though in many doctrines—perhaps in those which they regard as essential—I am far removed from their standpoint, yet a sort of Treaty of Passau has been silently established between us.* Besides, I like piety in women and have a horror of feminine cleverness.

A means to an end it may have been for Bismarck to profess here a belief in the Christian faith, but nevertheless there was probably a degree of sincerity about it. Through his marriage, he subsequently gained the trust of those who were to be instrumental in his rise to power. And a religious justification for actions has been a strong force for consolidation in the policies of many a major statesman. As one cynic remarked, 'If Bismarck believes in his God, God himself must be a Prussian.'

As if to vindicate this, although it probably had more to do with family influence, in the same year Bismarck was elected to the

* He refers here to the treaty which in 1552 allowed Roman Catholicism and Lutheranism to coexist, albeit grudgingly, in Germany.

Prussian United Diet. This was composed of three elements: the Liberals, the Centre and the Progressives. It was a key time both for him and for all of Europe. 1848 was the year of revolution, and he is known to have been involved in counter-revolutionary activities at that time. He was later to claim that for the next forty-three years of his political life he was striving towards German unity—although some historians believe that he was merely following, from one day to the next, a line of expediency. Whatever the truth, Bismarck's career now began to take off. In 1850 he was promoted to the post of Prussian envoy to the Diet of the German Confederation in Frankfurt. He was later to become Prussian Ambassador in St Petersburg, then in Paris, and then Minister-President. He was setting the stage for a performance

Bismarck in about 1855. *Joanne Street*

that was to establish him as the most dominant figure in European politics during the second half of the nineteenth century.

This is not to say that he was without opposition: on the contrary, his approach to his ministers was arguably one of domination, causing one member of the Progressive party to comment with misgiving: 'Bismarck—that is to say, government without budget, rules by the sword in home affairs, and war in foreign affairs. I consider him the most dangerous Minister for Prussia's liberty and happiness.' However, it is true to say that in economic affairs he followed a consensus policy of laissez-faire. The Progressive Party's fears were fuelled by a famous speech in which, while addressing parliament, he took an olive leaf from his pocket, claiming that he had intended to offer it to the house but that now he felt the time had not yet come. He went on: 'It is not through speeches and majority decisions that the great questions of the day are decided. That was the great mistake of 1848–9. It is by iron and blood.' The last three words, reversed, were to become famous—and for the Catholic faith, prophetic.

The 1860s brought dramatic international events which were to play an important part in the history of German unification. What came to be known as the Schleswig-Holstein question arose when Denmark and the Austrian–led German confederacy both put forward claims to the two duchies of Schleswig and Holstein, bordering the North and Baltic Seas. War was declared in 1863, and Austrian and Prussian armies invaded in February 1864, but disputes—probably orchestrated by Bismarck, whose real intention was to gain supremacy over Austria—arose between the invaders. Country by country, he isolated Austria, and in 1866 the brief and bloody Austro-Prussian War established that Austria lost her supremacy in German affairs. The combined duchy of Schleswig–Holstein was ceded to Prussia, and a new North German Confederation was established under Prussian leadership. Then, towards the end of the 1860s, came the crisis with France. After a revolution in Spain in 1868 in which Queen Isabella was driven out, a question of succession arose. Several European princes were offered the crown, until in February 1870 it was the turn of Leopold of Hohenzollern, a member of the Prussian royal house. Leopold immediately consulted William I, King of Prussia, who, after some hesitation and at the urging of Bismarck, gave his consent for Leopold to become a candidate for the Spanish throne. Clearly, such an expansion of Prussian influence would anger France, who would see it as an attempt to encircle her. Bismarck continued to manipulate the unsure Leopold, and, although on several occasions the affair seemed to have been peaceably settled, the French diplomats tried too energetically to push home their advantage. War was hastened by Bismarck's actions after a meeting at Ems on 13th July 1870 between King William and the French Ambassador, Count Benedetti. Informed by the King's secretary of what had transpired at the meeting, Bismarck published an account of the French reaction—the famous Ems telegram, worded in such a way as to make it seem uncompromising in the extreme:

After the news of the renunciation [of the Spanish crown] of the hereditary prince of Hohenzollern had been finally communicated to the Imperial government of France by the Royal government of Spain, the French Ambassador further demanded of His Majesty the King, at Ems, that he would authorise him to telegraph to Paris that His Majesty the King bound himself for all time never again to give his consent, should the Hohenzollerns renew their candidacy. His Majesty the King thereupon decided not to receive the French Ambassador again, and sent the aide-de-camp on duty to tell him that His Majesty had nothing further to communicate to the Ambassador.

It may be that Bismarck had planned a confrontation with France as far back as the mid-1860s, realising that such a war would bring South German states under Prussian control. Certainly, he later wrote in his *Reflections and Recollections*: 'All considerations . . . strengthened my opinion that war could only be avoided at the cost of the honour of Prussia and of national confidence in her.' In fact, France declared war first, on 15th July 1870. The Prussian victory was fast and decisive. By 2nd September following the Battle of Sedan, the French Imperial armies surrendered and 104,000 men, including their emperor Napoleon III, were taken prisoner. The fighting continued, but on 28th February 1871 a peace treaty was at last signed in the Hall of Mirrors at Versailles, where Bismarck had on 18th January crowned his king, William I of Prussia, as the first Emperor of a united Germany. Bismarck himself read the proclamation:

We William, by the Grace of God, King of Prussia, after the German princes and free cities have unanimously appealed to us to renew the Imperial dignity . . . hereby inform you that we regard it as our duty to the whole fatherland to respond to this summons of the allied German princes and free cities and assume the German Imperial title. May God grant us and to our successors to the Imperial crown that we may be defenders of the German Empire at all times, not in military conquests, but in the works of peace, in the sphere of national prosperity, free-dom and civilisation.

Kaiser Wilhelm thus presided over what might be described as Bismarck's greatest achievement: the foundation of the Second Reich, a new superpower with Bismarck as its Chancellor, which included Prussia, Bavaria, Saxony, Württemberg, the contentious acquisitions of Alsace and Lorraine, and eighteen other states. Otto von Bismarck, still Minister-President of Prussia as well as Chancel-lor of the German Reich, now became a prince. In order to consoli-date his work on German unification, he turned his attention to domestic policies which would unite the new state without damag-ing the ultimate powers of the Imperial government. As one of his supporters, Heinrich von Treishke, wrote: 'The core of the state is power. The state is not there for the citizen. It is an end in itself. Since the state is power, it can obviously draw into its sphere of influence all human activities.'

A portrait of Bismarck at this time shows a big man—it was often remarked, though, that his thin, reedy voice did not seem to match his large stature. He was still a man of excessive habits, smoking up to fourteen large cigars a day, eating huge meals and drinking far more than was good for him. He was, perhaps partly because of this lifestyle, growing increasingly irritable and intrac-table in his attitudes. Some of his words from his years as Chan-cellor support this—'I never forgive,' he once said, and on another occasion, after a sleepless night spent turning over his affairs, he declared, 'I have spent the whole night hating.' There was at first only one major source of opposition to his domestic policy: the powerful and—in Bismarck's view—dangerous Zentrumspartei, the new Catholic Centre Party. From 1873 he set out to destroy the Centre Party's power and influence; the struggle that resulted became known as the *Kulturkampf*.

The word *Kulturkampf* may be defined by the words 'cultural struggle', or 'conflict of civilisations'. It was originally coined by the noted Berlin pathologist and member of parliament, Professor Rudolf Virchow. He was one of a group of politicians and others who felt that the schools should be freed from clerical influence. Virchow was thinking of both Catholic *and* Protestant influence, but the contemporary climate and the turn of events both in the Vatican and in Germany were to dictate otherwise. Certainly, the debate over religious education was by no means limited to Germany. Between 1870 and 1900 many other European countries, among them France, Belgium and England, opened this matter to dispute. In Germany, however, the Chancellor used it as a touch-paper to ignite a greater struggle, which would unite the new nation against the Catholic minority. Thus the *Kulturkampf* has become identified as a campaign fought jointly by Bismarck and the German National Liberal Party, in the cause of state versus religious domination, against the Roman Catholic Church and, in particular, the new Catholic Centre Party. Wishing to create strength in a federal authority, Bismarck was prepared to cooperate with the National Liberals, who held the majority in the German parliament. He set out to legislate for the future of the unified Germany. A standard coinage appeared, the various legal systems of the hitherto separate states were unified, and the postal, military and civil services were now coodinated from Berlin. Most significantly and contentiously, many of the disparate foreign minorities who now lived—some of them unwillingly—under the German flag, found themselves subject to German laws which, particularly in the case of peoples such as the French in Alsace, directly cut across their own feelings of nationalism.

The Zentrumspartei represented the Catholic populace of many of these areas, and their power in the early 1870s was considerable and growing. During this decade more than a dozen political parties were striving for power in Germany, seeking the attention of nearly eight million voters. An examination of the votes cast in the national election of 1871 shows that out of those eight million, just over half exercised their right to vote giving the National Liberals a figure of 1,171,807. The Centre Party came second, with 724,179. By 1874, however, the gap had closed considerably. The number of eligible voters had risen to eight and a half million, of whom more than five million actually voted. Of these the National Liberals received 1,542,501 votes, while the Centre Party's share rose to 1,445,948. And this in spite—indeed, one may say, because—of Bismarck's battle against the Centre Party. But what were the real reasons for the enmity between the Chancellor and the Catholics, and what form did this 'struggle of the cultures' take?

In 1864 Pope Pius IX had published in his *Encyclica Quanta Cura* the 'Syllabus errorum', or 'Syllabus of Errors'. In it he declared it a gross and mortal error to accept that any pope 'can and must compromise and be reconciled with progress, liberalism, and modern culture'. This 'Syllabus' listed all contemporary doctrines that the Pope disapproved or condemned. And it contained most of the ideas that the Liberals—and Bismarck—believed to be essential elements of modern civilisation and of the state itself.

This was bad enough, but there was worse to come. In June 1870 the Vatican Council had adopted the dogma of papal infallibility. The effect of this was profound throughout Europe – even Gladstone, tolerant though he was, was moved to publish a pamphlet against the decree entitled *The Vatican Decrees in their Bearing on Civil Allegiance*. In Germany, perhaps Bismarck, and certainly the National Liberals, came to see in this dogma the potential for undermining everything they had so far achieved in their unification programme. What it could mean was that Catholics— German or any other—could find their allegiance to the state overridden by compulsory support for a pope's edicts. Here was a fundamental change in the relationship between Church and state, or so it seemed. Today we may see that it was only in the question of Roman Catholic dogma that such a claim to infallibility was to be used. In the early 1870s, however, it seemed like a return to the Middle Ages.

Given the already undeniable strength of the Catholic Centre

Party, the equation was not a difficult one to make. There had already been attempts to limit the influence of the Catholic Church on the independent German state of Baden, with the Baden Church Law of 1860 and the Elementary School Law of 1868. The year 1871 saw open confrontation in Baden between Church and state. Even as early as 1815, after the acqusition of the Rhine states, the largely Protestant nation of Prussia had been at odds with the Catholic population of these areas. Then, a compromise had been reached, but, in the event, it only postponed the struggle rather than solving it. Now, with unification, Bismarck saw the menace as a growing one. He saw Polish Catholics on one Frontier and the Catholic French on another, as well as some very reluctant converts to German unity at home, such as the strongly Catholic Bavarians. Thus it was that the Kulturkampf assumed a dramatic significance. That a cultural 'struggle' could occur over such an issue seems incomprehensible to many today. Yet, in the 1870s, as such it was perceived. Bismarck dramatised the whole issue in terms of a battle between priest and king that was older than Christianity, citing the struggle between Agamemnon and Calchas in Tauris with the powerful cry to the Reichstag, 'We shall not go to Canossa!'

The leader of the Centre Party was Ludwig Windhorst, a cool and capable parliamentarian, of whom Bismarck once said: 'Everyone needs somebody to love and somebody to hate. I have my wife to love and Windhorst to hate.' Bismarck proclaimed that Windhorst and his party were *Reichsfeinde*, or 'enemies of the state', a phrase he applied to anyone who opposed him. Windhorst's reply was characteristic: 'The Chancellor is not the state. Until now no minister has been so presumptuous as to call his opponents enemies of the state.' It was Bismarck's Germany of which the Centre Party was the enemies, rather than Germany itself. Windhorst stated in one of his speeches:

My loyalty to the royal house of Hanover will last until my dying day, and nothing in the world, not even the most powerful Chancellor of Germany, will be able to make me depart from it. But I remember the words of the Bible: obey them that have rule over you and submit yourselves, and I have done my duty as a subject to the best of my conscience

. . . It is easy to cling to the monarchical principle in fair weather; it is harder in foul.

Bismarck was in rampant and determined mood, however, and his great aim during the early 1870s was to crush the Catholics as a political force in Germany, by whatever means he could. In order to do so, he was to practise what has been called a 'policy of negative integration', in which he attempted to find a common enemy of the people, a conflict which would unite the majority against the minority. And he did have the support of the majority; he knew, for instance, that the Protestants believed the members of the Society of Jesus—the Jesuits—to be plotters and intriguers. In 1872, the Reichstag gave the government powers to dissolve the Society of Jesus, and to banish its members from Germany. In the same year Bismarck attacked the Catholic Church in Germany thus: 'The goverment cannot avoid the remarkable observation that the Roman Catholic clergy is national in all other lands. Only Germany makes an exception. The Polish clergy adhere to the Polish national movement, the Italian to the Italian . . . Only in Germany is there the peculiar phenomenon that the *clergy* has a more *international* character.'

The next year saw the climax of his campaign in the 'May Laws', introduced by the Prussian Minister of Religion and Education, Dr Adalbert Falk. Bismarck had taken Falk, a high-minded and high-ranking Liberal, from his position in the Ministry of Justice, and made him *Kultusminister*, replacing the existing minister in the Catholic division of the Prussian Ministry of Culture. He had instructed Falk 'to re-establish the rights of the state in relation to the Church, and with as little fuss as possible'.

Certainly, in many ways, Falk was the man for the job. He was a passionate believer in the new German state, and he supported the idea that it should be governed by a secular constitution, not influenced in any way by religion. The overall effect of the Falk Laws of May 1873 was that the Catholic Church in Prussia (representing two thirds of Germany) became much more subject to the control of the state. It was from now on to be the state that supervised Catholic education—and that included the education and appointment of the Catholic clergy. Only aspiring priests who had studied in Germany, and who had passed German examinations were to be admitted to the priesthood. It became compulsory for weddings to be conducted by state officials; church weddings could still be obtained, but it was legally meaningless unless a civil ceremony had also been performed. All religious orders, with the exception of the nursing orders—the state still had cause to recall the role they had played during the recent wars—were dissolved, and financial aid from the state to the Catholic Church was summarily ended. In addition, all Prussian Catholics lost their civil and legal rights. A Royal Tribunal for Ecclesiastical Affairs was set up by the government and immediately Pius IX wrote to the German bishops, telling them to ignore these new laws. Bismarck reacted furiously: forbidding the publication of the Pope's letter, he declared to the Reichstag that defeat in the struggle would mean that 'we non-Catholics would have either to become Catholics or to emigrate, or our property would be confiscated, as is usual with heretics'.

Perhaps, in the midst of all his planning and policy-making, Bismarck still remembered the day in Aachen when, as an arrogant youth, he had sought to defy Catholic dogma by refusing to bend the knee and had barely escaped with his life. In Aachen it had been by running into the arms of the Prussian infantry that he had been saved. Now he was enfolded by the might of an empire centred upon Prussia.

Bismarck's own prejudices played a strong part in his political thinking. As he himself said, he had been

> brought up to regard it as one of the most monstrous things that could occur in the political arena that a denominational party should form in a political assembly, a party against which, were all other denominations to adopt the same principle, one need only set the totality of a Protestant parliamentary group: then we should all of us be on an unequal footing, for we should be bringing theology into public assemblies to make it an object of political debate.

Turning to face the challenge from the men of the Zentrumspartei head on, he quickly extinguished any thought that there might be a compromise in his heart: 'On my return from France, I was unable to see the formation of this group otherwise than in the light of a mobilisation of the party against the state.'

In 1874, even more extreme measures against Catholics were

to follow. Dissident parish priests had their endowments confiscated, and bishops who remained rebellious towards the state could be exiled or imprisoned. The historian D. G. Williamson has commented that 'for the Catholics Prussia became a police state', and the phrase is an accurate one. Politically, however, Bismarck's bluster only served to strengthen Catholic resolve, and in the 1874 elections, as we have seen, the seats held by the Centre Party rose dramatically. As the British Ambassador in Berlin, Odo Russell, wrote at the time: 'The Roman Church has always derived strength from persecution, but it is impotent against the power of freedom and its blessings . . . Bismarck's anti-Church policy has compelled the German bishops to rally round the Pope and to suffer martyrdom for discipline's, obedience's and example's sake.'

Reaction was inevitable. On 13th July 1874 a young Catholic called Kullman, a travelling cooper and a member of a Catholic-organised working men's club, attempted to assassinate Bismarck. Wounded only slightly in the right hand, the Chancellor immediately tried to gain political mileage from the event, claiming it to be part of a conspiracy. In December of the same year a Bavarian called Jorg fuelled the flames of Bismarck's anger over the affair, by sarcastically claiming that the whole thing had been made too much of. 'You may try to disown this assassin, but none the less he is clinging to your coat-tails,' retorted Bismarck, launching another well documented attack on the Centre Party. The remark prompted the famous 'Pfui!' from Count von Ballestrem. The power of this insult in German is considerable, and Bismarck later said that, had he had a gun on his person at the time, he would have shot von Ballestrem there and then. This would have been unfortunate, as he would thereby have robbed Germany of one of its most highly regarded Presidents of the Reichstag, a post von Ballestrem was to hold twenty-five years later. Instead, Bismarck shook with rage and replied: 'Pfui is an expression of disgust and contempt. Don't imagine that *I* have not experienced these feelings. The only difference is that I am too polite to voice them.'

Between January and April 1875 the number of clergy imprisoned under the Falk Laws was 241. Without doubt the measures did effectively isolate the Catholics from the rest of the community, with churches—and even sees—standing empty.

We may see now that Bismarck, in pursuing the Kulturkampf policy, was following a line that was symptomatic of an attitude that pervaded much European thinking during the second half of the nineteenth century. It was an attitude that spilled over into foreign policy too, as leaders galvanised their peoples by appealing to their sense of national pride. The means by which this rallying to the flag was achieved became increasingly hysterical as the century moved towards its close. A strong spirit of strutting and swaggering Prussian feudalism was to last into the twentieth century, but increasingly its energies were harnessed to an expanding industry typified by giant concerns such as the Krupps steelworks. Ultimately it was the hysteria, synthesised with the two elements of feudal power and industrial growth, that was to lead to the catastrophe of 28th June, 1914, when the assassination of Archduke Ferdinand tipped the world into war. But for the sisters in the little Westphalian town of Salzkotten late in 1875, another tragedy was imminent.

3 Farewell to the Fatherland

To understand the implications of the anti-Catholic laws for Mother Clara Pfaender and her congregation, it is illuminating to quote the letter of some of the more pertinent ones. In June 1872 an early law proclaimed: 'Members of religious orders or similar groups may no longer be accepted as teachers in the elementary schools, and contracts now in existence are to be revoked.' The order of the Daughters of the Sacred Hearts of Jesus and Mary had expanded since its establishment, with sisters teaching in schools all over Germany. Now, with this law, came a major problem. Where were these sisters to go? To the motherhouse in Salzkotten? How would they be fed? Many still relied on charity for the survival of both themselves and their young charges, but in the present climate even this was difficult.

Then, in May 1875 it was decreed by the state:

All religious orders and similar groups are to be excluded from the territories of the Prussian state. New foundations are prohibited; those already existing are to be disbanded within six months; for foundations whose members serve to instruct and educate youth, the period of grace may be extended up to four years by the Minister of Culture, if no substitutes can be found. The property of suppressed foundations will not be confiscated by the state, but will be held in trust and managed by trustees.

The law thus dealt with one half of the sisters' vocational work. The other half, that of nursing, was preserved, but on the most insecure of footings:

Establishments of religious orders or similar groups who devote themselves exclusively to the care of the sick may continue; they may, however, be dissolved by the decree of the monarchy; meanwhile, the Ministers of the Interior and of Religion are empowered to permit them to accept new members . . . The continuing existence of religious orders and similar groups is dependent on the opinion of the government.

One consequence of this was that all sisters in Prussia were required by law to report monthly to police authorities. Furthermore, any transfers had to be formally requested, with detailed reasons for the transfer given in writing. And only nursing sisters —not cooks, housekeepers or other staff—were eligible for transfer, anyway. Nevertheless, because of the demand for nursing skills during the wars of 1866 and 1870–1, the congregation did manage to keep going, though this was not the case with other orders in Germany. Through clever interpretation of the laws as they were introduced, Mother Clara endeavoured to minimise their effect. One instance of her shrewd tactics may be seen in the part she played in the struggle for survival of her own elementary school. When the law of June 1872, referred to above, came into force, St Joseph's, the Salzkotten orphanage, contained one hundred and sixteen children under the care of their head teacher, Sister Ignacia, who was also principal of the orphanage itself. The June law forbade her both roles. But in response to a carefully worded request to the authorities from Mother Clara, the right to teach girls only was restored to Sister Ignacia, while the boys in the orphanage were taught by a lay instructor. Here, certainly, was a victory of sorts, but in the unstable atmosphere of the time the situation was liable to change without warning. And change it did.

In August 1874 Falk questioned the very existence of the orphanage. The boys were to be dismissed, while permission to continue with the girls would depend on certain conditions being fulfilled: 'The property of the congregation was to be transferred to the orphanage in order to ensure the orphanage's viability, corporate rights were to be obtained for the orphanage and new statutes were to be drawn up and submitted.'

That, however, was by no means all. What came next made the whole proposal unacceptable to the Salzkotten Superior: all instruction within the school must be given by lay personnel—which represented a direct contravention of the agreement Mother Clara had established in 1872. Representations were to be made to the Ministry by 1st November 1874. Mother Clara turned in desperation to Empress Augusta herself. It was widely known that the Empress felt an open distaste for the *Kulturkampf* in general, and a lasting gratitude for the nursing carried out by the Salzkotten congregation during the recent wars. By this time, however, Augusta was virtually powerless. Bismarck knew of her opposition to Catholic persecution, and disliked her intensely. Indeed in his book of memoirs, *Reflections and Recollections*, he was to attack her spitefully, and blame her for almost every setback in his career.

In the event, the state's requirements were met, and the boys left the orphanage. The closure of the school was ordered for 19th June 1875, although, after a formal request, the local authorities granted two more years of grace. In July 1876, the *Sauerland Herald* carried an official communiqué:

ANNOUNCEMENT

By order of the law of 31st May 1875, through the ministerial decree of 18th June 1876, the convent orphanage established by the Franciscan Sisters of Salzkotten is to close, and the termination date is hereby set for 31st March 1877. The respective foster-parents, guardians and other providers are, by the foregoing, charged with the responsibility of arranging alternative accommodations for the children as soon as possible.

Büren, 8th July 1876

The Imperial Magistrate

Another stay was granted until October 1877, which gave Mother Clara just enough time to propose another compromise which might maintain the orphanage in one form or another. And so it went on, in Salzkotten as, doubtless in other such establishments throughout Germany, varying only according to the severity with which the laws were interpreted. Finally, in the spring of 1880, defeat was admitted and St Joseph's closed. The house that had seen the determined care of children for so long,

under such trying conditions, was converted thereafter into a
hospital and home for the elderly.

Thus this particular struggle against the anti-Catholic laws persisted for nearly ten years, and it exemplifies the way in which
the *Kulturkampf* must have worn away at the will of those who
stood in its path.

In her fight against the laws, Mother Clara had a true ally in the
person of Conrad Martin, Bishop of Paderborn. He it was who
had supported her and her aims from the earliest beginnings of
the congregation, and he continued to do so now. Unfortunately,
this good friend of Mother Clara's was seen by the Prussian
government as an opponent, to be humbled at all costs, and it
was this campaign against Bishop Martin that was to make life
even more difficult for Mother Clara and her sisters. By implica-
tion, she was almost as guilty as he. And he had documented his
violent protest to the state's bullying legislation from the very
start, when he had written to the Ministry of State: 'If these drafts
are ever made law, I will under no circumstances, not even to
avoid the most severe penalties, ever be able to offer my consent
to the implementation of such laws.'

This was a burning of boats that seemed deliberately to pursue
confrontation. Thus, as the situation deteriorated, far from being
able to offer support to Mother Clara, he found his own position
beleaguered. The semi-official press branded him an enemy of
the state and of the Empire. As a result of his own opposition to
the laws passed by the new regime, he was affected to a greater
extent than anyone else by them. By the end of his life, Conrad
Martin could claim the dubious distinction of having run the full
gamut of the penalties laid down in the May Laws, from simple
imprisonment to the loss of his rights of citizenship. On 4th October 1874 this 'troublesome admonisher', as he had been called,
was committed to the district prison. In her book *The Burning
Seal*, Sister Brunilde Probst has left us a moving picture of his
imprisonment in Paderborn:

The episcopal city trembled with helpless agitation. On the
day of imprisonment a mass of people gathered in the streets
leading to the episcopal palace. After a long delay the con-
victed man, pale but erect, appeared at the entrance of his

house. Under guard he was led to the coach that would bring him to prison. It was almost impossible for the coach to start. Shoulder to shoulder, the crowd moved along in the same direction. After a painfully slow trip the coach finally reached its destination, and the otherwise rugged man climbed wearily up the high steps of the prison. There he beheld the flock of his faithful that looked like a densely packed herd of cattle. He glanced over the crowd sorrowfully. Then he stood erect and raised his hand in a farewell blessing. Weeping, the people remained on their knees as their Father disappeared behind the strong iron door.

On 5th January 1875, Bishop Martin was declared by the authorities to have been deposed from his office. This he refused to acknowledge, and as a result he was sent on 19th January to the prison at Wesel. From this point, things moved swiftly. Martin's story was to continue with a dramatic escape from Wesel, then flight into Holland. Sadly for him, the arm of German power was long, and the mind that informed it, unforgiving. The Dutch authorities, under pressure from Bismarck, expelled him, and his last years were spent in Belgium where, broken-hearted, he was to die on 16th July 1879. Shortly before his death, he wrote thus of this final indignity:

The Dutch government wisely gave no explanation for my expulsion, for they could give no legitimate reason for their actions against me. I have committed absolutely no crime against them.

They imposed the rule of expulsion not out of a sense of legitimacy, but because they gave way to pressure from Berlin. Nothing illustrates more vividly the untenability of the state of contemporary affairs than that so-called sovereign governments, in particular those of smaller countries, are no longer masters of their own decisions, but, out of self-preservation, have to bow to the power of foreign orders. Public or international questions are no longer so much questions of justice as questions of power.

Before his move to Wesel, Mother Clara had kept in close touch with Bishop Martin, and had visited him in prison on several occasions. Their friendship was a deep one, born of the same deep-seated beliefs and determination. She discussed all her affairs with him, as she had always done, and trusted his advice implicitly. She paid her last visit on 9th January 1875. On this occasion, he gave her a unique document. He also made her swear to keep it secret—a promise which was to cause her much trouble and anguish. The document read as follows:

> Under the present circumstances and for as long as I am forcibly prevented from governing the diocese, the venerable Superior-General of the congregation of the Poor Franciscans in Salzkotten is empowered, after consultation with the ecclesiastical Superior, if this is possible, to choose as confessors for the houses of the congregation in this diocese—when the term of the present confessors there is completed—such among the approved confessors of the diocese as she considers suitable according to her conscientious judgement, and those same confessors I hereby authorise to hear the nuns' confessions.
>
> She is similarly to be empowered to take suitable steps to receive new novices and to authorise the taking of vows, after consultation with the Reverend Moderator, again to the extent that this is possible.
>
> Paderborn, 9th January 1875
In the district prison
+ Conrad

With hindsight, Mother Clara realised that she had been given an impossible task: by honouring Bishop Martin's plea for secrecy about the plenary powers that the document gave her, she would appear in the eyes of the world, to be without authority to carry out the tasks cited in it. By failing to honour his plea, she would, in the eyes of the law, be seen to be a law-breaker herself by carrying out the very practice for which he was being punished; she would, in other words, become an accessory, and nothing would have been gained.

In the meantime, help was needed all over Germany, and in spite of all the problems of housing and feeding that they would bring with them, more sisters were desperately needed. There was no shortage of applicants to the noviciate, but if it was not to be allowed to receive new novices, the congregation would remain at a standstill. So with the approval of the District Moderator, Father Edward Klein, Mother Clara arranged a secret investiture. Thirteen novices made their vows on 1st July 1875—an event which, despite all attempts at secrecy, reached the ears of the authorities. Klein was charged with performing a role pertaining to a bishop, but was freed on a technicality by the civil court. But it was a loophole that did not remain open for long. From now on, Salzkotten was closely scrutinised, and the screws of the *Kulturkampf* tightened still further.

The fact that hers was an order dedicated to teaching as well as nursing was, the determining factor in Mother Clara's actions. If teaching was not to be permitted in the homeland, then the Word must be carried elsewhere. And she was not the sort of person to give up. Her faith enabled her to see positive blessings from God in the darkest hour. Also, her attitude to her religion was twofold: first, she had established a congregation to live in close contact with God, and had experienced a nourishing of the sisters' spiritual life. At the same time, she preached that those same sisters must be open to the needs of those around them, for it was in Mother Clara's nature to respond where she saw a need.

And it was not only within Prussia that need had arisen. This was a key fact: although it is possible to see the effects of the *Kulturkampf* as universally withering and stifling, Mother Clara's policy of expansion and positive response, of pushing back boundaries, was to lead in the long term to a worldwide network of spiritual care. The sisters had already established themselves in Lorraine during the Franco-Prussian War, and the link remained strong. At Metz, Mother Clara had taken over the Blandina Institute for girls, at the same time setting up an elementary school for boys nearby. In 1872 the city's Jesuit college had been dissolved, and the Franciscans from Salzkotten had taken over the building and converted it into a fine and spacious hospital. The order had also been received kindly in Holland, where collection trips for alms had met with a favourable response; here a seed of health care and education was planted that was in later years to grow strong and vigorous.

Perhaps the most exciting example of this expansion—and, to

the besieged sisters in Salzkotten, the strongest proof of the power of God working for them and for the Catholic religion— had come in 1872, when Bishop Martin had received a letter from an American priest, the Reverend E. A. Schindel, Rector of St Boniface Church, Carondelet, South St Louis, Missouri. Revd Schindel had appealed in his letter for sisters to help in the management of a new hospital there, which was nearing completion. Martin showed the letter to Mother Clara, and suggested that the Salzkotten nuns would be ideal for the task. Mother Clara readily agreed, and she did not have to search hard for volunteers. As it happened, a friend of Revd Schindel's, one Revd H. Brockhagen, was in Europe at the time, and it was agreed that he would accompany a small party of sisters to the New World. So, on the feast of St Francis Xavier, 3rd December 1872, Sisters Philomena Oldegeering, Mary Dorethea and Alphonsa Corman had set off. On arrival, Revd Schindel introduced them to sisters of Notre Dame who were already in charge of the school at Carondelet. They gave the Salzkotten sisters food and shelter and trained them in the use of English.

In 1873 the Hospital at Carondelet was completed, and the sisters moved in. In the meantime, Revd Schindel visited Salzkotten, met Mother Clara, and asked her if more sisters could be sent to build upon the foundations already established. Again, the response was enthusiastic. The second set of Falk's Laws had just been issued, and the future was becoming all too clear. Accordingly, a further eight sisters accompanied Revd Schindel back to Missouri: Benedicta Eickhoff, Adolphina Duechting, Ida Lukuschek, Ursula Brust, Euphemia Dziedziock, Isadora Gerdes, Engelberta Gramen and Anastasia Yolk.

They arrived in time for the dedication of the St Boniface Hospital on 7th September, and Sister Benedicta was appointed the first Superior. With the hospital full to capacity almost at once, the sisters were fully occupied in nursing, while their business affairs were managed by the Rector. It was a time of hardship, and a building debt of $40,000 added to the burden. As before in Europe, recourse had to be made to begging for alms to pay current bills.

The St Boniface Hospital was pleasantly situated. It was on high ground beside the Lemay Ferry Road in Carondelet, close to the Mississippi River, and it had a large park, with fruit trees and a thriving vegetable garden. In one crucial factor, however, it was lacking: situated as it was close to the water, it received the unpleasant and unsanitary fumes from a nearby creek. It may have been that mosquitoes bred here, and it is certain that right from the start patients and medical staff alike were prone to intermittent fevers. With a proportion of the nursing sisters almost always laid low, the burden of work on the others increasing and the worries of administration heavy on their shoulders, it soon became apparent that further help was needed. So in response to an appeal from Sister Benedicta, Mother Clara granted permission for a further eight sisters to leave Salzkotten for America on 15th July 1875.

They arrived in Carondelet on 1st August. It must have been a happy reunion, and a necessary strengthening of resolve and resource. As one of the sisters recalled, they soon became used to American customs and the way of life, and 'the thought, "We are among strangers" made way for the happier one, "at home"'. By September, expansion out of St Boniface had begun: three sisters had been sent to Cape Girardeau, Missouri, to develop a new hospital there at the request of the pastor of St Mary's Church, Revd Joseph Schmidt. This in turn led to the suggestion that they take over the school in the town, so on 5th September five more sisters sailed from Germany on the steamship *Weser*, arriving at St Louis on 5th October. Among them was Sister Theodora Brockmann, the new choir mistress of the school and an early chronicler of the order's Missouri days.

It was becoming clear that, as each new group of sisters arrived, the area in which work was found for them was increasing all the time. This in itself was good, and was what the Salzkotten congregation had always been renowned for. On the other hand, the sisters based in Germany had always had Salzkotten as their administrative and spiritual centre, a binding force from which they received both guidance and moral strength. And, of course, at the heart of the Salzkotten congregation was the powerful figure of Mother Clara herself. The time had arrived to recognise the need for a similar formal structure in America: a provincial motherhouse led by a trustworthy supporter of everything Mother Clara and her sisters stood for in the fatherland. Thus, over the next three months the Mother Superior watched and waited, pondering on which would be the next five sisters to make the crossing; and among them, this time, would be someone capable of carrying the torch and leading the young province as Mother Clara herself would wish it.

After much thought and prayer, she made her decision, (although she may have delayed the final choice of provincial Governess until the last minute). The sisters came from a wide area. Brigitta Damhorst was a local girl, aged twenty-seven. Her christened name was Elisabeth—nuns took another Christian name when they joined the order, as we saw earlier—and she came from the small town of Mastholte, eight miles from Salzkotten. (Her descendants still live in Mastholte, but no records exist of Brigitta today. Around 1925 the house in which she was born was burned to the ground, and nothing was saved.) Norberta (Johanna) Reinkober, aged thirty, was from Steindorf, and Aurea (Josepha) Badziura, at twenty-four the youngest of the sisters, was born in Neugarten. Both Steindorf and Neugarten were small communities in Upper Silesia, and no longer exist under these names now. After the Second World War this part of Germany became Polish, and today all the place names are Polish. When I asked some local people a few questions about the old days, I was met with the answers: 'There is nothing kept from the German time.' The fourth sister, Barbara Hultenschmidt, was thirty-two, and had been christened Thekla in the Westphalian village of Deleke—a tiny place some twenty miles west of Salzkotten.

About these four nuns nothing more is known. The *Kulturkampf* and two world wars have erased all but their names. Of the fifth, however, there is rather more to learn: she was the nun chosen by Mother Clara to become the provincial Governess in America, and her name was Sister Henrica (Catharina) Fassbaender.

Aachen has been historically one of the most important towns in Europe, as one might expect of a place situated where three countries meet—in this case, Germany, Holland and Belgium. It is Germany's most westerly city, was occupied by the French in 1794, and passed to Prussia in 1815. It has two names—Aachen for the Germans and Aix-la-Chapelle for the French. It is the Aix to which the 'good news' was brought from Ghent in Browning's poem—that undisclosed good news that has figured in the education of so many schoolchildren:

Then I cast loose my buffcoat, each holster let fall,
Shook off both my jack-boots, let go belt and all,
Stood up in the stirrup, leaned, patted his ear,
Called my Roland his pet-name, my horse without peer;
Clapped my hands, laughed and sang, any noise, bad or
    good,
Till at length into Aix Roland galloped and stood.

And all I remember is, friends flocking round
As I sat with his head 'twixt my knees on the ground,
And no voice but was praising this Roland of mine,
As I poured down his throat our last measure of wine,
Which (the burgesses voted by common consent)
Was no more than his due who brought good news from
    Ghent.

This heroic fiction was, according to Browning, set in the seventeenth century, but Aachen is far more ancient than that. Surrounded by gently sloping, wooded hills, it lies in a fertile basin, and enjoys a fine reputation as a health resort—a reputation already widespread in Roman times. The Roman 6th legion, the Victrix, was stationed on the lower Rhine from AD 70 to 120, and the remains of a vast bath built by the Romans during their occupancy have been found, linked to an elaborate aqueduct system. They called the place Aquae Granni, and appreciated the springs —the hottest in Europe, with a temperature of between thirty-seven and seventy-five degrees centigrade. Today, too, the hot brine and sulphur springs of Bad Aachen are noted for their efficacy in the treatment of gout, sciatica and rheumatism.

Aachen has always had a strong manufacturing bias, and in the last years of the nineteenth century boasted about a hundred textile factories as well as thirty making needles and pins, and fifty iron foundries and machine-shops. The business side of the city remains strong, with cloth and needle manufacture continuing alongside thriving glass, rolling-stock and chemical works. From a population of about one hundred thousand a hundred years ago, today that figure has risen to about a quarter of a million. During the Second World War, much of the city was destroyed, while many of the surviving buildings were badly damaged. Today's Aachen, like many European cities, is a masterpiece of reconstruction. It is a major centre for equestrian sport —appropriately enough considering Browning's poem.

Aachen was frequently the residence of the Frankish kings; it was a particular favourite of Charlemagne, who made it the capital of his dominions to the north of the Alps, and died here in 814. Although Charlemagne himself is reputed to have been able to read only with great difficulty he made Aachen rich and famous as a seat of learning and culture by gathering around him the greatest poets, thinkers and divines of his time. Sadly, little remains of the Carlovingian period, and even before the Second World War Aachen retained little from its ancient past. Today, the Rathaus, or city hall—a fine, well restored building—stands where Charlemagne's palace once was. The original Rathaus fell into decay during the thirteenth century, and the present structure dates from the fourteenth. The Market Tower and the Granus Tower remained as reminders of those great days, until both were virtually demolished by fire in 1883. From the time of Charlemagne's son, Louis the Pious, down to the accession in 1531 of Ferdinand I, younger brother of the Emperor Charles V, Aachen witnessed the coronations of no less than thirty-two German emperors and kings, and was known widely as the greatest free city of the Holy Roman Empire, as well as the seat of royalty.

This glory was often dearly bought. Aachen has frequently been besieged: in 1248, for example, Count William of Holland dammed all the streams during a six-month siege and drowned and starved the Aachen people until they gave in.

The chief remaining witness of those violent and glorious days is the cathedral. Comprising a central octagon to which was later added a Gothic choir, it dominates Aachen now, as it did when Catharina Fassbaender had her lessons in its shadow. This is the minster where Charlemagne was buried, although no one knows where. There is a legend that in the year 1000 the Emperor Otto III found his body seated upon a throne within the tomb, wearing a crown and holding a sceptre, with a golden gospel book open before him. It was as if Charlemagne were still alive, for no corruption was visible upon his body, except that the tip of his nose was missing. Otto took the book and the sceptre, and left the tomb, only to die himself two years later at the age of twenty-one. He too was buried in the minster, but in 1910, when his tomb was opened, his bones crumbled away to nothing. Subsequent historical research has given the lie to the tradition of Otto's discovery of Charlemagne. All that is mortal of him now rests in the treasury of the cathedral, within a magnificent reliquary. The minster was consecrated during Charlemagne's reign by Pope Leo III, in a ceremony of enormous pomp and grandeur. During the Middle Ages Aachen became the scene of many Imperial diets and ecclesiastical conventions, and in and after the seventeenth century a number of peace conferences were held in the city. At all of these events, the cathedral would have been the centrepiece.

In the distinctive octagon of Aachen Cathedral is a huge copper-gilt candelabrum made by one Wibert of Aachen, and placed here by Frederick Barbarossa to commemorate his coronation as Emperor in the year 1152. For the seeker after religious relics, the treasury contains items to stir the imagination: a robe claimed to belong to the Virgin Mary, clothing supposedly worn by the baby Jesus, and a piece of blood-stained material in which the head of John the Baptist was said to have been wrapped. On an impressionable child such as Catharina Fassbaender, receiving a Catholic education in a sympathetic environment, this place and these things would have had a seminal influence.

Catharina was born on 9th April 1847, the daughter of Karl Wilhelm Fassbaender and his wife Katherina (née Lennartz). Wilhelm Fassbaender was a teacher at the Parish School of the Holy Cross in Aachen. He had been born in 1821 in the little town of Altena, south of Dortmund, east of Düsseldorf and a few miles west of Salzkotten. He was a devoted educator of the young, taking his work very seriously. He had gained his first job on 5th February 1844 at the Parish School of St Michael in Burtscheid, some twenty miles south-west of his birthplace. He stayed in this post for less than two years, before taking up his Aachen position on Christmas Eve 1845. He was married twice: his first wife, Catharina's mother, died after sixteen years of marriage, and his second wife, also Katherina (née Lejeune), was his companion for his last twenty-two years. He had married Katherina Lennartz in 1845 or 1846, and Catharina, born when Wilhelm was twenty-five, was their first child. This first Katherina died about 1862, when Catharina would have been fifteen. As the eldest child, she was to show herself both strong and responsible. His two wives bore him a total of seven children. He was to outlive Catharina by rather less than ten years, dying on 30th July 1885 at the age of sixty-four, after a series of severe strokes. Judging by his obituary notice, his years in Aachen had brought him honour and affection:

His zeal and his devotion to his work, his true Christian conviction and honest piety, all won him the recognition and high esteem of everyone who was close to him during his lifetime, and assured for him in the afterlife the wages that God has promised his loyal servants: 'Whoever then will acknowledge me before men, I will acknowledge him before my father in heaven.'

His example was to be reflected in the life of his first child, who was baptised in 1847 at the Church of the Holy Cross in Pontstrasse, where she went on to take her first academic steps at the church school. Catharina's earliest reports, dating from 1853 when she was six, show us a bright and lively little girl, well behaved and academically able, though not exceptional. Her arithmetic was 'good' and her reading 'very good'. Her handwriting, on the other hand, was described as 'not particularly satisfactory' and her needlework was 'poor'. Further, she seems for some reason to have been absent from church—something that her head teacher thought worthy of comment. For she went on to say that she would make allowances for Catharina, who 'is in view of present circumstances exempt from attending church'. What these circumstances were we do not know, and it was undoubtedly nothing to do with any lack of enthusiasm, since her report stated that in religious instruction she was 'good', and at Bible history 'very satisfactory'.

The report for the following year, dated 16th September 1854, 'for the schoolgirl Fassbaender, Catharina, Class 1', shows an improvement all round. She had started French now, and was good at it, she had a 'pleasing' singing voice, and her handwriting had improved. Her grasp of arithmetic was growing stronger all the time, and her church attendance was now regular. The only criticisms for this term were that 'her domestic application could be greater', and that 'Catharina must be quieter during classes'. From the Parish School of the Holy Cross she moved on to the Ursuline Institute of St Leonard in Franzstrasse, on the southern side of the city.

Clearly, from her earliest years Catharina was brought up with the Church as a major force in her life. The St Leonard Institute still exists, although the original building was destroyed during the Second World War. Its history is long and venerable. At the beginning of the twelfth century funds were donated by a local nobleman, Berthold, for the establishment of a convent in Aachen, and in 1144 that aim was achieved and St Leonard's was born. In addition to its function as a place of worship for nuns, the newly established convent was to be a rest-station for pilgrims. Through the centuries, it has flourished and put its spiritual stamp on Aachen. Records tell us that at the end of the fourteenth century the convent chapel was being rebuilt. From 1603 to 1608 —during a long period when ownership seems to have changed quite frequently—the Jesuits owned it. In 1625 came a key moment in its history, when the convent passed to an order of sisters from Vise, a small town on the German-Belgian border, some twenty miles from Aachen. It was these sisters who, just a year after taking up occupancy, began a school for girls.

In 1634 disaster struck, when the convent was nearly destroyed by fire. It was ten years before rebuilding work could begin, and when it did, such was the devastation that three more years elapsed before the building was once more able to carry out its function. The next major change happened in 1794, during one of the most turbulent periods in the history of Aachen, when the institute became a French hospital. Thus it remained until 1805, when the city council department responsible for looking after the interests of the poor re-established the convent as a boarding school. Although this function seems to have prevailed there was further reorganisation in 1827, when we find the convent listed as a 'girls' school. From 1848 to 1878—which includes the period when young Catharina Fassbaender was studying there—the convent was in the hands of the Ursuline sisters, and after that it became a secular school. After the destruction of 11th April 1944 the school moved to the Jesuitenstrasse, where it remains to this day. Only a part of its present name, Gymnasium Sanet Leonhard

(St Leonard High School) survives as a reminder of the establishment that the future Sister Henrica would have known.

After leaving school, Catharina Fassbaender appears to have worked for a number of years in Aachen as a shop assistant. Then in January 1867 we find her leaving her first employer, who gave her the following reference: 'I hereby certify that Miss Catharina Fassbaender has worked in my business for the last three and a half years to my greatest satisfaction, and that during this time she has always conducted herself in an exemplary fashion in every respect. I should therefore like to wish her a fitting placement.' That placement was with the Scholl sisters, whose shop Catharina worked in until shortly after her twenty-second birthday in April 1869. Again, the testimonial was a glowing one: 'I the undersigned certify that Fräulein Catharina Fassbaender has worked in our shop for the past two and a quarter years, and that during this time she has conducted herself in all respects in an exemplary manner, so that we can now recommend her with confidence.'

After the Scholls' shop came one more brief period of employment, in the establishment of Wilhelm Oethgen, who found her 'agreeable and trustworthy—in spite of her young years, I have always been able to leave the shop in her care.' She left in January 1871. Two months later, and just three weeks before her twenty-fourth birthday, she made the most momentous decision of her life: on 18th March she entered Mother Clara's Salzkotten congregation as a postulant. By the September she was a novice, and on 11th November 1872 she took her temporary vows.

For the next three years Sister Henrica, as she had now become, grew in maturity and moral standing in the eyes of her Mother Superior. Although no one could fully share the burden of responsibility that Mother Clara carried on her shoulders during those difficult years, the young nun from Aachen was a constant support and delight to her. Thus, when in late 1875 it became clear to the foundress that the American houses, increasingly disparate, urgently needed a strong force to unite them, her choice was a proud but sad one. Five more nuns were to leave for the New World, but this time there was a crucial difference—for among them would go a new leader for the American mission. In the words of Mother Clara's biographer, Sister Brunilde Probst:

Among the Sisters was one who according to the plan of the Foundress would guide the American Province with wise circumspection. For it became more and more evident that it was too difficult to guide the daughter-houses in America from Salzkotten. Therefore, Mother Clara fostered the plan of uniting these American houses into an independent province. With watchful eye, she tested her daughters for a period of time to discern the one whom she might one day appoint as Provincial Superior.

Her choice fell upon Sister Henrica Fassbaender. Intelligence, prudence, motherliness and piety were the excellent qualifications which Sister Henrica possessed. Indeed, the commission was hard for both Mother and daughter. They were truly devoted to each other. Mother Clara lost in Sister Henrica a promising source of strength for work in the fatherland, but the welfare of the community surpassed all personal considerations and desires on the part of the Superior General.

On 2nd December, the day of departure from Salzkotten for the port of Bremerhaven, four of the nuns, including Sister Henrica, pronounced their perpetual vows, and one, her temporary vows. The five sisters recommended themselves to the prayers of those left behind, and the nuns of the motherhouse began a period of adoration before the sacrament to plead for a safe journey—a task they intended to perform until word came that the travellers had safely arrived in America.

The first leg of that journey would take them through Bremen. Perhaps Sister Henrica thought, as she made ready for departure, of Bremen's link with her own home town. The bishopric at Bremen had been founded by Charlemagne himself; it was a city heavy with history, and an appropriate first stage on the journey to the New World. From Bremen the five nuns would follow the River Weser by train to Bremerhaven, the daughter-port of Bremen (Bremen itself is some sixty-five kilometres from the sea). In the sixteenth century the Weser began to silt up, but it was not until 1827 that Bremerhaven was founded. In 1875 there was no alternative to Bremerhaven, but latterly the Weser has been dredged, so that ocean-going liners can reach Bremen itself.

From the front steps of the motherhouse, Mother Clara watched as the carriage took the sisters away. Then, with a heavy heart, she returned to her study. There on her desk was an envelope. She opened it, and found it contained a poem, written in Sister Henrica's strong copperplate hand:

The last page of Sister Henrica's poem of farewell, 'Lebe Wohl', in her own hand. *Franciscan Sisters*

Farewell

Now the solemn hour of departure is at hand,
And my heart, deeply touched, throbs with fear;
'Tis bleeding as though pierced by many a spear,
For in bitter pain we leave you and our land so dear.

I leave—yes, depart gladly and in peace—
In obedience to your wishes, O Mother most dear;
Though distant, I know that your prayers will ne'er cease,
For your love will follow—hov'ring ever near.

Yet, poor nature doth press its human rights so—

Clinging in anguish to you and the fatherland blest;
Thus, from a torn heart, these hot tears do flow,
Mingled with many a sigh from my burdened breast.

But oh! as once again before you I kneel,
Allow these tears of departure free rein—
Thus consoled, I shall depart; for I shall feel
Your precious blessing coming to us o'er the main.

Yes, bless me Mother! God can and will heed
The prayerful blessing your fingers trace on me;
I need not fear—God knows best my every need—
Is he not ruler over land and sea?

For me beg the courage, the strength, and the power
That holy zeal for his honour within me may be born;
That humbly his glory I increase in each hour,
While striving his Holy Will to perform.

May I never fall into self-complacency vain,
Forgetting the promise and pledge I now raise;
To please God alone, I seek! His Will shall reign—
E'en though my work from others gain praise.

O pray that this office upon me now laid
Shall not too heavy for my weak shoulders prove;
May I learn to bear all with soul unafraid
While for God's highest honour, I labour with love.

Now farewell! Receive as a last little cession
My heart with filial gratitude aglow;
In fidelity to obedience, this last possession,
My consecrate heart, into your hands I bestow.

Farewell! Farewell! For I must now depart,
Yet will remain in spirit ever close to you!
Enclosed for ever within Jesus' Sacred Heart,
Your joys and sorrows will be mine too!

Farewell! also to you, my Sisters fond—
Ever preserve in your hearts your love for me!
Thus, uniting more firmly the consecrate bond
That binds our hearts for all eternity.

Farewell! Hallowed spot, where so oft I have knelt;

Farewell! Our convent chapel, so dear!
For here in they sanctuary oft have I felt
God's plea: 'Draw nigh to me here!'

Farewell! Holy Statues—perhaps for ever!
You who so peacefully down upon me gaze,
As though you'd say: 'You too must endeavour
Your eyes to Heaven always to raise!'

Farewell! Farewell! You hallowed rooms—
Where I have lived so happily without pain;
Farewell! You gardens and all you lovely trees—
Farewell! Farewell! and Auf Wiedersehen!

Dedicated to our dearly beloved Venerable Mother
at our departure for America
by your loving daughter, grateful unto death,
Sister M. Henrica
Salzkotten, 2nd December 1875

How moved Mother Clara must have been at these simple words expressing so much anguish and love. Towards the end the words, 'Lebe wohl', toll like a mournful bell, as the young sister, able to bear the sacrifice of separation only through the strength afforded her by her vows of obedience, forcing herself to face the inevitable, wrings out her farewells. The omens—if the pain of personal loss could be set aside—were good. Sister Henrica would give strength and unity to the American houses, and as the *Kulturkampf* in the homeland tightened its grip, would establish a bright future on the other side of the Atlantic. Furthermore, Sister Henrica would be going to friends, for she would be greeting again the sisters who had gone before her. There surely could be no cause for worry . . . after all, the crossings from Bremerhaven to America were becoming almost routine for the Salzkotten sisters. And maybe there was also a good omen in the name of the ship that awaited the five nuns at Bremerhaven—the *Deutschland*.

4 'American-outward-bound'

The North German Lloyd Company owned a large fleet of trans-atlantic steamers—at one time it numbered fifty-three, although in 1875, twenty-nine vessels were registered—and claimed proudly that it had not lost a single passenger since beginning operations in 1857. The company took seriously its responsibilities regarding safety at sea, claiming their emergency precautions were more than adequate, with ample lifeboat facilities on all their vessels. The pride of their fleet was the steamship *Deutschland*. She had made many voyages between Germany and New York and was an exceptionally well equipped ship, claiming to carry in the region of a thousand lifebelts. One hung on the wall above the head of every first- and second-class passenger as they slept, while the 'tween-deck' area, where the steerage passengers slept, was said to be roofed with lifebelts. In addition there were eight large lifeboats, seven metal and one wooden, with air-tight compartments—in all, a reassuring statement of security for any of the 113 passengers* who might have felt nervous about an Atlantic crossing in December.

Although not registered by Lloyd's of London, the *Deutschland* was entered in the *Liverpool Underwriters' Book of Iron Vessels*. She was a British-built ship, from the Caird Yard at Greenock, where she had been launched on 30th May 1866. John Caird had founded his engineering and foundry business in Greenock during the early years of the nineteenth century. Then, in 1840, his company secured the contract for four paddle-steamers. His origi-

---

* The numbers of crew and passengers on the *Deutschland* vary considerably in the many contemporary accounts. The overall total ranges between 206 and 219, with the number of passengers quoted as being between 107 and 119. The figure of 113 occurs most frequently, and I have therefore followed it here.

nal plan was to subcontract the work on the hulls, but he changed
his mind and opened his first shipyard, the Cartsdyke Mid Yard,
in order to take on the full job. Here the *Deutschland* was launched
twenty-six years later, and Caird and Company stayed until 1867,
when they commenced operations at the Westburn East Yard on
the Clyde. Then in 1871 they opened the Westburn West Yard,
and maintained the two until 1922. John Caird died in 1888, and
in 1916, Harland & Wolff acquired the company. Caird's had
produced their first steel-constructed vessel in 1859, and hulls
produced in their yards were considered first-class. Up to 1922
the yards had produced about 360 ships, and well over eighty of
those were for the P & O line; in fact, so long was the association
between line and yard that Caird and Co. became known as 'the
P & O yard'.

In the 1860s, though, it might equally have been called the
'North German Lloyd yard'. The *Deutschland* was the sixth
steamer built for the firm, the others being the *Bremen*, the *New
York*, the *Hansa* the *America* and the *Hermann*. Shortly after the
Deutschland was finished, yet another steamer, the *Union*, was
launched by Caird for the Bremen company, and an eighth was
already laid down on the slips. The career of the *Union* was
destined to be short indeed. Completed in the spring of 1867, she
was wrecked on the north coast of Scotland in 1870. At the time,
the Franco-Prussian War was at its height, and German vessels
were forced to take this hazardous route to avoid confrontation
with French cruisers. In addition to the North German Lloyd
commissions, Caird's were also building two vessels for the Hamburg America Company, to be employed for a similar purpose:
the emigrant trade was clearly a profitable one at its peak, but
there would be signs by the mid 1870s that it was slowing down.
The *Deutschland* was equipped to carry eighty first-class passengers, 120 second-class, and six hundred steerage. On her last
voyage her pay-load was a fraction of this number—fortunately,
as it was to turn out.

When on Wednesday 30th May 1866 the *Deutschland* was
launched 'gracefully' from Caird's Westburn West Yard, the formal ceremony was conducted by Miss Caird, the eldest daughter
of the firm's owner. The local paper, the *Greenock Advertiser*,
reported: 'The launch was highly successful, and the steamer

which was built under the superintendence of Captain Wessels
and Mr Janssen, engineer, was taken to the Victoria Harbour,
where her machinery will be put on board.'

This happy occasion was able to take place in spite of a strike
by shipyard workers on the Clyde, which at the time had shown
no signs of reaching a conclusion. The *Greenock Advertiser* of 31st
May 1866 stated:

No change has taken place in the relations between the employers
and employed in the shipbuilding trades, which have done so
much towards promoting the commercial prosperity of the city.
The only prospect of a speedy termination being put to the struggle
seems to be in the hope that the men may at the eleventh hour aban-
don their demands which their masters characterise as 'unreason-
able'. In a struggle where capitalists are banded together against
labour, and determined to remain unanimous as the Clyde
employers seem in this instance emphatically to be, it is not difficult
to tell in whose favour the beam must ultimately turn.

This industrial unrest does not seem to have hindered the fitting out of the *Deutschland*, which had been completed by late
September. She had been formally handed over to the owners on
the 28th of that month, and again the *Advertiser*'s reporter had
been there:

The Directors of the North German Lloyd, of Bremen, the
owners of this magnificent steamer, recently completed here
by Messrs Caird and Company, her builders and engineers,
took a cruise down the river yesterday, and expressed themselves satisfied in the highest degree with the vessel and her
machinery. She left the Tail of the Bank shortly after ten
o'clock, being on board Mr Freirchs and Doctor Pletzer, Directors, Mr Overbech, superintending engineer at Bremen; Mr
George Bailey, agent for the company in London, Captain
Wessels, the Commander, Mr Caird, Mr Miller . . .

Powered by two direct-action engines generating a total of 600
horsepower, the *Deutschland* was 320 feet long and 38 feet deep,
with a beam of 42 feet. Her registered tonnage was 2,500 gross,
1,971 net, and her construction had included five bulkheads. She

could boast 72-inch inverted cylinders with four-foot stroke, Krupp's shafts, surface condensers, variable expansion gear 'and all other modern improvements'. As with many vessels of her time, she carried sail by way of augmenting her engine power. She was also powered by a single screw—a factor which was to prove significant.

As far as public accommodation was concerned, she was sumptuous. The main saloon was panelled with bird's-eye maple, and with pilasters of oak inlaid with rosewood; there were gilt capitals, and the ceiling was decorated in white and gold. On the walls of the saloon were eight oil paintings of pastoral scenes, specially commissioned by North German Lloyd from the Hamburg artist, F. Hunten. The cabins were said to be 'fitted in a very superior style, and contain every requisite for comfort'.

On that first cruise down the Clyde, the completion of another successful deal between owners and builders was celebrated in fine style, as 'the party sat down in the saloon to a sumptuous dinner' before returning to the Caird anchorage after a six-hour round trip. The next day, 29th September, Captain Wessels took charge of her formally, and she sailed for Bremen. Her maiden voyage to New York took place on 14th October. From then on, the *Deutschland* was in the headlines from time to time—as when, on 15th June 1869, King William paid a state visit to Bremerhaven, and came aboard to inspect the luxurious interior of North German Lloyd's pride and joy. In February 1872 she was the first vessel to grace the new dry dock at Bremerhaven, and in 1874, during a refit, she was installed with a modern integrated engine.

By 1875 the *Deutschland* was a veteran of many Atlantic crossings, and for her crew of ninety-nine plus three pilots, Saturday 4th December of that year had an air of routine about it, as she eased out of Bremerhaven. Immediately before this trip, the ship had been laid up for a number of months at Bremerhaven because of slackness of trade on the transatlantic run. Also, she had been undergoing repairs, for early in 1875 she had been the victim of an accident that could have proved serious. She had lost her propeller in the Atlantic, but had been rescued and towed back to Southampton for repair by another steamer from the same shipping line, the *Braunschweig*. Thus the passengers on the *Deutschland* could now feel assured that the vessel was equipped with the very latest in engineering. She had been fully inspected in dry dock during September, ships' engines were examined as a matter of course after every voyage, and her compasses had been checked and adjusted at the beginning of November.

Up until her December sailing the *Deutschland* had been under the command of a Captain Ludewigs. Then a week or so before departure one of North German Lloyd's inspectors had suddenly died and Ludewigs was promoted to this prestigious desk job at very short notice. So it was only on 1st December, four days before sailing, that Edward Brickenstein, who had returned from a transatlantic crossing on 13th November as master of the steamship *Rhine*, had been given the job of taking the *Deutschland* out.

Brickenstein had been born in 1830, in the little Schleswig-Holstein town of Rantzau, east of Kiel. His father had been the owner and director of the local Institute for the Education and Instruction of Young Gentlemen in Rantzau, but it seems that young Edward attended not this establishment, but a nearby Protestant grammar school. Although there does not appear to be any history of seafaring in the Brickenstein family, it would seem that the sea was definitely in Edward's blood—and it is hardly surprising, given the geographical situation of his birth. From Kiel he could look out across the bay to Denmark; from Lübeck not far to the south, there was the prospect of the Mecklenburger Bay and the Baltic Sea; while further south, but still close enough to capture the youthful imagination, lay the giant port of Hamburg.

As soon as he left school he enlisted as a seaman, before serving on the Rheder Fritze and Berdes lines as first mate. Such was his efficiency and conscientiousness that before long he was offered the command of one of the line's sailing ships, and he held the post for a considerable time. But steamships were rapidly taking over from the time-honoured sailing vessels, and new lines were opening. One of them, North German Lloyd, was looking for responsible officers for their Atlantic operation. Brickenstein, warmly recommended by his former employers, took up the post, initially, of first officer, then of captain, of one of the company's older steamers. Again, his progress was swift, and he advanced to newer and larger ships within North German Lloyd until he was appointed Master of the Caird-built *Hansa*. The company declared itself 'satisfied with him in every respect'. It was true that the *Hansa*, while under his command, had lost her rudder once while in mid-Atlantic, but on that occasion, Brickenstein had behaved with commendable coolness and had successfully brought her into harbour at St John's Newfoundland, without further mishap or danger to passengers. Then, in about 1873, he had been given the captaincy of the *Rhine*, on which he was to remain until he took over the *Deutschland*. With sixteen years' experience as a master of vessels, and eight years in charge of North German Lloyd ships with no losses, he was a man whose judgement could be trusted.

It is a measure of his standing within the company that, when the emigrant trade began to fall off in 1874 and North German Lloyd laid up several of their ships, serving redundancy notices on many crew and giving officers compulsory leave, Brickenstein was retained, along with a handful of other elite officers. At the age of forty-five he could be said to be at the height of his powers, a popular man with crews and passengers alike. His parents, still alive in 1875, could look on his steady rise to the rank of captain with pride.

With him on the *Deutschland* were five officers, all of whom had masters' certificates, and a crew of ninety-four hands, many of whom had made the voyage numerous times before, while the ship's purser, Benning, had been carrying out his duties on the *Deutschland* since her maiden voyage. The ship's Fourth Officer, Otto Tramultz, had distinguished himself some years earlier as one of the members of the German expedition to the North Pole aboard the *Germania*—this ship was later wrecked off the English coast. Of the three pilots on board the *Deutschland*, two had to negotiate the tricky Weser estuary, and the third to take the ship from the Nab light up Southampton Water to her first and only port of call en route for New York. The English pilot was Charles Dore Harvey, making his 121st trip as a pilot on a run such as this. On this occasion, both of the Weser pilots had opted to stay aboard once off duty, and travel as passengers as far as Southampton, where the ship was due to take on board more passengers and the English mail for New York—a job that North German Lloyd had done for fourteen years. On leaving her home port, the *Deutschland* was described as being 'moderately, not deeply, laden, having room for about 600 or 700 tons more of cargo'.

The grave of the drowned nuns in St Patrick's Roman Catholic Cemetery, Leytonstone, photographed shortly after the funeral. *Franciscan Sisters, Daughters of the Sacred Hearts of Jesus and Mary*

Above: The first Salzkotten mother house, established in March 1863. *Franciscan Sisters*

Above right: The barn which served as the nuns' chapel in the early days at Salzkotten. *Franciscan Sisters*

Below: Mother Clara Pfaender. *Franciscan Sisters*

Below right: The cathedral at Paderborn, in whose diocese the Salzkotten foundation was situated. *Franciscan Sisters*

The second mother house in Salzkotten, shortly after completion in October 1872. *Franciscan Sisters*

The interior of the church built for the second mother house. *Sean Street*

Conrad Martin, Bishop of Paderborn. *Franciscan Sisters*

In addition to the five nuns from Salzkotten, the other 108 passengers comprised some Americans going home, and a Russian family, but mainly German emigrants bound for a new life in the New World. It was not long before a number of friendships between passengers of various nationalities were struck up. As the *Deutschland* stood at the quayside, Adolf Hermann, a young German travelling on his own to Cincinnati, had met Anna Petzold, eighteen years old, born in Germany but living with her parents in New York. She was going home after visiting her sister and brother-in-law in Bremen, and as she was also travelling alone, her relations, having met Adolf and feeling him a man to be trusted, asked him to watch over Anna during the voyage. There was also a Swede, Olaf Lundgren, travelling second class; he had recently had a narrow escape when he had sailed on the ill fated *Schiller*, which had gone down with heavy loss of life off the Scillies.

Up until recent months, the shipping line had enjoyed a booming trade—and this was not due only to people's need to escape persecution, as in the case of the Salzkotten sisters. It was a time of social expansion in Europe, with the Industrial Revolution encouraging many to travel more, in pursuit of pleasure or of work opportunities. Travel was the keynote of the age, with rail and sea transport pushing back or demolishing geographical barriers. In the twenty years between 1850 and 1870 the amount of railway track in existence rose from less than five thousand miles, most of it in Britain and America, to just under half a million— and 176,000 miles of that were in Europe. Not far behind in terms of growth was shipping, fuelled by the recent developments in steamship engineering; it was this that made transatlantic trade and travel viable for the first time for many people.

Thre was a new middle class at the hub of the economy, and education had become a growth industry. There were many who were either displaced or galvanised into mobility by the sweeping social changes in Germany—and not solely because of religious differences. Some felt dissatisfied by the lifestyle brought about by the growth of the new European urban world: towns had become factory civilisations. Governments had begun to export their proletariats as part of a policy of developing colonialism. The desire to escape the old life had combined with the fast-growing nineteenth-century European lust for exploration and exploitation of other parts of the world. By 1870 huge areas of the globe were under the control of one or other of the major European powers.

It is an ironic fact that, while Catholics in Germany were enduring the Kulturkampf, the North American Indians were going through their own crisis of displacement at the hands of European emigrants. In 1876, while the St Louis mission was consolidating its position at Carondelet, elsewhere in the United States the Plains Indians under Sitting Bull were defeated, and white settlers moved into the Midwest up to the Rocky Mountains. The end of the North American Indians as a race with a traditional heritage of territory came ten years later with the abolition of tribal land.

Everywhere, it seemed, an expanding world brought its human cost. Goods as well as people made the journeys, as the export and travel bonanza continued from its European centre, for manufacturers and financiers were amassing the great fortunes that were to result from the advent of truly international trade. But undoubtedly the most dramatic symptom of this mobility—in that it spread colonial pretentions and developed a more cosmopolitan society nearly everywhere—was emigration. True, at the time that Sister Henrica and her sisters made their journey, the trade was quiet; of North German Lloyd's twenty-five transatlantic ships only seven were making the crossing, whereas in better times the company had had thirteen vessels regularly plying the Atlantic between Bremerhaven and New York alone, with a further six crossing from the German port to Baltimore, and six more between Bremen and New Orleans. But the lull in transatlantic trade in the early 1870s was a temporary one, occasioned by a period of uncertainty in Europe. The fact remains that between 1850 and 1914 more than forty million people left the Continent, most of them heading for America, Latin America and Canada.

Most passengers on board emigrant ships such as those operated by North German Lloyd travelled steerage class rather than first or second cabin class—most, but not all. And among the second-cabin-class passengers aboard the *Deutschland* were the Salzkotten travellers. Cabin passengers enjoyed a certain amount of comfort, privacy and luxury, and for the sisters it was a justifiable indulgence. They would have received reports from the sisters who had gone before them as to the conditions they were likely to encounter; they had already travelled some ninety miles to Bremen from Salzkotten, weighed down with the sadness of their parting from their Reverend Mother and the other sisters of the congregation. Ahead lay the tedium of a long and inevitably unpleasant Atlantic December sea crossing, to be followed by another tiresome overland journey to Carondelet. Perhaps, as they boarded the *Deutschland*, they reflected on the fact that the River Weser, about to bear them towards the open sea, was a Westphalian river that flowed through towns and villages not far from Salzkotten.

The weather as they drew away from the Bremerhaven quay at 3.30pm on that Saturday was fine. The passengers, some waving happily, others with tears in their eyes at leaving the fatherland, watched the docks of Bremerhaven on either side of the river slip past. Captain Brickenstein had had bad reports of the weather ahead, and for a time the ship stayed moored in the river before proceeding towards the sea. She soon got under way again, but shortly afterwards mist began to build up, and the pilot needed all his skill to put the ship into open water. By the time the Weser estuary began to widen around the *Deutschland* the mist was becoming an impenetrable fog, and when the pilot handed back control to Brickenstein, the Captain decided it was unsafe to continue: he would anchor for the night. And there at the mouth of the Weser through the Saturday night the *Deutschland* stayed. It must have been another trying hold-up for already homesick passengers, knowing that Germany was still so close at hand.

As Sunday 5th December dawned, the weather changed again —dramatically. The fog had now gone, blown away by a north-easterly gale which cut the sea up into a rough grey switchback, giving the passengers a distressing lesson in what being at sea could mean. Flurries of snow fell at intervals. None the less, at about 7.30 that morning Captain Brickenstein decided to press forward, perhaps reasoning that a moving ship is less at the mercy of the waves than a static one. The First Officer August Lauenstein, remembered the ship moving forward, with a 'stiff north-easterly breeze'.

At 9.30am the *Deutschland* passed the key buoy, the point where the Weser gives way to the open sea. Moving away from the river now, Brickenstein steered for the Borkum lightship—a westerly course. 'As she left the river she was making about twelve knots, and she more or less retained that speed through Sunday.' Eyewitnesses stated later that she passed the lightship at a distance of just under a mile on her port side. The time was half past one on Sunday 5th December.

But Brickenstein was soon confronted by infinitely worse conditions, and the gale increased, bringing with it more driving snow, this time continuous. Once again visibility fell, and the Captain became navigationally blind. Yet he knew these waters well— surely well enough to realise that he must steer his ship out into the North Sea into the deep middle channel to the south. To cling to the Dutch coast in the vain hope of shelter would be to court the disaster of running aground on one of the treacherous shoals which lay off shore. But how far to go? Part of the answer would be given in the soundings taken as the ship progressed; anything under twenty fathoms meant he must be off course. The *Deutschland* had hugged the coast of Holland as closely as her Captain had dared, but now, off the island of Vlieland, Brickenstein was steering a south-westerly course.

Throughout Sunday conditions deteriorated, and by nightfall the gale-force winds had increased still further, bringing driving snow. Brickenstein's own word for the weather at this time is simple but eloquent: 'thick' is what he was to call it, at the Harwich inquest hearing. It was a word that was echoed by others present at the time—and one used regularly by mariners from the east coast of England to describe precisely the weather he was experiencing on the *Deutschland*. Progress was inevitably agonisingly—but, as it transpired, deceptively—slow, and conditions for the passengers at this time can only be guessed at. Perhaps the Captain believed himself to be too close to the Dutch shoreline, and so continued to drive the ship in the dead straight south-westerly course in an effort to reach the relative safety of open water. Lauenstein, First Officer, remembered Brickenstein's conversations with him at this time:

> The Captain spoke to me on deck about the course of the vessel. He spoke about the wind and the weather. He sent me down to look at the chart. He told me to look at the chart after every watch—about every four hours. We thought we were off Terschelling* about 4 o'clock. I spoke to the Captain

* Another of the islands off the coast of Holland.

about it . . . He said he thought we were about eighteen
miles off. The snow was not falling very thickly at this point;
sometimes you could see the lights of passing vessels. No
suggestion was made by myself or the pilot that we should
follow a different course.

None of the inquiries, at which Brickenstein was present, ever
successfully cleared up the mystery of the fact that by the early
hours of Monday 6th December the *Deutschland* was hopelessly
lost on one of the most dangerous seas in the world. As conditions
worsened, the gales and snows were joined by a deadly ally: a
devastatingly powerful current that pulled all with it as if towards
some storm-driven vortex. Those attempting to navigate the
Deutschland would have realised by now that, wherever the ship
was, there was little they could do that would have any real reffect
on her direction. The truth of the matter was that she was beating
a course almost diagonally across the North Sea, heading for the
east coast of England where, some thirty miles out, close to the
northern approaches to the Thames estuary, lay waters notorious
for their deadly sandbanks.

These sandbanks are grimly obvious on a sea chart. Sadly, with
snow and fog blinding both himself and his look-outs, Brickenstein would have seen little similarity between a chart and the
reality he was facing that night. The Thames estuary banks, running roughly parallel to the coast, reach out into the North Sea
like long fingers. Nearest to the shore is the Gunfleet, a sandbank
that dries out at low water and is visible from Clacton and Walton
on the Naze, on the Essex coast. Next come the Barrow sandbank,
the Sunk Sand and the Long Sand. Beyond all of these, some
thirty miles off shore, lies the Kentish Knock. With the exception
of Galloper, it is the outermost shoal at the mouth of the Thames,
bleak and remote in the fairest weather, while in gales the con-
flicting currents form a maelstrom in which, at depth of a mere
fathom or so at low water, a ferocious sea will pound a ship to
pieces in no time. Indeed, these remotest sandbanks stretching far
out into the North Sea form a network of treachery which has
regularly claimed the lives of unwary travellers. In 1826 J. W.
Norie published his *New and Extensive Sailing Directions for the
Navigation of the North Sea*, in which he referred to these 'dangerous shoals, namely, the Inner and Outer Gabbards, the Falls, the

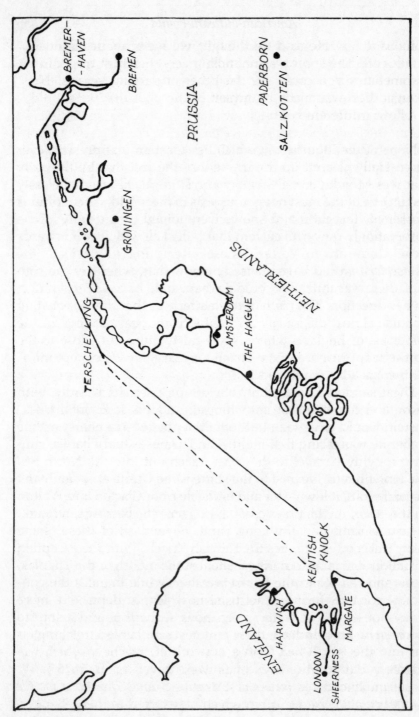

The North Sea, showing intended and actual courses of the SS *Deutschland*.
Jemma Street

Long Sand, and Kentish Knock; the two latter may be considered
to be connected with the sands that so greatly impede the
entrance to the Thames, but the others are separated, and lie at
a considerable distance from them.'

As she proceeded in what was now approaching a force 10
storm, the *Deutschland* must have passed very close to—and probably between—the Inner and Outer Gabbard sands, and Galloper. Had she struck any of these distant banks, the catastrophe
that was soon to come would without doubt have been worse,
even, than it was. Just how narrow the margin of error was—and
is—for navigators may be judged by another glance at Norie's
observations:

> The Galloper is a very dangerous shoal, having in some
> places, not more than six feet of water; it extends 5½ miles
> N.E. and S.W., and is not a mile across at the broadest part,
> which is near the middle . . . The Channel between the Gal-
> loper and the Long Sand Head is about 10 miles wide, and
> has from 20 to 17 fathoms in it. On the east side of the Gal-
> loper are 12, 16, 18, and 20 fathoms, at 3 miles distance are
> 27 fathoms coarse sand with small dark stones; near to the
> south end are 14 fathoms, the ground stoney; about three-
> quarters of a mile without the north end are 14 fathoms, with
> coarse stones; and close to this end are 9, 8, and 7 fathoms.

For any vessel striking such a shoal, on a night like that of 5th–6th
December 1875, the end would indeed be swift.

At 4.00am on Monday 6th December the *Deutschland* stopped
to take soundings, and then was put on half speed. The English
pilot, Harvey, went on deck at this point and joined the Captain
on the bridge. Captain Brickenstein's own account of these last
hours shows a master and crew in a state of increasing confusion,
as, unknown to them, the Kentish Knock sandbank loomed ahead
of them. The accounts all agree, though, that the Master of the
Deutschland kept cool:

> Every two hours, soundings were taken, and between
> 4.00am and 5.00am we cast the lead three times. From
> 4.00am, also, we went half speed. (At half speed we should
> have been going at about 9½ knots an hour.) The lead was

cast about five or seven minutes before the ship struck, and we then found seventeen fathoms of water.'

It was Lauenstein who, as First Officer, was in charge of casting the lead, and he confirmed this account exactly. He had seen Brickenstein on the bridge throughout the night, staring out into the blinding storm and the fog. Whenever a steamer took soundings, the engines would be cut and she would heave to. Effectively, therefore, she would be drifting at such times, and so it was at this point that the lead was cast for the last time:

Soon afterwards, at a little after five o'clock, we saw the breakers. I don't think we had gone two miles after casting the lead when we saw the breakers. The vessel had no sails set, she was under steam alone. There were at that time four look-out men on the bridge and two in the bow, but the weather was so thick that they were of little use. When we took the last cast of the lead, the vessel was stopped, and was merely drifting with the wind.

After this last attempt, Lauenstein had joined the Captain, shortly before the breakers were sighted, indicating the presence of a sandbank.

Ironically, the *Deutschland* must have passed close to the Knock Edge light, the warning beacon for the sands, and probably left it on her port side. A light was seen, but was misinterpreted—and anyway, it was too late, since Captain and look-outs alike were blinded and helpless. It must have been only a minute or two before Brickenstein understood the full gravity of their situation: 'Then we saw the breakers. I immediately ordered the steamer to go at full speed astern, but had hardly given the order when the screw broke, and the vessel was left at the mercy of the wind and the waves. Then she struck on the sands. It was then high tide.' The First Officer agreed:

I saw him telegraph into the engine room, 'Full speed astern'. There were a few revolutions of the screw afterwards, but then it broke. The screw did not last long enough to influence the course of the ship, and she was really drifting ahead when she struck. The wind was right astern. Her headway

was not stopped, and after twice touching gently she struck
the sand. The screw did not break by touching the sand; it
broke while the vessel was still moving ahead. If the screw
had not given way, she might have been saved.

The allegation that the propeller sheared at this crucial point was
borne out by the chief engineer of the *Deutschland*, Rheinhold
Schmidt, who had served on the ship for four or five years. He was
in the engine room at the time she struck. Schmidt's timetable of
events, however, seems to be rather different from Brickenstein's:
'The propeller broke about a quarter of an hour before the ship
struck; the engines had to be reversed, and were working about
four minutes astern before the propeller broke. I can think of no
reason for this to have happened. Later, Schmidt added that he
believed the propeller had struck something. The moment of disaster was easy for him to spot: suddenly, no longer emitting their
normal regular rumbling tone, the engines started to race. An
engineer of his experience would have read all too easily the signal
that that change in sound was sending him.
   The breaking of the propeller was not an unusual occurrence
at the time, and was usually attributed to metal fatigue. As we
have noted, this was a replacement propeller for the one the ship
had lost earlier the same year. As a direct result of the *Deutschland*
disaster, measures were to be taken which would ultimately lead
to the introduction of twin screws—a piece of technology that
might well have saved Brickenstein's ship, had he had it. Some
fourteen years previously, the breaking of the screw had nearly
sealed the fate of Brunel's giant *Great Eastern* as she floundered
out of control three hundred miles off Cork in Ireland, en route
from Liverpool to New York. The *Great Eastern* was many times
bigger than the *Deutschland*—double the length—and could
carry an astonishing four thousand passengers, and in addition
to her single screw she carried sail and paddles. Two critical
factors of difference between the *Great Eastern* experience and
that of the *Deutschland* were, first, that the crew of the Brunel
ship knew where they were, and second they were not stranded
aground.
   Brickenstein claimed that he had not expected to make Galloper, the outermost shoal, until six-thirty that morning, so the
fact that he struck a sandbank at five was evidence, if evidence

were needed, of how far he was out in his reckoning. The one piece of navigational technology that would have been available to him at this time was not carried by the *Deutschland*. This was the patent log, a device which, trailed in the wake of a vessel, gave an indication of the number of miles travelled—although, as both Captain and First Officer agreed, in the circumstances even this would have been useless. August Lauenstein recalled:

> We didn't know where we were when we saw the breakers. Snow was falling and the weather was very thick. As to the patent log, you can't use it when you're heaving the lead every quarter of an hour, because the line would foul the propeller. We had an English pilot on board, but he was not in his own waters, and would have had no knowledge of the navigation where the vessel struck. His duties would not begin till he got into his own waters.

This English pilot, Charles Harvey, was on board to steer the *Deutschland* through the Solent and up Southampton Water, not to negotiate the shoals round the Thames estuary—an area where, after all, the *Deutschland* should never have been anyway. Brickenstein agreed: 'We had an English pilot on board, Mr Harvey, but he did not have charge of the ship. He would only take charge when we made the Nab, and would then take us into Southampton. He was on the bridge at the time we struck, but gave no directions. All directions were given by me.'

Harvey remembered coming up on deck at four o'clock, while the ship was stationary, and taking soundings. And he was present when she struck, an hour later:

> She took the land forward, and slewed round with her port side to the sea. Shortly before she struck, I saw a light [the Knock Edge, presumably], which I took to be a fixed and not a revolving light. The Captain as well as myself was looking out, and we both saw it, but the snow came, and we lost sight of it. We thought it might be the Hinder [a light on the Dutch coast], and at about three miles distance. When we saw it first, it was about two points on the port bow. The head of the vessel was at this point slewed to port. As we

went round we lost sight of it; it was abeam when I last saw it.

Although the Captain, his First Officer and his chief engineer agreed broadly on what had happened, one anonymous witness held a different view regarding the severing of the screw. Quoted in *The Times* two days after the accident, he agreed on most points, but maintained: 'The sea was very rough, blowing hard from the east-north-east, thick with snow. The lead was cast every half-hour. We found 24 fathoms and then 17 fathoms. Immediately afterwards she struck, ship going dead slow. The engines were turned full speed astern, and immediately lost propeller. The ship was then driven further up.' Interestingly enough, it is this account that is most often quoted even though all members of the crew who were directly involved recall otherwise. It would certainly seem that the ship was drifting without power or mechanical means of propulsion at the time of running aground; whenever the propeller went, the result would have been the same.

Driven by the merciless current, the *Deutschland* was now hard aground on the Kentish Knock. Before finally settling, she slewed round with her port side broadside on to the huge seas then running, thus catching the full force of the waves breaking over her. It was high tide, but she was caught, with no means whatever of getting herself off. The crew went below immediately to ensure that everyone was wearing a lifebelt. One seaman recalled that the sea 'washed over us fore and aft, carrying away much of our gear'.

There was nothing the Captain and crew could do but signal for help, and pray that it might come before waves broke the vessel up completely. And given the force of the storm then raging, that would not be very long. She would soon break her back on the sandbank, and thus become a 'dead' ship, unable to rise and fall with the tide. When the next high water occurred, the sea would simply engulf her. Lost as they were, the crew must have had by now some grim understanding of their general location. Without doubt, they had hit a bank far out in the North Sea, but still far to the West of their intended position. The navigational works available at the time would have enabled them to make a short list of the possible shoals upon which they could have foundered. Norie's *Navigation of the North Sea* was already fifty years old by the time of the wreck, but it was still broadly accurate in its stark description of the bank that had in fact claimed the *Deutschland*:

> The Kentish Knock is a dangerous and extensive shoal, lying in nearly a S.W. and N.E. direction, its length being 6½ miles, and its broadest or middle part 2 miles . . . Close to the south-eastern side of the sand, which is steep-to, are 5,6,8, and 9 fathoms, the ground generally soft and muddy; very near its northern extremity are 10 and 11 fathoms, and between it and the Long Sand 8,9,10 and 11 fathoms; there is a passage between it and the Long Sand two and three quarter miles wide, but no vessel will attempt to run through without the greatest necessity.

A glance at a map of this area of the North Sea will show the remoteness of the Kentish Knock: south-east of Harwich and almost due north of Margate, it is nearly twenty miles from the nearest point on the English coast. But even this is misleading, for between the Knock and land in almost every direction are other deadly shoals, and deceiving currents to go with them, so that distances in nautical miles taken as the crow flies may bear little relation to the tortuous route the navigator of any sizeable vessel would have to take to reach the Kentish Knock.

The nearest of these banks to the *Deutschland* was the Long Sand, which Norie identified as separated from the Knock by just under three miles of deeper water. Had the ship refloated, Brickenstein would have found himself within this narrow corridor; thus, even had the *Deutschland* not stuck fast, there is a strong likelihood that she would have ultimately come to grief on the well named Long Sand itself. On modern navigational maps of the area there is, even today, a wreck symbol on the edge of this channel, on the western side of the Kentish Knock, close to the very spot where the *Deutschland* foundered. The shoal has continued to take its toll. Thirty years after the wreck and eighty years after Norie, the *Admiralty North Sea Pilot* still gave an awesome picture of the Knock, for all its matter-of-fact language:

> Kentish Knock, a dangerous sand bank south-eastward of Long Sand, and separated from it by a channel named Knock

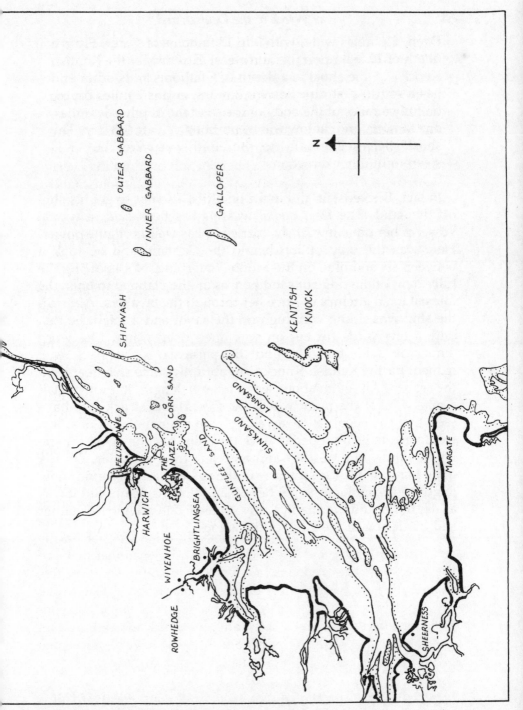

The Thames Estuary, showing sandbanks. *Jemma Street*

Deep, 2½ miles wide, with 9 to 13 fathoms of water. From a depth of 10 feet upon the north-east extremity of the Kentish Knock . . . the shoal to a depth of 5 fathoms at its other end has a south-west direction for 7 miles, and is 2 miles broad; on fully 4 miles of the body of the sand the depth is less than one fathom, and, at low water, portions of it are left dry. The shoal shelves gradually to the south-westward, but it is steep-to in other directions.

In fact, Brickenstein did make one final attempt to get his ship off the sand. The *Deutschland* was, as has been said, a typical vessel of her time, in that she carried sail as well as engine power. Here was the only option left to the Captain, and he took it between six and nine on the Monday morning. Not knowing the full extent of the ridge of sand he was on, he planned to hoist the foresail in an attempt to force her through the breakers. After all, the ship was sitting very high on the sand, and it might be that only a few yards further on was open deep water. The word 'knock' is Celtic for 'hill', and this particular sandbank is well named, for the Kentish Knock rises abruptly some sixty feet from the seabed. Although about seven miles in length, it is only a half a mile wide at the point where the *Deutschland* struck. We have seen that the shoal fell away sharply on several of its sides; this would create its own perils, once the ship was damaged, for she might simply slip off the sand and sink in deep water. On the other hand, while the structure of the vessel was still sound, now might be the moment to get her off and floating again. But it was a false hope, and the attempt only succeeded in driving her higher and harder on to the edge of the Knock.

5 At the Mercy of the Waves

The first rockets were fired from the *Deutschland* at 5.15 on that Monday morning, almost as soon as she struck. By the time daylight came, however, the powder was wet and the guns would not fire. Those on board could only hope that someone, somewhere, had seen their distress signals, and would, when the storm abated, come to their aid. In the meantime, they must try to ride out the storm. Because of the lack of visibility, which had made it impossible for Brickenstein to see the warning light marking the Kentish Knock, he could not have known, either, that he was relatively close to two lightships, the Sunk and the Cork. But the Kentish Knock, nearly thirty miles from the east coast of England, would have been a bleak and lonely place in such conditions, and hopes of a signal reaching shore would have seemed forlorn indeed.

Meanwhile, Brickenstein seems to have made another questionable decision: he apparently gave an order to attempt the launching of some of the ship's lifeboats. This was foolhardy indeed—and, as he himself recalled, in the event, disastrous: 'One of the boats was cast off and dashed away by the sea soon after we struck. Three others were stove in.' According to an eyewitness, one of the boats, 'in [the] charge of the Fourth Officer [Otto Tramultz] contained seven or eight persons, while the other contained Quartermaster [August] Beck and only three or four persons. But both filled.'

The boat that had been 'dashed away by the sea', according to Brickenstein, and which the other witness said contained 'three or four persons' plus Quartermaster Beck, in fact contained just two others: a male passenger and a seaman called Forsenstein. Miraculously, this boat was to survive the storm and reach Sheerness after some thirty hours in the water, coming ashore at Garrison Point. Sadly, of the three men, only Beck, a married man from Bremerhaven with two young children, lived to tell the tale:

> In the morning, the ship being about to break up as we thought, the Captain told us to lower the lifeboats. I and two seamen got into one, but in lowering it the heavy seas twice capsized it, and we were each time thrown into the water. We managed to get back into the boat, which righted, but were dismayed at finding ourselves adrift, as the rope fastening us to the ship had broken. We endeavoured to pull back to the ship, but were not strong enough in the heavy lifeboat to make headway against the raging sea. The last I saw of the ship they were endeavouring to launch all the boats. The sea was very wild at the time, and the ship laboured heavily. I got up a small sail, and drifted before the wind, but my two mates were soon helpless because of the blinding snow and the piercing cold. One died the same night and the other the next morning. On the Monday I saw several ships and made distress signals, but none came near me. On the Tuesday morning I passed a lightship and called out again, but I suppose they did not hear me. I saw a light on shore, and luckily I managed to steer my boat to it.

Beck was later to add that at the time the order to man the boats was given there was considerable panic among the passengers, particularly the women, and there followed a wild rush to get into the lifeboats, of which the *Deutschland* had ten. After the failure to launch them, clearly, Brickenstein had thought better of it and ordered the passengers back. As a crewman recalled: 'No other boats were launched, the sea being too rough, but the rest were kept in readiness. Ultimately, however, the sea stove in and washed overboard all of the boats.'

Something of the force of the storm may be gathered from the fact that the rope that Beck reported as having snapped would have been a good three inches thick. When the boat had then drifted away, the sailing gear had remained intact. There were, however, no provisions on board of any kind. One of the other men in the boat, the passenger, had injured his head on a hoist as he jumped into the boat, and it was he who was the first to succumb to the cold, his injury reducing his resistance still further. He died at about three o'clock on the Monday afternoon. With just the two of them now in the boat, August Beck recalled doing all he could to keep up the spirits of his companion, seaman Forsenstein, and he advised him to move about to keep his blood circulating. He also tried to cheer him by telling him that they were near land, massaging him with what strength he had, to warm him up. He later remembered those fearful hours, in a graphic account of his battle to keep Forsenstein conscious:

> He was a youngish man, and hadn't got inured to the hard-ships of the sea. I coaxed and bullied him to move, so as to keep the blood going in his veins, but all to no purpose. He dropped down at my feet, looking up in my face with a dumb, helpless expression that gave me a chill all through, for I knew it meant nothing but death coming. I tried my best to warm him, but I dared not leave my post for the purpose; so there he lay, and never stirred, and I only knew he was dead when the boat gave a lurch to leeward and he rolled over, so that I caught sight of the sharpened features and open, lifeless eyes. The night was coming on, and I could not sight land anywhere, and the cold was something awful.

The tiny boat was first seen by an artilleryman on sentry duty at the naval barracks in Sheerness. The sighting was made at about six o'clock on the Tuesday morning, when the man, looking seaward over the parapet of the fort, saw a boat beating against the beach at the foot of the barracks. It was dark, and the sentry thought at first that the little vessel was empty. Nevertheless, he raised the alarm, and he and two other men went down to the shore, and found Beck and his companions. The two dead men were huddled in the bow of the boat, half clad, one wearing only a coat and a pair of canvas trousers. Both corpses were almost black with exposure to the cold and the salt water. The living man was crouched in the stern, and answered questions feebly in broken English. He was lifted gently from the boat, and carried to the infirmary. The corpses were taken to the barracks stables, and thence to the Duke of Clarence Hotel at Sheerness, pending an official inquest. Beck ruefully remembered that before the ship had sailed, 'my wife did say she believed we were going to make an unlucky voyage of it'.

Beck seems to have become something of a local celebrity in Sheerness; while he was recuperating at the barracks hospital there, he was showered with gifts from members of the public and treated as a hero. Seamen and townspeople made a collection for him, and W. H. Vile, Master of Arms of the royal naval barracks, presented him with the sum of £13 raised by the Captain, officers and men, while residents of the town provided a further £7. Beck was so touched and delighted with his reception that, even after he had been declared fit by the doctors, he delayed his departure from Sheerness so as to spend more time with his new comrades.

To return to the stranded vessel. From the accounts of several passenger witnesses, the first thing that many knew of something unusual happening was a loud grinding, cracking noise. It was thought at one point that this was the sound of the ship striking the sand, but in fact it was the screw breaking—in other words, it was the sound they heard before she struck. Many passengers came on deck, having hurriedly dressed, to find out what was going on. However, there seemed at first to be no real cause for alarm. The crew were calm, and there was a lightship just two miles off. Brickenstein and his crew assured their charges that there was nothing they could do; these assurances, added to the cold and the wet, persuaded people to return below decks.

By daybreak on Monday the seas were breaking over the ship alarmingly, and, having jettisoned some cargo, Brickenstein set as many men as possible to working the pumps. Most of the cargo that was shed at this point seems to have been taken from the foreholds by the crew, assisted by male passengers. The intention was to lighten the bows, in the hope of making it possible for Brickenstein to swing the *Deutschland* into the wind, thereby avoiding the danger caused by the ship taking broadside the full strength of the gale and the high-running seas. Later the jettisoned cargo began to come ashore: at Kingsgate, between Margate and Broadstairs on the Kent coast, three hundred and sixty cases of gloves were washed up, and near Herne Bay a case of silk; also, a poignant note in a bottle, cast overboard shortly after the ship struck: 'We are ashore one hour, every minute terrific thumping. One boat and passengers already gone. D. J. Behring, Mrs Behring, Bremerhaven. I believe we are lost. I depart in peace with my God, and without anxiety. Love to friends, children and mother-in-law. D. J. Behring.' In the list of survivors, Mr Behring's name appears; Mrs Behring's does not.

As the morning of Monday 6th December progressed, the weather improved somewhat. It became clear, although still very cold. In spite of this, a good spirit seems to have prevailed on board, with passengers and crew enjoying some good-natured banter as they worked on the pumps. The *Deutschland* carried a complement of three steam-pumps and five hand-pumps, and all were now working at full stretch, with the men joking about who was the fittest among them and the ablest at operating the hand-pumps. Indeed, it appears that at one point there was almost a party atmosphere, as copious amounts of food and drink were served and the look-outs scanned the horizon for signs of approaching help. After all, it was only a matter of time before they would be rescued, surely? They were close to the main shipping lanes on one of the busiest routes in the world. In fact, several passing vessels were seen, at least two of them steamers of not inconsiderably size. Every method was used to attract their attention.

At about 11.00am a steamer was sighted. When they first saw her, she was four or five miles away, to the south-east. It appeared that she had been attracted by guns firing from the lightship, and she was now bearing down on her rapidly. Then, for no apparent reason, something happened to change the mind of the strange ship's captain. She had come to within half a mile of the scene, soon she would be close enough to see in detail, and yet now, with the raging seas breaking over her, she was turning away. And not a single sign of recognition! Was she a passenger ship or a cargo vessel? It had been impossible to say. The ship vanished over the horizon.

Within an hour, another vessel came within sight of the *Deutschland*—a brig this time, driving between the Kentish Knock and the Long Sand. For three hours they watched her beating about; at one point she appeared to be picking something up: perhaps it was one of the *Deutschland*'s boats that had broken free? But she did not approach the wreck. It transpired later that the brig was the *Ino* of Newhaven, on her way to Weymouth under her master, Captain Thomas Key, with a cargo of deal. Having made the Haisborough Light off Cromer on the Norfolk coast, she had steered a course that she hoped would take her clear of the Kentish Knock. But being a light vessel and standing high out of the water, the wind had taken a hold of her, driving her to the west into the deadly waters between the Long Sand and the Kentish Knock, through which 'no vessel will attempt to run . . . without the greatest necessity'. As the early winter dusk approached, she too moved away and out of sight. No communication had been received from the brig throughout the three hours of her close proximity to the stricken steamer.

Another night was looming on the Knock for the *Deutschland*. Notwithstanding the strenuous efforts of the men on the pumps, she was still shipping water, and Brickenstein feared that if she were to slip astern off the bank now, instead of floating off she might go down like a stone. With this in mind, he cast both his anchors. The ship was safe—for the moment. Yet the Captain realised that the coming night, with a rising tide and the weather closing in again, would bring the greatest threat. Having taken on so much water, she would not rise with the tide, and as the sea came up, she would be engulfed. He must attract attention to the plight of his vessel. The rockets and most of the signal guns's powder was fairly dry, so by five o'clock, as the darkness intensified, the crew were able to launch more distress signals. Everyone watched as flair after flair rose, burst and fell. They waited.

Then, at precisely twenty past five, a shout went up. There to the south-east of them came an answering rocket! It was the Sunk lightship. And then came another, more distant flair, from the Cork lightship, nearer to shore. In turn—although the passengers and crew of the *Deutschland* would probably not have seen it— came a third acknowledgement, this one from the coastguard station at Harwich. In fact, the lightships had known that a vessel was in trouble on the Kentish Knock for some time. All day they had been firing maroons to alert possible rescuers of the emergency, but such was the screaming of the gale that it would have carried away the warning sounds. Now, with the return of darkness, the rockets' visual rather than their audible aspect came into play. Perhaps, after more than twelve hours grounded in this terrible place, here at last was hope for those aboard the *Deutschland*! Indeed, that very evening two Great Eastern steamers, the *Claud Hamilton* and the *Richard Young*, bound for

Rotterdam and Antwerp respectively, *did* leave Harwich. But what the people on the *Deutschland* did not know was that Harwich had no lifeboat.

The night came on, and the seas rose. The *Deutschland*, on the west edge of the Kentish Knock, was lying bow down, stern up, and Brickenstein could see that at high water she would be wallowing in four fathoms; her stern would be some five feet clear, but her bow would be completely submerged. Anyone below decks would have little hope of survival. The Captain had no choice; he gave orders for the hatches to be battened down, and at 2.00am on Tuesday 7th December, in spite of the worsening conditions, he ordered all passengers to come on deck. Now the class system of first-cabin, second-cabin and steerage passengers was forgotten. Many, from all classes, were already gathered in the aft saloon, which was still clear of the water. Most of them now answered the summons and came up to face the biting cold, their only real hope of surviving the night. According to Brickenstein's statement at the inquest, the rear saloon filled with water an hour later, and for anyone left inside there could be no hope. And not everyone obeyed his order. Some, such as those already severely weakened by their ordeal, felt unable to move, and convinced that death would come to them all anyway, resolved to stay below and meet it without a struggle.

By now, word had reached various points, among them Ramsgate on the Kent coast. At six o'clock on the Monday evening a small fishing smack had sighted the *Deutschland*—or at least a light that the captain believed to come from a ship. But the weather was so appalling, that he dared not investigate. Instead, he sailed on towards his home port, arriving at Ramsgate at about 9.30pm. He told the watchman at Ramsgate what he had seen, and then reported to the harbour master that rockets were going up from the Kentish Knock. What he omitted to say was that he had seen a ship too. The harbour master did nothing. Later he stated that the cruising ground for the Ramsgate lifeboat was the Goodwin Sands, and that the Kentish Knock was out of their area. He recalled that in seventeen years of service, the Ramsgate boat had been called to the Knock only seven times, and several of those occasions had been wild goose chases. In the event, given the distance it would have had to travel, the Ramsgate lifeboat would probably have been too late.

On the *Deutschland*, the situation was rapidly descending into nightmare. The deck structures offered few places of refuge; as many passengers as possible crowded into the wheel-house. One survivor, Hermann Egner, remembered that from the relative security of the rigging he had watched the number on deck decreasing with every heavy wave that broke over the ship. Like Egner, most of the crew and some of the stronger emigrants climbed into the rigging, where they found a degree of safety as long as their numbed hands could maintain a grip in the fierce cold. As Brickenstein said, for many people this was not very long: 'Many fell off, chiefly from cold and exposure, and some of the bodies were swept through the broken glass into the cabins.' Among the first to fall was the ship's purser, Benning. Although a strong man, he was fatigued by the long hours of ceaseless struggle, and at about 3.00am on the Tuesday he was seen to fall silently into the sea.

One second-class cabin passenger, George Sauer, saw a young steward fall from the rigging: 'He must have struck something, for I saw him swim with his head under water and away from instead of towards the ship. His chum ran down and called to him, 'Swim this way!', but he took no heed, and soon sank out of sight.'

Sauer's story, which was confirmed by others—as well as Brickenstein's and Egner's—tells graphically of the rapid deterioration in conditions that led passengers to take to the rigging. As early as 3.30pm on the Monday, steerage passengers had begun coming into the main saloon, reporting that their quarters were filling with water.

About 12.30 Tuesday morning I saw that the ship was filling very fast . . . I got up on to a table and from there into a skylight, and sat waiting. The nuns were sitting below me on the table. All at once a window burst open on my left and a deluge of water flooded the cabin. About 2.30am, when the water in the cabin was a foot higher than the tables, the steward said to me, 'It's about time to get out of this.' I looked at the skylight, and found that a covering of canvas prevented it from being opened. I told the steward to take out his knife and cut the cover. He did so, and we were the first to get out. I was washed across the deck by a wave, and then I looked up to the masts and asked if there was any room there. I got no answer, and thinking 'It's every man for himself', I clung to the mainmast, which was crowded. All this time there were fearful cries from the first cabin, and I could see those who came out of the skylight being washed off into the ocean. It was cold—dreadfully cold.

Passengers and crew were being washed from one end of the deck to the other, then swept off into the boiling sea. At one point a sailor tried to save a drowning child. Secured by a rope, he climbed down from his safe position in the rigging towards the child. As he reached the deck, a huge wave dashed him against the bulwarks of the ship, decapitating him. In the grey light of morning, his headless body, still attached to the rope, was seen swaying to and fro with the waves. Adolf Hermann, the young German whose friendship with Anna Petzold had in the few days at sea blossomed into a shipboard romance, pulled the eighteen-year-old on to the deck and dragged her up into the rigging. He had found a bottle of whisky below decks, and a sailor near him had some black bread, ham and cheese. It was as they hung there precariously that Benning the purser, who was above them, had lost his grip and plunged to his death, almost taking Anna with him as he fell. His body had hit her shoulder, but Hermann's arm had been firmly round her waist, and she survived.

Hermann later remembered a moment of humour, amid this scene of tragedy and terror. With one arm round Anna and the other hand clinging to the rigging, the task of opening the whisky bottle was not easy. Unable to remove the cork, in the end he solved the problem by knocking the top off the bottle. Now came the challenge of finding Anna's mouth as the ship pitched and rolled in the darkness. After several attempts, he heard her quiet voice below him: 'You're pouring it down my neck!' In the end, they both managed to drink. By now Hermann's feet were in danger of being frost-bitten, and several friends pounded them in an attempt to bring back some feeling.

One man, about to shoot himself, was dissuaded by a woman who told him to be brave and not die a coward's death. Less than five minutes later, she was herself washed overboard. Hermann went on: 'A Swiss who had told me he had lived sixteen years in China was hurled from his perch in the rigging as soon as he arrived there; and a boy forced against the rail had his leg torn off while extricating himself.'

A young passenger from Cleveland, Ohio, one W. Leick, saw that stewards and crew were tying rope around their waists, and decided to do the same. 'There was a steerage passenger sitting on the saloon stairs; he had tied up his bedding, which he thought he could save. I asked him for a piece of the rope, but he refused, so I whipped out my knife and cut a piece away, which I tied round me as the others had done. That piece of rope saved my life.' When the time came to take to the rigging, Leick went up with a man called Theodor Teidemann; several times he seems to have lost consciousness but, having tied himself to the rigging, he did not fall. He recalled looking down and seeing people being washed about: 'One man was in a sitting posture and he was not making any apparent effort to save himself. Perhaps he was dead already. Anyway, he went overboard. I saw two little children swept about in the same way.'

Helplessly, Brickenstein watched the horrific scene all around him. For some it was too much to endure: one man hanged himself behind the wheel-house, and a woman died by the same means below decks. Another man hacked at his wrists with a pen-knife, 'working the knife to and fro in the wound until his strength failed him and he fell down dying'. He had preferred to die a relatively painless death by bleeding. 'The shrieks and sobbing of women and children were agonising,' one survivor remembered later. These cries from the flooding saloon and cabins would have risen up to those in the rigging. At one point, unable to bear it any longer, a sailor leapt 'nimbly down the rigging', reached the poop deck, and attempted to rescue some of the half-drowned people floating about in the saloon. He managed to catch one little child by the clothes, but before he could secure him a wave carried the boy out of his grasp, 'and his shrieks were hushed in the roar of the waters'.

Among those who remained below decks were the nuns from Salzkotten. It was said that they had decided upon this course deliberately, considering that, given the limited space on deck and on the ship's superstructure, there would not be room for everyone, and therefore some must sacrifice themselves. Throughout the emergency, according to the traditional story, they had been occupying themselves in ways appropriate to their calling: caring for the sick and frightened and for the children, praying with the distressed, and generally helping in whatever way they could. Henrica Fassbaender might have thought fleetingly of Mother Clara and of the peaceful gardens at Salzkotten, but realist and leader that she was, she would have quickly erased any such thoughts and got on with the task in hand.

On 11th December, the Harwich correspondent of *The Times* was to report thus the incident that furnished Gerard Manley Hopkins with the inspiration for his ode, 'The Wreck of the Deutschland': 'Five German nuns, whose bodies are now in the dead-house here, clasped hands and were drowned together, the chief sister, a gaunt woman, six feet high, calling out loudly and often, "O Christ, come quickly!" until the end came.' In fact, though, the reality may have been rather different. There is no doubt that, when the order came for all passengers to come on deck, the nuns declined to do so; that *four* of the five were later found drowned in their cabin; and, as we noted earlier, that the fifth, Sister Henrica Fassbaender, was never found. According to one report, when, at about midnight, it was becoming clear that the passengers would have to be brought up on to the deck and into the rigging, Sister Henrica was pulled through a skylight by a member of the crew; but as she was brought up, she fell, and just as she righted herself a colossal wave broke over the wreck, bearing her into the sea. She was never seen again.

Here, however, a certain amount of confusion subsequently arose. A later *Times* report speaks of the four bodies brought ashore: 'One, noted for her extreme tallness, is the lady who, at midnight on Monday, by standing on a table in the saloon, was able to thrust her body through the skylight, and kept exclaiming, in a voice heard by those in the rigging above the roar of the storm, 'My God, my God, make haste, make haste.' Although it has often been accepted that accounts of the incident mainly lead to the conclusion that the 'tall, gaunt nun' and Sister Henrica Fassbaender were one and the same person, the eyewitness accounts cast doubt on this assumption, and it may be that the tall nun was not Sister Henrica at all. The earlier *Times* report which refers to the 'chief sister, a gaunt woman, six feet high' may in fact be wrong, because the account just quoted which mentions the presence of one 'noted for her extreme tallness', was written after the reporter had seen the nuns lying in state.

The reporter from the *Daily News* also saw the bodies after the event, and while their personal identities remained unknown, 'with respect to one there can be no difficulty in the way of identification, for she is of the extraordinary height of six feet two inches. There is another who is five feet ten inches in height, and broad in proportion.' Basing his account on interviews with survivors, this reporter claims that the tall sister is the nun who, 'thrusting her body half-way through the skylight of the wreck, [had added] tenfold to the horrors of the fearful night by crying in a loud voice for the quicker coming of death'. We also have *Times* accounts which support the claim that one of the nuns was pulled through the skylight before being swept away.

Previous accounts of the wreck by the *Daily News* had shown the incident in a rather less heroic light:

> There were five nuns on board who, by their terror-stricken conduct, seem to have added greatly to the weirdness of the scene. They were deaf to all entreaties to leave the saloon, and when, almost by main force, the stewardess (whose conduct was plucky in the extreme) managed to get them on to the companion ladder, they sank down on the steps and stubbornly refused to go another step. They seemed to have returned to the saloon again shortly, for somewhere in the dead of night, when the greater part of the crew and passengers were in the rigging, one was seen with her body half through the skylight, crying aloud in a voice heard above the storm, 'O my God, make it quick! Make it quick!'

This account was reproduced verbatim in the *New York Times*, and it may well be here, in this report, that the answer lies. Leick of Cleveland reported:

> At about one o'clock on Tuesday morning the Doctor came into the saloon and shouted, 'When the water rises all the men must get into the rigging, and the women on the tables or the rafters of the skylights.' Soon afterwards the head

steward came down and called out, 'All on deck!' Most of us
went out, but some persisted in remaining in the cabins and
the main saloon, among them the five nuns. The stewardess
at last induced the Sisters to come up to the entrance of the
companion, but she was herself struck by the sea at this
moment and swept across the deck and back again. The nuns
fled back terrified into the saloon.

Then the stewardess, whom Leick praised for her courage, clut-
ched the grating of one of the skylights and hauled herself up;
and when the water had run off the deck she got on to a seat and
pulled a tarpaulin over herself, staying there all night. One report
states that she succeeded in pulling Sister Henrica through the
skylight, only to lose her to the sea immediately afterwards. The
other nuns, seeing this, retreated again, and it was one of these
who later cried out to her God.

Adolf Hermann knew that the ship contained 'five Roman
Catholic nuns from Paderborn . . . they prayed aloud that God
would send them a speedy death, and so end their misery ['*Ach
Gott! Mach es nur kurz, wenn wir schon sterben müssen!*'].' He
remembered hearing and seeing the nuns in the saloon, and commented on their apparent resignation; one, he recalled, had said,
'Well, it's useless to resist God's decree, I will do nothing.' And
it was Hermann who later heard the tall nun 'shrieking through
the skylight, and when she was silenced the cry was taken up by
a woman wailing from the wheel-house, "My child is drowned,
my little one, Adam."' This may be the child whom the seaman
mentioned earlier had vainly tried to save from the saloon.

Leick remembered 'one of the nuns, a very large woman, with
a voice like a man's . . . half way up through the skylight and
shrieking, "*Mein Gott! mach es schnell mit uns! Ach Christ! mach es
schnell mit uns* [Give us our death quickly]!"'. Later, Leick claimed,
when morning came and the waters receded, he was able to
return to the saloon

to fetch my valise. I wish I had not. The sight was fearful.
Everything was covered with the oil and grease from the
engine room. The five nuns [He clearly states *five* nuns] and
other dead bodies were lying about on the floor. One of the
nuns had been washed into my stateroom and her arm was

lying across my valise. I called to the sailor who had offered
to get it, 'Never mind, don't touch it', but he pulled it out.

Several other reports state that when survivors were able to peer
down into the flooded cabins, they 'saw the nuns floating about,
face upwards, all dead'. On 9th December the *New York Times*,
which wasted no time in obtaining as full a picture of the wreck
as possible, stated: 'At daylight on Tuesday, the five nuns were
seen floating, face upward, dead.' These reports provide us with
another possibility: that all five nuns did indeed die together, but
that one body, that of Sister Henrica Fassbaender, was washed
out of the saloon sometime between the rescue and the return of
salvagers the next day. Accounts spoke of this happening to other
bodies that were later recovered miles from the Kentish Knock,
although many corpses lost in this way were never found.

There is yet another possibility, one that was put forward by
the newspaper *Weser Zeitung* in a report that was later published
in the *Kölnischer Zeitung*. The story—which seems to appear
nowhere else—was evidently written in response to the previous
reports that the nuns had not wanted to leave the saloon, and
that their cries of lamentation had contributed to the horror of the
occasion. This account suggested that those early reports were
false and reflected anti-Catholic feeling, and went on to quote
other examples of liberal papers having prejudicially reported the
actions of Catholic sisters while being quick to report favourably
on those of Protestants. The papers based their story on eyewitness accounts, as did the others, but with a dramatic difference:

> Two members of the ship's crew, one Protestant and one
> Catholic, report that as soon as the order was given to leave
> the ship's rooms, the sisters went straight away on to the
> deck with the other passengers. They heard no specific cry of
> lamentation from them. In fact, one [Sister Henrica?] climbed
> calmly and bravely into the rigging, and nothing more was
> seen of her, so that it is supposed that she fell into the sea,
> as only the bodies of four of the sisters were found in the
> cabin area. These four went back down into the cabin area
> with most of the other women, when conditions on deck
> made it impossible for them to stay there. There was certainly
> hour-long lamentation from the women in the saloon, but it

is ridiculous to speak of a particular wailing from the sisters, as it is much more likely that they remained the calmest of all.

This account, therefore, might even suggest that the famous cry was not made by any of the nuns! And of equal interest is the mention of the nun climbing the rigging, and then being seen no more. The persuasiveness of this argument is undeniable, answering as it does in such a plausible way the question of Henrica Fassbaender's disappearance. It is strange, however that no other eyewitnesses put forward this story.

By eight o'clock on the Tuesday morning, the sea had begun to abate. Wearily those left alive climbed down from the rigging, or emerged from the fragile shelter of deck structures, to which they had clung throughout the night. At about ten, a small vessel was sighted. At first it was thought to be yet another passer-by, but it soon became clear that this time help really was on the way. It was a small steam paddle-tug, the *Liverpool*, captained by a sixty-year-old veteran of these waters called John Carrington. She reached the wreck at 10.30am. The nightmare was all but over.

Carrington had captained the *Liverpool* since her arrival in Harwich from Sunderland four months previously. She was a sixty-horsepower dual-purpose vessel: during the summer months she was to be used for pleasure trips, while in the water she would earn her keep as a tug, doing the job for which she had been built. But the *Liverpool* was not the first vessel to attempt to rescue the *Deutschland*. Since Harwich had no lifeboat, it had long been understood that rescue in these treacherous waters was very much in the hands of local east-coast sailors and fishermen: the fishing smacks and steam-tugs were skilfully mastered by brave men who understood the seas off Harwich as no one else could hope to.

Thus it was that when the first rocket signals reached land on the Monday evening, they were sighted by a smacksman, Henry Mills Cook, who owned a first-class smack from Rowhedge in Essex called the *Aquiline*. Cook nicknamed 'Fud', was a well known east-coast character, with a reputation for making irreverent fun, particularly when it came to outwitting the customs auth-

orities. As late as 1900 he was known to have been involved
in smuggling activities in the Walton Backwaters, up the coast,
between Walton-on-the-Naze and Harwich, and was said to have
got the better of the authorities on one occasion by playing drunk.
Rowhedge boasted a fleet of some eighty smacks, many of which
were involved in the salvage trade up until the 1890s. The long-
evity of the apparently frail little craft was quite remarkable.

The *Aquiline*, though, was one of the largest smacks on the
Colne. For many years she was a familiar sight, lying at Anchor
Quay at Rowhedge, instantly identifiable not only by her size, but
by the distinctive flag fluttering proudly from her high topmast—
a white gamecock on a black ground. At public holidays, festivals
and Sundays, another pennant was added; Margaret Leather,
whose family have been well known on the Colne river for generations, described this in her book *Saltwater Village* as 'a large blue
pennant with a yellow scalloped edge and a white letter 'A' in
the centre of it'. The *Aquiline* was still registered as late as 1919,
although she had been sold away from her Colne River base
during the First World War, and as recently as 1955, according to
Hervey Benham, her rotting hulk was to be seen on Peewit Island
in Pyefleet Creek.

A smack such as the *Aquiline* would have had nothing but sail-
power—mainsail, staysail, jib and topsail – to pit her against the
storm. It was an unequal contest, and in the brave attempt to
reach the wreck, the *Aquiline* sprang her boom and crippled her
mainsail while negotiating the shallow maelstrom over the sands
surrounding the wreck. In the event, she did not come within
sight of the *Deutschland*. To continue would have been sheer folly,
particularly as all that was known at this stage was that something
was aground on one of the outer shoals. Cook found shelter in
Walton Backwaters, where the crew attempted to refit the boom,
but the winds were still ferocious and, reluctantly, they had to
admit defeat. Despite this setback, Harry Cook was determined
to get help. He rowed to the hamlet of Great Oakley, waded
ashore, and set off on the five-mile walk to Harwich.

Wearily he trudged into the town, weighed down by wet
clothes and heavy seaboots, and arrived at the Harwich Coastguard Station only to find that the news had already been received
by telegraph from Sheerness, after the recovery of August Beck.
Nevertheless, Harry Cook had a better idea than anyone else on

land of the location of the distressed ship, and as the crew of the *Liverpool* made ready to put to sea, he was able to pass on this valuable information.

At that time, Harwich had two steam tugs, of which the *Liverpool* was one, both belonging to John Watts who had been mayor of Harwich no less than seven times, and his son, Walter. Walter Watts, and his skipper, John Carrington, who lived in Church Street, Harwich, had reported for rescue duty at the coastguard station on Monday evening. However, conditions, in port as out at sea, were deteriorating fast, and they considered it inadvisable to venture out. It was later suggested that the sixty-year-old Carrington had been overly cautious in his appraisal of the situation, but it must be said in his defence that his decision was probably sound. To take his ship out would have been to risk both vessel and crew. Throughout Monday night, however, Carrington and his crew were not idle, and although it was agreed that the following morning was the earliest time that any effective rescue attempt could be mounted, nevertheless steam was raised and maintained throughout the night.

At the first sign of improvement in the weather, shortly before six o'clock on the Tuesday morning, the *Liverpool* sailed, with John Carrington at the helm and Fud Cook to help with navigation. By first light she had reached the Cork lightship. Carrington was desperately seeking any indication that might send him in the right direction, knowing that for whatever was aground out there, after such a night as this time must now be running out. His account of the search and finding of the *Deutschland* betrays something of his anguish and frustration:

Myself and five hands were on board the whole night, waiting for the slightest lull . . . It was very dark [when] the weather was sufficiently moderate to make any attempt to reach the sands from which the signals were supposed to have been made, and we at once started for the Cork lightship for information. This ship we spoke to and were informed by those on board that the signal was from the Sunk lightship, about seven miles distant. We at once made for and spoke to the Sunk lightship, and were then told that our course should be South by East, as there was a steamship on the Long Sand distant from the Sunk light about five miles. We then proceeded to the Long Sand, without being able to discover any appearance of a vessel, although we made every exertion to do so. The time was now nearly 8 o'clock, and we then continued our course down and round the Long Sand, and made for the Kentish Knock lightship, she having a signal half-mast. We had just at this time discovered a ship on the sand. We spoke to the lightship, and asked if they had the crew of the ship on board their vessel, as we had not seen any person or apparent life on the vessel on the sand, although we had on board (and used) a powerful field glass for that purpose. They informed us that they believed the crew were either on board or had left the ship, as they had not seen anything since the signals, which had ceased late the previous night. We then proceeded down and round the Kentish Knock again, and in between the Knock and the Long Sand, we found the ship.

It was one thing, however, to find the ship, and quite another to get alongside and take off survivors. The sea was still angry and wild, and the risk of smashing the *Liverpool* against the *Deutschland*—or of running aground herself—was high indeed. In the end, John Carrington manoeuvred his tug as close as he dared, and moored in three fathoms. His next move considering the conditions, required great bravery on the part of all concerned. Acting swiftly, he launched the *Liverpool*'s lifeboat:

I gave directions to the engineer and mate, whom I had placed in charge of the boat, that as there appeared to be a large number of women on board, they were to allow only the women to be brought off at first; and the boat at that trip brought nine persons, women and children only. We again sent out the boat, and nine more women were brought on board the 'Liverpool'. I then ordered soundings to be taken off the depth of the water between the wrecked ship and mine, and on the return of the third boatload of women (with one man who jumped in as the boat was leaving), being told that there was still three fathoms of water, I at once took up anchor and lay alongside the wrecked ship.

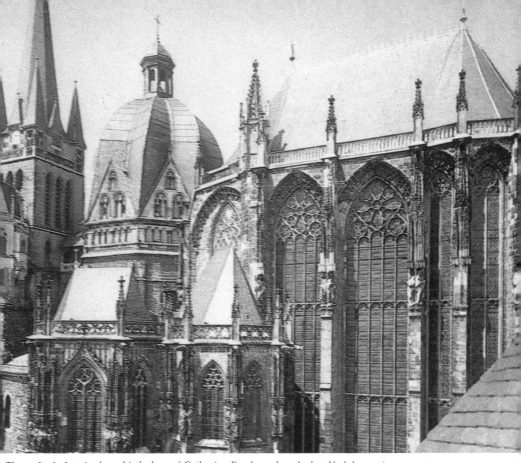

The cathedral at Aachen, birthplace of Catharina Fassbaender. *Aachen Verkehrsverein*

The Ursuline Institute of St Leonard, Aachen, where Catharina Fassbaender was a pupil. *Museen der Stadt, Aachen*

Unterrichts- und Erziehungs-Anstalt
der
Ursulinen zu Sanct Leonard in Aachen.

Schuljahr 186_1_

Sommer=Halbjahr.

Schul=Zeugniß
für
Catharina Faßbender

Schülerin der ___ ten Klasse ___ ten Abtheilung.

Betragen

gegen die Lehrerinnen:	gegen die Mitschülerinnen:	außer den Lehrstunden:
gut.	_gut._	

	Aufmerksamkeit.	Häuslicher Fleiß.	Fortschritte.
Religionslehre	_gut_	_gut_	_gut_
Biblische Geschichte	_gut_	_gut_	_gut_
Deutsche Sprache	_gut_	_gut_	_gut_
Französische Sprache	_recht gut_	_recht gut_	_recht gut_
Englische Sprache	_sehr gut_	_sehr gut_	_sehr gut_
Allgemeine Geschichte	_gut_	_gut_	_gut_
Geographie	_gut_	_gut_	_gut_
Naturkunde	_gut_	_recht gut_	_gut_
Rechnen	_recht gut_	_sehr gut_	_recht gut_
Schönschreiben	_gut_	_auszeichnend_	_gut_
Zeichnen	_sehr gut_		_recht gut_
Gesang	_vorzüglich_		_vorzüglich_
Handarbeit	_gut_		_auszeichnend_
Ordnungsliebe	_recht gut_		

Schulversäumniß.	Kirchenversäumniß.	Zu spät gekommen.	Versäumte schriftliche Arbeiten.
1 Tag mit Entschuldigung 1 ohne	_keine_	_nie_	_keine_

Besondere Bemerkungen:

Catharina erhielt unter 21 Wochen: 6 Billets im Betragen,
14 ,, ,, Kirchenbesuch,
20 ,, ,, Fleiß und
17 ,, ,, in der Ordnung.

Aachen, den _9. September_ 1861.

Der Religionslehrer:

Th. Linden

Die Vorsteherin der Anstalt:

Maria Hartzheim

Unterschrift des Vaters oder dessen Stellvertreters:

Catharina's school report for the summer term, 1861. _Franciscan Sisters_

The SS *Deutschland* in Bremerhaven. This rare photograph is the only known picture of the ship before the wreck. She is seen in dry dock, probably during the autumn of 1875. *Arnold Kludas*

The *Deutschland* aground on the Kentish Knock, as she appeared to the *Illustrated London News* artist on the Thursday after the wreck. On the right, the tug *Liverpool* is seen approaching. *British Library Newspaper Library*

The *Liverpool* taking passengers off the *Deutschland*. From the *Illustrated London News* of 18 December, 1875. *British Library Newspaper Library*

'Wreckers at work in the saloon of the *Deutschland*', as observed by the *Illustrated London News* artist. *British Library Newspaper Library*

Sailors are often men of profound belief. Many feel, when danger threatens, that they are not alone, that some unseen force acts at certain moments in their favour. They believe, in short, that God is on their side at such times. Certainly, the crew of the *Liverpool* felt the hand of God at this crucial moment. As Carrington made his vital run in towards the *Deutschland* for no apparent reason the winds died, the seas fell, and in relatively quick time the tug was able to take off all the remaining survivors—in all, one hundred and fifty-five souls, including twenty-two women. Part of the *Deutschland*'s bulwark had been washed away, so Carrington's men improvised a fender using hawsers, to cushion the two ships as the *Liverpool* swung and bucked against the grounded vessel. It worked. In addition to the tally of survivors, the *Liverpool* was able to recover twenty-five mailbags.

It was a remarkable end to a daring rescue. Carrington later recalled that he had never seen worse conditions in nearly fifty years at sea, forty of which he had spent specifically in salvage and tug work, among the most dangerous of all maritime occupations. It was in many respects a triumph, but it came too late for the forty-four passengers and twenty crew of the *Deutschland* who had died between 5.00am on Monday 6th December and 10.30am the next day.

At Sheerness in the Thames estuary, as soon as Quartermaster August Beck had been washed ashore with his two dead companions—at the very time when the *Liverpool* was engaged in delivering the *Deutschland*'s survivors—frantic attempts at launching a rescue operation were set in motion. When Beck had told his story, the master attendant immediately ordered the naval steam-tug *Locust* to fill up with coal and to proceed to the Kentish Knock. The master of the *Locust*, Joseph Flood, accompanied by two sick-bay men from the naval hospital, set out at 2.15 on the Tuesday afternoon. It is easy for us, in this time of instant communication, to see the futility of this action. Even this sizeable vessel—281 tons and 100 horsepower—was forced by 6.30pm to seek shelter near a bank called the Tongue Sand, where she lay all night. Rescue attempts often used to come to nought, frustrated by haphazard signalling techniques, by vessels' lack of speed, and by the elements themselves.

Eventually, on the Wednesday morning, the *Locust* was able to continue, at one point sighting a corpse floating in the sea. At first they thought it must be from the wreck, but closer inspection showed it to be too much decomposed to be the result of a recent accident. In Flood's words: 'It would have fallen to pieces if taken out of the water.' Soon after 10.30am the *Locust* arrived near the wreck, only to find the *Liverpool* in attendance, and various officials including Captain Brickenstein, engaged in the mournful task of removing bodies. A lifeboat was sent by the *Locust* to the *Deutschland*, and the master of the tug offered assistance to her Captain. Brickenstein apparently said that he 'might help the *Liverpool*', but Carrington is reported to have declined the offer, saying that 'as he had taken the living, he would take the dead'. The *Locust* steamed back to Sheerness.

It had been a similar story at Broadstairs. At eleven o'clock on the Tuesday morning, the Captain of the steam-tug *Dreadnought*, lying off the Foreland of the Isle of Thanet in Kent, had spoken with the owner of a smack who had told him that he had that morning passed a large brig-rigged screw lying on the Kentish Knock, with people in the rigging and the sea breaking over her. The smacksman was on his way to alert the Broadstairs lifeboat, three and a half miles away. To save time, the tug raced off to spread the word, and efforts were instantly made to launch the lifeboat. Tragically, the storm had washed up a bank of shingle off the lifeboat station, and it proved at first impossible to get the boat over the bank and into the water. Finally, however, after an hour and a half the boat was launched, and the *Dreadnought* towed her out. By the time they set off it was between one and two in the afternoon; the journey took nearly five hours, and when they reached the neighbourhood of the Knock it was quite dark. The Broadstairs men went straight to the lightship, only to learn that all survivors had been taken off that morning. Thus, after close on seven hours of toil they returned wearily to Broadstairs, without even setting eyes on the *Deutschland*. No one could have done more.

For the survivors themselves, the return journey to Harwich aboard the *Liverpool* was fraught with danger. The seas were still running high, and the tug was grossly overloaded with passengers, mailbags and as much other cargo and personal luggage as she could carry, stacked in every available corner of the small deck. She must have made a bizarre picture as she paddled back into Harwich harbour. One eyewitness recalled that, with her crowded decks, she resembled a pleasure-steamer on a day trip. She berthed at the Corporation (or 'Ha'penny') Pier, and the survivors were taken to the Great Eastern Hotel, mercifully just across the road from the landing point.

Harwich from the Harbour, 1860. *Leonard Weaver*

Among those awaiting the *Liverpool* when she docked was a reporter from *The Times*. Over the next week he was to be busy filing story after story, many of which were to anger the local fishing communities. For now, though, he was simply trying to ascertain the facts of the accident – which was no easy task. His first reports, which began to appear on Wednesday, 8th December were published in quick succession. There was no time for sub-editors in London to amend his copy, and continual updates in the story made previous reports redundant. The first ones tell of the landing at Sheerness of August Beck. They are fragmentary in the extreme, based as they were entirely on Beck's assumptions of what must have happened to the ship after he and his companions left it, but they give a dramatic sense of a tragedy unfolding: 'A boat came ashore this morning from the *Deutschland*, steamer, with Quartermaster named Beck, August, and two dead men in her. Had been in boat 38 hours . . . General

cargo and passengers . . . Not known what has become of ship
or the rest of passengers and crew . . . Steamer struck on sandbank in North Sea. One boat left ship before [Beck] . . . Number
of passengers and crew 150. He thinks all the rest are lost.' His
report of later the same day is more ordered and more hopeful,
although details were still very sketchy:

> The North German Lloyd steamer, Deutschland, of Bremen,
> Captain Brickenstein, from Bremen for New York, with emig-
> rants, grounded on Kentish Knock on Monday morning dur-
> ing a gale from the north-east, thick with snow. Part of the
> crew and passengers were landed here today by the tug
> Liverpool, of Harwich, and placed under the care of Mr
> Oliver John Williams, the North German Consul at Harwich.
> About 50 of the crew and passengers are drowned.

The *Times* reporter then goes on to list some of the cabin passengers known to be missing, and includes the simple phrase, 'five
nuns'.

First reports had given the impression of a much greater catastrophe. At least, now, it was known that there was a large number
of survivors. Sorrow and relief combined among those waiting for
news. In New York, William B. Fundling, who ran a perfumery
business at 156, Front Street, was at first told that his wife Bertha
and two-year-old son Theodor were among those missing. Later
he was to hear that the child had been saved. His wife had been
drowned. There was good news for Dr Petzold from his daughter
Anna. She telegraphed a message to North German Lloyd's New
York office, saying she was safe. What Dr Petzold did not yet
know was that romance had blossomed between his daughter
and young Adolf Hermann. After a short time recovering in Harwich, the couple had proceeded to London, where Hermann
revealed: 'Instead of losing by the shipwreck, I found my own
happiness in resolving while there with her in the rigging to make
her my wife, should we be rescued.'

Among the crew, the Polar hero, Fourth Officer Otto Tramultz,
did not survive the ordeal. A boy of fifteen did survive, while his
brother-in-law, in whose care he was, did not. A young German
woman lost her father, mother and brother, while a man travelling
with his sister saw her die of exposure, having tied her to a mast to

stop her being swept away. In the end, he was forced to cut her lifeless body free and see it float away. An American businessman, who had left 1,500 dollars on board, learnt that his wife, whom he had believed dead, was among those saved: neither knew of the other's safety until they met on the tug bound for Harwich. But even as help arrived, the wreck was to claim one more victim. Mr G. Gmolch of New York was to receive a telegram from North German Lloyd's agents in Bremen, Messrs Osoelrichs and Company, that his wife Anna was among the passengers who survived, but that his little daughter Paulina had not. Mother and child had been travelling to New York in steerage class, planning to join the child's father, who had gone on ahead to make preparations for their new life together. As the *Liverpool* reached the shelter of Harwich harbour, little Paulina died in her distraught mother's arms.

On Wednesday 8th December, two days after the disaster, Carrington took Brickenstein back to the wreck, and the task of recovering the bodies began. The *Liverpool* arrived at nine that morning, finding the *Deutschland* apparently in much the same condition as they had left her the day before. Her two masts and funnel were still standing, black and stark against the sandbank, and eerily her sails still flapped loose in the high winds. Indeed, conditions remained so bad that Carrington could not bring the *Liverpool* alongside, and so a boat was launched, under the charge of his mate and Brickenstein.

The chief officer and the engineer, with some sailors from the tug, among them Richard Stanley and Thomas King, rowed across to the ship. It was low water, and the decks were dry. There were at first no bodies to be seen, but when they went below they found in the saloon eight women, among them four of the Salzkotten nuns, a man and two children. The first of the sisters to be recovered was found lying face downwards, in the middle of the saloon. The body of another was found in a different position; according to the *Essex Telegraph*, 'having apparently reclined her head upon her hands on the table [she] had fallen so that she lay leaning over the stool, with her head resting on some wreckage'. The two other sisters' bodies were also brought up, and laid with the rest on the deck of the *Liverpool*. Then, in the forward cabin, they found a dead seaman. In all, they recovered twelve bodies on this first trip back. As the tug sailed away from the *Deutschland* on that dark December day, she left a ship lying in four fathoms and rapidly settling into the sand, the relentless action of the sea starting to break her up, aided by the sails, still up and fluttering and constantly rocking her to and fro, working her down into the Kentish Knock.

At every high tide, bodies were swept out of the grounded ship. Some were washed up on the beach at Sheerness, and one was later identified as that of a woman who had been seen the previous day lying dead in her berth. She must have floated out through a companionway or a skylight, together with many others who were never found.

What a sad sight the tug must have made as she steamed into Harwich at 9.00pm, her flag at half-mast and a row of blanket-covered bodies on her aft deck. The *Liverpool* made other return trips to the *Deutschland*, but on Saturday 11th December she had to turn back to escort another ship, the *Conrad*, which had got into difficulties near the Knock, towards the safety of harbour.

The Great Eastern Hotel, Harwich, as it was in 1889, where the survivors of the wreck stayed. *Leonard Weaver*

Most of the survivors were accommodated and treated at the Great Eastern Hotel in Harwich, until they had recovered, or alternative plans were made for the continuation of their journey to New York. The Great Eastern would have been well qualified to cope with the sudden emergency: it had been built on Harwich quay ten years earlier to provide hotel facilities for passengers travelling to and from the Continent on railway steamers, at that time a thriving industry. In 1883 the steamer services were transferred elsewhere, and the building ceased to be an hotel. During the First World War it served as a military hospital, and then, until local government reorganisation in 1974, it was the town hall of Harwich. Since that time it has gone through yet another metamorphosis, and today stands converted into flats. In December 1875, however, it provided a haven for the survivors of the *Deutschland*, and many later spoke warmly of the way they had been looked after during their unscheduled visit.

Meanwhile, the shipping line was doing all it could to enable them to resume their journey with the minimum of fuss. Arrangements were already in hand for berths to be made available on the *Mosel*, the next North German Lloyd ship out of Bremen for New York via Southampton. On Saturday 11th December forty-eight of these passengers left Harwich by rail for Southampton, to meet the *Mosel* the next day. They were seen off from Harwich station by civic dignatories, Captain Brickenstein, and a number of local ladies who had been caring for them. A gift of nine shillings was presented to each passenger on behalf of the wife of the local MP, together with a parcel of 'useful sundries' for the journey; plus, for each person, £1 7s 6d that had been raised by public subscription. As they took their seats in the carriages of the 1.05 for London en route for Southampton, they were given oranges as a parting gift. The local reporter wrote: 'As the train drew slowly out of the station, hats, handkerchiefs and hands waved adieu, and the German women called for three cheers for the Harwich ladies.'

Only three survivors now remained in Harwich—two men and a woman. One was still suffering from frostbite to the feet, and his companion had stayed on to look after him. The third person was the tragic mother of Paulina Gmolch, the little girl who had died as the *Liverpool* entered Harwich harbour. She refused to leave until the funeral of her daughter had taken place.

*

In contrast to the scenes of appreciation and thanksgiving at the station that day, the same *Essex Telegraph* reporter painted a graphic picture of the mortuary, which lay behind the Three Cups Hotel, adjacent to the Church of St Nicholas:

> As we enter a man is measuring the bodies for coffins, and they are being searched. Turning to the left the first body is that of one who in life was a bonny girl. Although completely attired save her frock, it was apparent that her attire had been hurriedly put on. Round her neck was a muffler. Her age somewhere about fourteen years. Eyes open, but countenance peaceful . . . face a good deal bruised, hands firmly clenched.

Then the reporter comes to the first of the nuns:

> Her head is still covered, and to some extent her face, by the white hood. Her hands repose across the body, which is attired in apparel of a very expensive kind—a characteristic of that worn by the other deceased nuns. The countenance is somewhat less pale than most, but so peaceful, that it were not difficult to believe she sleeps . . . Another nun, with both hands clenched, and a full, fat face—that of a Dutch woman, we fancy—which wears a happy expression, but is exceedingly pallid, completes the bodies ranged along the left-hand side of the mortuary, their heads to the wall. Part of the hood is missing.

Some of the bodies showed signs of the violence of their deaths: some had glaring, terror-filled eyes, and others had dreadful head wounds. One woman in particular, with eyes unnaturally wide open and hands clenched hard, shocked the reporter. He then came to a nun who, we must assume, was the one who had made the cry that so many had recalled: 'A masculine-framed nun, with features in harmony, and the oldest of the four; and the youngest, whose countenance betokens peacefulness, complete the ghastly spectacle.' As the 1.05pm train left Harwich with its survivors, perhaps many did not know that the bodies of the four nuns were also on board, bound for their last resting place in Leytonstone

Roman Catholic Cemetery. Their elm coffins had been taken to the station by farm cart, and despite attempts at concealing what was happening, inevitably the scene had attracted a number of onlookers.

Also on that day, the body of Julius Grossman, a Hamburg man, was being taken by cart from the mortuary to the Great Eastern Railway Company's pier, where it was shipped aboard the steamer *Zealous*, bound for Rotterdam en route for Hamburg. Two survivors, George Weiss and Carl Meyer, chose to return to their homeland. Meanwhile, the grim task of photographing the dead for identification purposes took place, a duty carried out by one Mr Basham, who had the coffins brought outside into the daylight, two or three at a time. They were then leaned against a wall, and the face, shoulders and arms of the victims were exposed. The *Essex Telegraph* reporter, who had so assiduously chronicled every macabre detail of the story, was appalled at the crowds who gathered around to watch, and thronged the mortuary itself.

The burial of the dead was carried out in two services. On 14th December, several bodies were buried at sea from the coastguard vessel, HMS *Penelope*. There is no record of the number, but it is likely that some twenty-two victims were sent to a watery grave. In addition, two men were buried where their bodies had been washed ashore, one in Margate and one in Sheerness.

The funeral of fourteen victims was conducted in Harwich on Thursday 16th December. The *Essex Telegraph* of 21st December reports the event:

> The funeral of the ill-fated German people evoked such general indications of grief that the few survivors who were amongst the mourners . . . were unprepared for any such expression of sympathy and respect. From half past nine to ten on Wednesday morning the peal of eight bells of St Nicholas church chimed in the manner customary prior to the commencement of funerals in Harwich.

The short journey from the mortuary to the church was led by Captain Carrington and his First Officer, a number of local dignatories, the German Vice-Consul Oliver Williams, who was also a Lloyds agent representing German maritime interests. The coffins, borne by marines and seamen from HMS *Penelope*, were followed by relatives of the dead, some of whom had arrived only just in time to make formal identifications. The crew of the *Liverpool* brought up the rear. At the church door they were met by the Revd T. O. Reay, the vicar of nearby Dovercourt, who was deputising for his Harwich counterpart the Revd S. Farman Jnr, who was away in the Midlands on business. When the coffins had been laid out against the altar rail, the service, before a packed church, began. After the psalms, came the first hymn:

> Brief life is here our portion;
> Brief sorrow, short-lived care;
> The life that knows no ending,
> The tearless life, is there.

Then came the lesson, from chapter 15 of the First Epistle of Paul to the Corinthians, followed by the second hymn:

> Jesus lives, no longer now
> Can thy terrors, death, appal us;
> Jesus lives, by this we know
> Thou, o grave, canst not enthrall us.
> Alleluia

The organist A. M. Warren, played the *Dead March in Saul*, and the procession moved off once more, Lieutenant Hailstone and the men of HMS *Penelope* bearing the coffins to two waiting wagons, one supplied by Mr Bull of the Three Cups, who also ran a farm, the other by Vice-Consul Williams. It was usual for farmers to be taken on their last journey in their own wagons, and it is likely that this mode of transport was thought best in view of the large number of coffins to be transported. The whole town seems to have turned out—to attend the funeral, to stand silently by the roadside or to join the procession as it passed on its way through Harwich and Dovercourt to Dovercourt Cemetery. All the Harwich shops closed as a mark of respect. As the cortège neared Dovercourt church, the passing bell rang out.

Fourteen graves had been dug on the northern side of the cemetery, under the supervision of Alfred Chaplin, the parish clerk and sexton. There were nine in one row, and five in another.

Because of the nature of the soil and the number of bodies, a large communal pit had been dug, into which the coffins were lowered one by one 'amidst a silence which might almost be said to have been felt' by the crowd. The coffins were numbered, with a view of the exhumation of any particular body when photographic identification had been completed. And it would seem that they were in fact subsequently removed and reburied elsewhere, as there remains no trace in Dovercourt Cemetery of the *Deutschland* dead. Paulina Gmolch, being a Catholic, had a separate funeral conducted by the Catholic priest for Harwich, Father Parkinson, and she was buried in an unconsecrated part of the cemetery. Captain Brickenstein attended the funeral: 'Among those present both in the church and at the cemetery were the ladies whose assistance since the landing of the survivors has been so valuable to the Vice-Consul.'

The next day, the Captain wrote a letter to the Mayor of Harwich, expressing his appreciation for the help and care that so many had given to the survivors:

Before leaving Harwich permit me to tender to you, your fellow-townsmen, and adjacent residents, my most sincere and heartfelt thanks for all the substantial kindness and sympathy shown to myself, my crew, and passengers, since landing here from the wreck of my vessel.

To the ladies, especially I desire to express my gratitude for their personal attention to the wants of all, but more particularly to those passengers of their own sex, and although it is difficult for me to know whom to thank the most, I cannot forbear to mention the names of the Mayoress, Mrs Reay, Mrs Cox, Miss Firbuan, Mrs Jarvis, Mrs Pye, Mrs Bull, Mrs Dunlop, Mrs Williams and daughters, Mrs Freshfield, Miss Runnioles, Miss Chambers, Mrs Wells, Mrs Hardinge, and Fräulein Richter. All hearts will carry with them to their distant homes memories of these kind friends, and when they tell of the hardships they have endured, they will also speak with gratitude of those whose kindness will never be forgotten. I cannot close this letter without reference to the solemn scenes . . . when the remains of my late fellow-voyagers who were recovered from the wreck were conveyed to their last resting place. And when the loved ones far away who live to mourn their loss shall hear how tenderly these last rites were performed amidst the sobs and tears of all around, they will feel they have the sympathy of many true English hearts.

But the mental suffering of the survivors was by no means over. As those remaining travelled to Southampton on Monday 13th December, news was just beginning to filter through of another disaster—concerning this time the very ship they were expecting to board, the *Mosel*. At first the news was as sketchy as the *Deutschland* story had been, but piece by piece, a new saga of horror built up. On Saturday 11th December the *Mosel* had been on the point of departure and the Bremerhaven quay was crowded with people, just as it had been on the previous Saturday when the *Deutschland* had pulled away. Suddenly, ship and shore had been rocked by a massive explosion. The first reports were stark: killed and maimed —170 persons. On Wednesday 15th December, the *Times* carried the first facts of the story:

A Mr Thomas, from Dresden, a passenger in the North German Lloyd steamer, 'Mosel', has owned himself the proprietor of the dynamite chest which exploded on shore just as it was about to be sent on board. Thomas is likewise stated to have confessed that he meant to leave the vessel at Southampton, and that the chest was so prepared as to explode after a week's voyage, when he expected the ship to sink. It appears that Thomas in such a case would have become entitled to a large indemnity from Insurance Companies, and that the goods on which the claim was to be based and which were to be insured for above their value were intended to be shipped at Southampton.

On being discovered, Thomas (or Thompson, as he seems also to have been known) shot himself, but was stated to be still alive. A local Bremen newspaper, the *Bremer Nachrichten* pointed out in its issue of 14th December that, had Thomas succeeded in taking his life before his confession, the source of the explosion might have remained a mystery, with the criminal himself simply being listed among the missing. North German Lloyd, reeling from this second disaster, quickly put into operation plans for another liner to take the *Mosel*'s place. Thus the *Salier* with her master, H. C. Francke, set off for Southampton after a delay caused by heavy fog in the Weser estuary, and picked up the *Deutschland* passengers on the morning of Thursday 16th December. After this new setback, the state of mind of those who had already experienced the Kentish Knock can only be guessed at.

On board the *Salier* were sixty-four passengers from the *Deutschland*—nineteen cabin and forty-five steerage—and eighty-nine from the *Mosel*. What a strange and terrible crossing it must have been, beset as they were not only by fog and snow but also by a rumour that another of Thomas's exploding devices had been placed on board. In New York, the tension became unbearable, with the agents watching for the *Salier* three days before she was due, and frantic relatives and friends besieging the shipping office at all hours of the day and night. When she finally docked in New York on 3rd January 1876, the cabin-class passengers were looked after first, and were housed in hotels or made their way to the homes of those who had been awaiting them for so long. Steerage passengers had to wait rather longer before being allowed to disembark, but at last they could now begin to believe that the ordeal was at an end. At long last, an exhausted Captain Francke and his officers retired to rest.

For others, however, the story was by no means over. As the *Deutschland* lay an irredeemable wreck in the North Sea, finally broken in two by the incessant waves, a period of questioning was about to begin. In Berlin, the National Liberal Party unanimously signed an interpellation in the Reichstag asking the government for information about the disaster. In addition, a motion was carried that was to provide the machinery for full government inquiries in future into the loss of German ships. During the past months, a number of German steamers, of which the *Deutschland* was the latest, had gone down, and an official response to the catastrophes was now called for. In the meantime it was deemed appropriate that the *Deutschland* inquiry should be handled by the British on the German behalf. But a new storm of controversy would shortly break over the wreck and its aftermath.

6 Burial in a Foreign Land

By Saturday 11th December, five days after the wreck of the *Deutschland* and the day of the *Mosel* explosion in Bremerhaven, the *Times* reporter was building up a picture of the Kentish Knock tragedy from eyewitness reports. He also remarked on the progress of those who had come through the ordeal:

> Most of the surviving passengers and crew left Harwich today. One engaging little girl, of German parentage, but American born, passed the terrible night of Monday in her father's arms, but seemed little the worse now for the cold and exposure, and, with the happy forgetfulness of childhood, laughed and chattered as though she had passed through no such terrible ordeal. Two or three passengers are still suffering from cold, and are confined to their beds at the various hotels. There is no case of illness however.

The German Vice-Consul in Harwich, Mr Williams, had been informed by the Consul-General in London that the Imperial foreign department in Berlin had agreed to defray all disbursements for the relief of passengers, and that everything was to be done for their comfort and maintenance.

The reporter from *The Times* went on: 'The bodies of the four German nuns were removed today for interment at a convent of the Franciscan order, to which they belonged, near Stratford [London]. They were from a convent in Westphalia.' And another report tells us:

> Four of the five nuns who perished in the wreck are to be buried in Leytonstone. When their deaths became known it was resolved by the authorities of the Roman Catholic

Church in London to give them solemn burial. For this purpose two Franciscan Fathers were despatched to Harwich, and the bodies were brought to London . . . There will be a solemn Requiem Mass at the Franciscan Church, Stratford, after which their bodies will be interred in St. Patrick's Catholic Cemetery, Leytonstone.

It was Father Francis Verhagen, the Superior of the Franciscan friary in The Grove, Stratford, East London, who, with one Thomas Jansen, went to Harwich to take custody of the bodies and bring them by the 1.05 train to London on Saturday 11th December. The friary had been established two years previously, and consisted in 1875, as it does today, of eight residents. By a curious coincidence, the building now known as the Friary had already had an association with exiled nuns. On 21st September 1870, a group of French sisters had moved into the premises, then known as 2 Eden Villas and owned by the diocese of Westminster. The group had been founded as the Servants of the Sacred Heart by Father Victor Braun, a priest from Lorraine, and had nursing and educational aims similar to those of the Salzkotten community. The group's expulsion from their homeland had followed defeat to Prussia's forces in the war, and the sisters had stayed at 2 Eden Villas until 1873. They renamed it the House of Our Lady of the Sacred Heart. It was an ideal location, since it backed on to the Catholic church of St Vincent de Paul in Grove Crescent Road, later to be rededicated to St Francis. Father Braun quickly established himself in the Stratford community, as did the nuns.

Meanwhile, the then Archbishop, Henry Edward Manning, had been seeking to establish a Franciscan house in London. Manning had succeeded Cardinal Wiseman as Archbishop of Westminster in 1865. He was a zealous supporter of the doctrine of papal infallibility, as well as being devoted to all things Franciscan. Born in 1808, he joined the Church of Rome quite late, in 1851, but his subsequent progress was remarkable. Even as an Anglican his commitment was to the Franciscan ideal, and later, as a Catholic, he edited the first English edition of *The Floretti*, or *Little Flowers of St Francis*. He was made a cardinal in 1875.

Manning first expressed his desire for a London Franciscan congregation to the canonist and theologian, Father Anselm Knapen, in Rome during the Vatican Council of 1870. Two years later, Manning wrote to the Guardian of Gorton Friary in Manchester, where Father Anselm was based, suggesting that he should propose someone to act as Superior at the new establishment, which would be based at Stratford in East London. Father Willibrord, Guardian of Gorton, sent Father Anselm and Father Francis Verhagen to London to discuss the idea. It was, as Manning said, an attractive proposition: a newly built church, with a school beneath it, and adequate housing and stabling. On the other hand, Bird, the builder of the church, was still owed £3,935, of which £2,000 would have to be found by whichever community of friars took over the living from the nuns currently in residence as rent-paying tenants.

Father Anselm and Father Francis reported back to their Superior, and a certain amount of bargaining between the friars and the nuns then ensued. Finally, on 23rd April 1873 an agreement was reached, and on 21st June three Franciscan priests and a brother arrived to found the friary. Leading them was Francis Verhagen himself, and with him came Brother Patrick Dalton from County Limerick, Father Alfred Murray, a New Zealander who had until recently been chaplain to some Franciscan nuns at Taunton in Somerset, and Father Malachy O'Loughlen from Devon, who had previously been at the friary in Glasgow. They inherited an area bounded by Bow Bridge to the west, Leytonstone church to the north and the Barking Road to the south and east, and containing a still-growing population of eight thousand, of whom between 1,500 and 2,000 were Catholics. The nuns of Our Lady of the Sacred Heart moved out, by mutually happy arrangement. They had been approached by a priest in nearby Homerton to undertake work there, and anyway they needed more space. They continued, however, to maintain a presence in Stratford, through parish visiting, for another forty years.

The Church of St Vincent de Paul was now rededicated at the suggestion of Archbishop Manning to St Francis of Assisi. Father Francis Verhagen, the new Superior of the friary, was a Dutchman with a German background. On his arrival he met Father Thomas Jansen, a German priest who had been visiting the Ursuline Sisters of Upton, based at St Angela's, Forest Gate, probably with the intention of learning English. Father Francis and the German became close friends, and when he learned of the Salzkotten nuns' death Jansen suggested to the Stratford Superior that they should bring the bodies to London, with a view to finding a suitable place of burial.

Father Francis and Father Thomas arrived in Harwich expecting to find five bodies to take back to Stratford. It was only when they reached the mortuary where the bodies of those so far found were being kept, that they learnt that one sister was missing, presumed drowned.

On arrival in London on the Saturday evening, the train carrying the four simple elm coffins was met at Stratford station by two hearses. From there, the remains were escorted to the school hall beneath the Church of St Francis in Grove Crescent Road by boys and girls from Stratford's Catholic schools, and the nuns of the Convent of Jesus and Mary, which was situated at Park House, in The Grove, almost opposite the present friary. It was these nuns, assisted by sisters from the Sacred Heart at Homerton, who prepared the Salzkotten nuns for their lying in state and burial.

In this task, a key role was played by Mary Broadway, a young woman who worked for Tillett's Laundry in the Romford Road. The story of this girl is in itself remarkable. The daughter of a local couple, William and Elizabeth Broadway, she was just nineteen and had only recently been received into the Catholic Church. It seems that her family were greatly opposed to her conversion, and since she was a minor, it must have taken courage and determination to maintain the strength of her convictions. But Mary seems to have had a strong and unusual personality. The register at St Francis's Church tells us that she was baptised there on 8th July 1875 by Father Arsenius Marten, OFM. She had been greatly moved by the poverty of the friars in Stratford, and seems to have spent much of her wages in buying food for them. When Father Francis had decided that the nuns' bodies should be put on public display, he then approached Mary with Smith's, undertakers of West Ham, to arrange the grimly practical job of laying out. At this time, the bodies were, of course, still clothed in the habits the sisters had been wearing at the time of death. Mary had the task of, first, removing the sea-bedraggled garments. Next, she took them to Tillett's laundry, and had them cleaned and ironed; she also washed the white waist cords from the habits. Finally, she dressed the corpses in their clean clothes. At this she was occupied throughout the Sunday morning; by the

afternoon, just eight days after the *Deutschland* had left Bremerhaven, the sisters were lying in state in the spacious pillared
school hall below the Stratford Franciscan church. While she was
doing this job, Mary had found that each nun carried a little
leather bag around her neck, containing written and signed 'forms
of profession'. It was ultimately by reference to these documents,
which carried the number assigned to each nun in making her
profession, that formal identification was made. The bags Mary
placed in the nuns' joined hands, with their rosaries.

Mary Broadway's long life was as colourful as her personality
and her London accent, and it is worth diverting from our story
for a moment to consider her. At the time of her father's death,
some years after the events of 1875, her stepmother contested
William Broadway's will, in which he had left his daughter
money. It took a court case for Mary to claim her legacy, and here
again her strength of character was to have an unexpected effect
upon at least one who encountered her at that time. Mary later
recalled meeting the judge in the case, a Mr Justice Hawkins, one
day as she was coming out of St Francis's Church. Thinking he
was coming to tell her that he was rescinding his previous judgement, she tried to escape, only to be stopped by him with the
words: 'Don't run away, Miss Broadway. I would like to thank
you. What you said in court about your religion made such an
impression on me that I am now under instruction, and am in
fact just going to Mass.'

Hawkins, later Lord Brampton, never forgot Mary Broadway.
On one occasion, years afterwards, while in conversation with
Bishop Burton of Clifton he happened to mention her, to be told
that she was now a nun herself in the Bishop's diocese. She
had made her profession on 15th October 1882, when she was
twenty-six, in the presence of the Revd Paul Stapleton, Prior of
Woodchester, near Stroud in Gloucestershire. Here, at the Convent of the Poor Clares, she spent the rest of her life as Sister
Mary Pascal. She died on 28th May 1947 at the age of ninety, full,
to the very last, of the determination and East End good humour
that had marked her whole life. It is recorded that when the
priest, at her deathbed, said, 'and now I am going to give you
the last blessing', she sat bolt upright and responded in a strong
voice, 'That's ever so kind of yer, Father.' She always remembered
'Judge 'Awkins', as she called him, as well as the macabre func-

tion that she had performed at the very start of her career, in the dim lower room beneath St Francis's Church.

Today, that room is used as a parish hall, but it is little changed, and it is not difficult to imagine what it must have been like in 1875. As to the church itself, more changes are visible. Over the altar, one of the treasures of the church, not present at the time of the nuns' funeral but well worth going to see, is a painting of St Francis by Vincenzo Carducho. Looted from a Franciscan church in Spain by Napoleon's troops, it was sold in Paris in 1921, then purchased by a Colonel Bigge, who left it to a Scottish family called Stewart. Then, in 1926, it was presented to the Stratford church by the Stewarts as part of the seven-hundredth anniversary commemoration of the death of St Francis. Thus it was at last restored to its original function as the centrepiece of a Franciscan church. The church at Stratford is also notable for the baptism, in 1899, of Alfred Hitchcock! One wonders whether he ever knew of the *Deutschland* association—or perhaps even considered the subject as potential film material. It is sad that the architect of this neo-Romanesque church is unknown—and surprising, considering its relatively recent origin. At a time when Victorian Gothic was very much the popular style in ecclesiastical architecture, this building goes against the trend. The sense of grace and space is what first impresses the visitor today.

As the bodies lay in the school hall, awaiting the service, lighted candles were placed around the coffins, which were displayed on a raised dais, and flowers and wreaths were set at the nuns' heads and feet. Their faces were said by many eyewitness to express 'calmness and resignation'. A reporter from the *Stratford Express* wrote:

> The faces of the deceased wore a placid aspect, and there was nothing to indicate the sad manner in which death had occurred. It having become known that they were to be seen at any time, of course crowds (Protestants as well as Catholics) flocked to see them . . . the stream of visitors was continuous, and in the evening after vespers, the Rev Father Jansen preached an impressive sermon to a large congregation, in which he alluded to the kindness he had received at Harwich, and the readiness and charity with which the

dead bodies of the four women who had devoted their lives to the salvation of men, had been received in a strange land. He advised his hearers to look beyond the corpses and the coffin, to the altar and the cross which spoke of satisfaction and forgiveness, and argued that their deaths were saintly deaths, because they had lived saintly lives. Now that they had been sent here, they must receive them as sisters and give them their prayers.

In one detail only, the *Stratford Express* reporter was incorrect: one of the bodies displayed a fresh cut on the right hand. Otherwise, there was indeed no evidence of the ordeal the sisters had been through. Upon each breast lay a cross of white flowers, gifts from the Ursuline Sisters of Upton.

On Monday 13th December, the day of the funeral, the coffins were carried up the narrow stairs of the school hall and into the church. The building was packed to capacity, and the crowds outside were enormous. Press coverage of the wreck and its aftermath had been extensive, and in any case, Cardinal Manning had agreed to preach the oration. Manning's presence was significant: clearly, he saw here an opportunity to make a political stand, to voice solidarity with the beleaguered Catholic Church in Germany, and at the same time to make a point with the authorities in England. No less than fifty priests attended; Father Francis was chief celebrant, the deacon was a Spanish priest, named as Father Hogan, and the subdeacon, an exiled German, one Father Gabriel.

For the people of Stratford, this must have been an extraordinary event. The friary in The Grove had only existed in its present form for two years when the *Deutschland* was wrecked, and the funeral, bringing with it the presence of a figure of the stature of Cardinal Manning, would put the place firmly on the map. What must the atmosphere have been? Fortunately, we have a recollection, albeit written some time afterwards, in the form of an article by Father Edwin Whitsker OFM. He and Father Francis met some years after the event, when they were both in Manchester. Father Edwin's main interest in the affair stemmed from the fact that his own father, a German, had been expelled from the Black Forest as a result of the Kulturkampf. The account of the funeral was published in *The Franciscan Monthly* of March, 1897:

We can imagine once again the little church draped in black, filled to suffocation within, while thousands outside await the funeral. Catholics and Protestants were intermingled, alike to shed a tear, or offer a prayer over the strangers, to whom the hospitality of the tomb was about to be given.

Before the altar are four bare coffins, with flowers and many lights. The sisters lie within clad in the habit of their Order, their joined hands still holding the rosary. More than fifty priests stand by, with eyes fixed on the coffins of the holy victims.

At the beginning of the service his Eminence, Cardinal Manning, who had kindly promised to preach, entered the church accompanied by Monsignor Searle. Before occupying the temporary throne prepared for him, he knelt in prayer a while in front of the coffins. After the last Gospel the Cardinal –Archbishop, in cope and mitre, ascended the altar steps, and turning, faced the coffins. Here the scene became indes-cribably pathetic. For several minutes his Eminence stood facing the coffins; he then ordered the sacristan to take the lids off, and descending from the suppedaneum, visited each coffin in turn.

This, the first time Cardinal Manning had seen the sisters, clearly moved him greatly. The blend of political and religious persecution and natural tragedy, all within the solemn theatre of the church, served to generate a virtually overpowering emotion. As Father Edwin recalled: 'The Cardinal's emotion became visible; we won-dered whether he would be able to speak. Again he ascended the altar steps, and with that voice of peculiar feeling which many of us remember so well, began a discourse of unusual tenderness.' Manning's eulogy undoubtedly caught the feeling of the time:

It is impossible for me to find words worthy of this occasion, knowing that nothing I could say would increase in a single degree, the natural piety and Christian charity which fill your hearts. If anyone among you is unmoved by this sight so beautiful and yet so sad, my words will not affect him. And yet, I do not know whether sadness or joy should fill your hearts. Why grieve for these worthy women, whose lives were consecrated entirely to the service of our heavenly

Father? Why weep at a glorious death, which has just broken a career entirely dedicated to God? I think I see in this circumstance the fulfillment of those words of our Saviour: 'I was a stranger, and ye took me in'; for never until this day have you seen these poor creatures. Again, as our Saviour said: 'Whoever shall leave father, or mother, or sister, or house, for my sake, shall receive a hundredfold.' And behold! In a strange country, these unknown, shipwrecked sisters are welcomed in the great family of the Holy Catholic Church, by their brothers and sisters in Jesus Christ, in a dwelling filled with that tender sympathy natural to man, with sanctifying grace and Christian charity.

But there is more still. They were daughters of our Seraphic father, Saint Francis; humble Tertiaries, having consecrated their poor and tranquil life to the service of the sick and dying, and now they have been received by the family of Saint Francis, by the Fathers of their Order. And I know that amongst those who are listening to me there are many Tertiaries. They, like myself, will understand that a threefold bond unites us to these holy sisters—the bond of nature, the charity of the Catholic Church, and the sweet domestic love existing in the great family of Saint Francis.

What can I tell you about their lives? What do I know? I know but few details concerning them. In the land of Germany, where Christ's faith has taken such deep root that it resists the most violent storms, they had a happy and a peaceful home, the centre of innumerable good deeds. They spent their lives in humble and tranquil work, administering consolation to the sick and dying, teaching children the fear and love of God and his Holy Mother. Why is their country no longer a home for them? I will not answer the question. My answer would be a discordant note and would wound your feelings. However, it is but too true; their country is no longer a home for these poor women. Forced by a sad necessity, they were going into exile to ask strangers for a home. Compelled to embark without delay, they were obliged to face the perils of the sea in a cold season. You probably know, as well as I, the details of this sad catastrophe. Last Monday, at five in the morning, still dark, in a heavy fall of snow, the vessel followed its course peacefully and securely. The passengers were still at rest, not fearing the least danger, when all at once a terrible shock awoke them. The vessel had struck on a sand-bank, and in a single instant, peace, and confidence, and security fled, to give place to the dire anguish of despair—the vessel was lost without hope.

Many wrecks have happened on our coasts—in few have the victims been kept so long in suspense, in few have the circumstances been so heart-rending. Since five o'clock in the morning of that fatal Monday until Wednesday evening [Here the Cardinal's chronology is awry], the unfortunate passengers watched vessels passing in the distance, unable to come to their aid. Signals of distress followed one another without ceasing. The signals were answered but no help came. Oh! how dreadful must such an agony have been. And these holy souls, these good sisters, were so resigned in the tranquility of their confidence in God, that they showed not the smallest sign of agitation or fear. They remained quietly in their cabins and when at length they were asked to mount the riggings, as a last chance of safety, they refused—they were already prepared for the great voyage of eternity—life and death were the same to them. When at length a means of escape was at hand they allowed others to take their places and save themselves.

Can you imagine the horror of their position during the anxious hours of waiting? What terrible scenes around them! The agony, the despair, the piercing cries of their fellow-passengers! The roaring of the tempest, the terrifying cracking of the vessel; and nevertheless in such surroundings a divine calm pacified the souls of these holy victims. Why then should we weep? More than fifty others met their death in the same shipwreck, and we can confidently hope that the calm resignation, Christian hope, and peaceful joy of these holy women served as an example for those who shared their dangers in those long hours of agony. How many acts of faith, how many acts of contrition, how many acts of submission to the divine will, how many acts of hope and confidence in the love of Jesus Christ, must these sisters have offered for themselves and their companions in misfortune? How powerfully must their example, like an eloquent voice, have strengthened the courage of those who are no longer, and united them all in a general preparation for death.

It is interesting to speculate on what the effect on the same congregation would have been, had the famous poem that was to be inspired by the wreck been read in place of Manning's rather florid oration.

After his sermon, Cardinal Manning pronounced the absolution. To continue Father Whitsker's account:

> The congregation passed by the coffins, and viewed the glorious remains of these noble Tertiaries. The lids were fastened, and the coffins covered with palls. The funeral procession was then started: cross and acolytes, and servers, followed by the schoolchildren on foot, four hearses, and numberless coaches. It is estimated that forty thousand people lined the streets from Stratford to Leytonstone.

The order of the procession was precisely recorded. After the cross-bearer came a long train of servers, as well as boys from Catholic schools in Stratford. Then came girl pupils, and then the former occupants of 2 Eden Villas, the Sisters of the Sacred Heart, now of Homerton. With them walked the nuns of Jesus and Mary from across The Grove in Stratford.

The figure of forty thousand seems extraordinary, even given the great interest aroused in the public imagination by the wreck of the *Deutschland*. Other reports claim about four thousand people formed the procession—and it must be remembered that Father Whitsker's account was written nearly twenty-two years later. All the same, it was based on the eyewitness statement of Father Francis Verhagen himself. Whatever the number, the point is well made: Stratford and Leytonstone were linked that day by a black ribbon of sorrow. The presence of children in the procession—they had also met the coffins on their arrival in Stratford —would be looked on askance today. It does not seem to have excited comment at the time. The Catholic journal *The Universe* took up the description:

> All the way the windows of the houses and shops were thronged with people, and with the exception of a few 'tosses of the head' on the part of several persons on seeing the cross

borne in procession, the utmost respect and even sympathy were manifested by all. Several of the police force were also at the funeral, but their office was a sinecure, for nothing occurred to call for their interference.

The journey from the Stratford church to St Patrick's Roman Catholic Cemetery at Leytonstone is about two miles. The procession would have set out from Grove Crescent Road and turned left into The Grove; then left at Maryland Point into Leytonstone Road. Continuing for about a mile, the cortège would then have turned left into Langthorne Road, and reached the main cemetery entrance and mortuary chapel some four hundred yards further on. Here Father Francis carried out the burial service. *The Universe* continues:

> Arrived at the cemetery, the coffins were placed on the shoulders of several men, and, preceded by clergy and acolytes bearing lighted tapers, they left the mortuary chapel and advanced towards the newly opened graves. Here the final office was chanted in the most impressive manner, the bodies were lowered into the earth, and then, in conclusion, all knelt down to offer up a prayer for the eternal repose of the souls of those nuns, as yet unknown, who were drowned in the wreck of the Deutschland.

In stark contrast to the pomp and dignity of the nuns' burial, the violent sequel of the *Mosel* explosion in Bremerhaven was continuing to unwind. The *Weser Zeitung* explained what had happened:

> The 'Mosel' was ready to commence her journey on Saturday morning. The steam-tug 'Simson' lay under her bows, having to pull the 'Mosel' through the ice into the Channel. At the last moment two wagons came on from Lloyd's Hall, one with mail goods, the other with passengers' luggage, both to be shipped. The whole was taken towards the steamer by carts, and when the last of them, with four cases and a barrel, was unloaded in front of the 'Mosel', a stupendous explosion took place.

The effect of this was dramatic: because the quay was so thronged with people, both passengers and those seeing loved ones off, the human devastation could hardly have been worse. A witness who had been standing under the gangway remembered a huge report, and the air filling with black lumps. Such was the cloud of dust and smoke that for a time he could not see anything on shore at all. Thinking at first that one of the ship's boilers had exploded, he flung himself to the ground. He quickly found himself covered with sand, broken glass, timber, and—to his horror—pieces of human flesh and bones: 'in large reeking pools of blood you might see here an arm, there a calf, intestines, a mutilated bust'. The damage to the ship herself was considerable. Not one skylight was left intact, cabins had been crushed by the pressure of the explosion, portholes had been forced inwards, and the whole ship was 'smeared with blood, and stuck over with pieces of flesh and other human debris'. The front of the navigation cabin had been completely stove in.

One family, the Etmers, were seeing their emigrant son off to California. The father, mother, son and son-in-law were all killed outright. The daughter-in-law lost an arm, while her baby had a hand blown off. The cart that carried the explosives completely disintegrated, the horse that was pulling it 'having all four feet blown off near the hooves'. It was said that a hole six to seven feet deep had been left in the quay, looking as though 'the earth had been rammed down from above'. The tug crew escaped relatively unhurt, being below the level of the quay, although the *Simson*'s deck was wrecked.

The *Weser Zeitung*, in common with other newspapers of the time, spared no imagery in bringing its readers a full picture of the horror on Bremerhaven quay that Saturday. The final toll was 128 dead and 156 wounded, and the disaster left fifty-six widows and 135 orphans. On the Tuesday after the explosion, forty corpses were buried in Bremerhaven, together with several wooden chests filled with unidentified fragments of bodies.

At 4.25pm on 16th December, William Henry King Thomas, the American who had admitted to planting the explosive trunk, died in hospital. His wife had arrived at his bedside twenty-four hours earlier. His suicide attempt had been a determined one; after his wound had been bandaged, he repeatedly removed the dressing until his strength was so diminished that he could no longer do so. At first it had been thought that he was insane, and that the explosion had triggered something in his unbalanced mind that made him claim it as his work—such guilt complexes are not, after all, unknown. What lent plausibility to this idea was Thomas's deathbed claim that there was a second case containing explosives; yet when the supposed second suspect case was examined, it was found to hold nothing suspicious. (It is conceivable, though not likely, that the explosion had ignited both containers together.) It soon became apparent, however, that this concept of an unhinged innocent could not apply to Thomas. Here was a cold, clear-headed man whose greed had made him stop at nothing. At first he had claimed that he had accomplices in New York. Later, however, he denied that anyone else was involved, and no evidence was ever found to prove that this second statement was untrue. In his confession, he had given his home as Brooklyn, New York. He was thought to be about thirty-five years of age.

As the facts clarified, Thomas began to emerge as something of a colourful character. He had registered under the name Thomassen, but when questioned about the discrepancy had claimed that he had changed his name to avoid being prosecuted for running the blockade during the American Civil War, when he had captained a vessel called the *Old Dominion*. Taken to America at the age of two, and a naturalised American, he had been born in Beckholt, Westphalia. In fact, he had links with both ends of the Salzkotten story—for later investigations showed that after the Civil War he had boarded for a time at the Southern Hotel in St Louis, close to where the first German nuns were to settle. Clearly he was a man people remembered—perhaps he had the same sort of charisma and style as that famous fictional blockade runner, Rhet Butler. He was recalled vividly by staff at the Southern Hotel as a 'stout, well built man' with sandy hair and whiskers. And it is hardly surprising they remembered him, because he had at one time placed $70,000 in US bonds in the hotel safe.

From St Louis he went to Highland, Illinois, where he stayed at the Highland House Hotel and handled his money 'in a loose manner'. It was here that he met one Miss Paris, the daughter of a well-to-do milliner. They fell in love and quickly married, after which Thomas returned with his new bride to St Louis, and bought a house from one Mr Derby on the corner of Fifth and Olive Streets. The couple had four children, the youngest still a baby at the time of the Bremerhaven incident. It is clear that throughout his time in St Louis and Highland he was being watched with regard to his blockade-running activities, and there were even rumours that a detective who was on his track had been paid 5,000 dollars in hush money. During the Civil War he seems to have lived in Virginia, but had been in Europe since 1866, living in Leipzig, then in a suburb of Dresden, where he seems to have been held in high esteem. From these bases he made occasional trips back to America. Twice during 1875 he was there, the second time without his wife's knowledge. At this stage he appears to have lost all his money, and desperation was strengthening his resolve. After his second trip to America, he had written to his banker, telling him that arrangements had been made to clear all debts in December.

All the evidence indicates that Thomas had planned with considerable care the campaign that nearly ended in the destruction of the *Mosel*. In October 1875 he had spent a week in Liverpool, apparently weighing up whether or not to put his plan into practice there. Perhaps he had finally picked Bremerhaven because he considered that the new German state had enough enemies to make such an explosion as he planned appear to be the possible work of any one of them. During the time he spent in Bremen preparing the barrel that was to contain the explosives—a period of about two weeks—he stayed at the Stadt Bremen Hotel, and was working with two barrel-makers in a hired coach-house owned by a Dr Florke. These barrel-makers, Delvendahl and Luben, were, like his landlord, completely unaware of his plans, and it was they who unwittingly constructed the barrel. It seems extraordinary that neither of them apparently sensed suspicious circumstances. Delvendahl had made the original barrel, consisting of two compartments, using a section of a larger barrel in which there was a flap. It would seem that one compartment contained the explosives, while the other held the timing device. Luben later modified the barrel, and it was finally sealed by a journeyman cooper, before Thomas took it to the Lloyd's storeroom in Bremerhaven and calmly instructed the staff there that the barrel should be kept warm.

He had imported the explosives from America, having had them originally delivered to his Brooklyn home. As to the clockwork igniting device, for some two years he had been working with a mechanician by the name of Fuchs from Bernburg in the province of Anhalt in South Germany. The device was designed to work for ten days silently, at the end of which time a lever would strike the explosive with the force of a thirty-pound hammer. Thomas had ordered twenty similar pieces of equipment from Fuchs, who had first met Thomas in the spring of 1873. Throughout the operation, Fuchs had believed the device was for a peaceful purpose: Thomas had told him that he owned a silk goods manufactory in America, and wanted a machine which, after ten days, would with one stroke break a thousand threads. Whether Fuchs was incompetent, or whether Thomas had set the device incorrectly, will never be known.

The character of the perpetrator of such a malicious act clearly provided the press with a good story. The *Bremer Nachrichten* stated: 'The criminal is said to give the impression of a hardened sinner, making his statement in a cunning and calculated manner. He is of clear and sound mind, and there is no trace of insanity in his statement.' The paper went on to give an account of Thomas's attempted suicide:

> The three doctors who were summoned, Dr Rothe, Dr Brickenstein [apparently no relation to the Captain of the *Deutschland*] and Dr Luce, found Thomas in his shirt sleeves lying stretched out on the sofa of the stateroom. He was breathing with difficulty, was unconscious and his face was spotted with blood. The doctors saw a significant head wound, and after a superficial examination thought they could see brain tissue mixed with blood.

By this time it was 5.30 on the afternoon of the explosion and Dr Rothe arranged transport to take Thomas to the camp hospital that had been set up to deal with the injured. It was clear that the man was very badly hurt, although at this time the source of his injury was a mystery, the gun being found only some two hours later. Even though the injury did not match those of the other victims, it was felt that he must have received the wound in the explosion. It was curious, of course, that the Captain had reported Thomas's stateroom doors to be locked, and that they had had to be forced before he had been found in this condition. With some difficulty, eight men carried the corpulent Thomas in a blanket down the slippery gangway from the *Mosel*. The bullet was found and removed, at the hospital on Monday 13th December. Even as his treatment began, rumours were spreading that the *Mosel* had been blown up deliberately by smuggled explosives. William Thomas would not be able to make his confession for some hours, but already his name was being linked to the crime, because of the circumstances of his discovery in the stateroom and the subsequent finding of the bullet.

The investigation that was later to find Thomas guilty was led by Inspector Schnapel of the Bremerhaven police. In the meantime, there was a mass funeral for the victims: the press described the town as resembling 'an enormous house of mourning. Every ship and hotel is flying its flag at half mast.' An appeal for the dependants of those killed and injured was quickly set up, asking 'our prosperous townsfolk to help alleviate the need' of the families 'of emigrants, labourers and manual workers who will be plunged into great hardship by the death or mutilation of their breadwinner'.

While some of the German papers were drawing the conclusion that Thomas's crime was the natural result of 'the mercenary civilisation of America', the *New York Times* reports of the explosion were suggesting the implementation of certain measures at shipping ports which have, in the latter part of the twentieth century, become all too familiar in airports around the world:

> A rigid inspection of all goods shipped on board steamers and all baggage not accompanied by its owners would not only render any such attempt abortive, but would put a stop to the practice of shipping dangerous articles under false names. There is no doubt that Dynamite, Phosphorus and other chemicals which cannot be openly shipped on board passenger vessels are often carried without the knowledge of the ship owners. The travelling public must be protected against such dangers, and it is the duty of the companies to take active measures to prevent the possibility of their recurrence.

When the third North German Lloyd steamer, the *Salier*, arrived at Southampton the following Saturday bound for New York with the survivors of the two tragic disasters, the German Consul was able to assure Southampton magistrates that the cargo of the ship had been 'strictly examined to ascertain that there were no explosive substances on board such as the culprit Thompson [Thomas] had endeavoured to get placed on board the *Mosel* at Bremen'.

What Thomas could not have known was that, had his plan succeeded, he would probably have killed those who had so narrowly escaped death on the *Deutschland*—although it seems unlikely that this would have moved him unduly. In fact, it was later learned that he had originally intended to travel with his deadly cargo on the *Deutschland*, but that he had not been in possession of the explosives in time to meet the sailing. It would seem that one way and another, fate had earmarked the *Deutschland* as a doomed ship. While the official inquiry was to satisfy itself that there were no suspicious circumstances in her loss, she would, had Thomas had his way, have been the victim of a man-made disaster much worse than the tragedy on the Kentish Knock.

On the day that the news of Thomas's death was reaching the world, the *Daily Telegraph* was reporting what it referred to as 'an astonishing article' in the leading Berlin commercial journal, the *Boersen Zeitung*. The vitriol of this paper's attack on the English people, and the residents of Harwich in particular, makes every extravagant claim made by other papers during the *Deutschland* case fade into insignificance:

The steamer was wrecked almost within the shadow of St Paul's. A large number of the passengers miserably perished before the very eyes of Englishmen who contemplated their struggles with the utmost tranquility of soul. To the human compassion aroused by this frightful fact is added the indignation which has been caused by English subjects in every German heart wherever it may be by this heavy insult to his national pride, to the atonement of which insult absolutely nothing has hitherto been done. In this case the State and Justice are not concerned with a single vile criminal, but a nation is opposed to a nation, the German Empire against the British nation. The matter can and must be regarded in no other light if Germans are not again to be hurled back to the deepest degradation of national thought and feeling. We have waited to express our judgement upon the ghastly facts of the 'Deutschland' affair until the details reached us, in order not unjustly to pronounce upon the indifference of the English population towards the stranded ship. The population of Harwich contemplated the 'Deutschland's struggle with the waves for four and twenty long hours, and answered the signals for help in a manner surpassing the most brutal cynicism, and without offering the least assistance, finally advancing the ridiculous excuse that no lifeboat was at hand. Even admitting this, one cannot but be penetrated with the most profound astonishment that the inhabitants of Harwich were as unacquainted with the use of the telegraph or other plentiful means of communication as though they had been natives of Honolulu or Otaholta, whom they resemble in other respects. All means of communication were disregarded in order to surfeit upon the German's death-struggle as though they had been man-eating Patagonians, inhabitants of that England stuffed with civilisation which attempts to react in a most vehement manner to every wrong done to its subjects, whether in civilised or uncivilised countries. England will not be surprised if we demand the strictest account from her for the brutalities committed by the Harwich population and the local authorities towards the 'Deutschland'. A simple judicial proceeding cannot atone for this tremendous offence. The English Government must acknowledge and apologise for this wrong in the most positive and emphatic manner. It must give guarantees against such occurrences for the future. The most entire satisfaction must be given for this grave neglect towards Germans of the 'Deutschland', against which the Harwich population has sinned. But the nation of the 'Deutschland', mighty and great as it has grown, which feels herself wounded in the most inward heart of her national pride, and which is also great and mighty enough to obtain for herself the satisfaction which, if not accorded willingly, the authority of the German Government will be equal to procuring for the German people satisfaction in full that is due. We do not bring back from France's bloody fields only an increment of territory and a war indemnity, but also the consciousness of our national might and power, which we

Thomas Barnard (1816-1896), a Rowhedge man, and skipper of the *New Unity*, one of the Colne smacks involved in the *Deutschland* salvage operation. *John Leather*

Anchor Quay, Rowhedge, as it is today. This village was the home of many of the Colne fisherman, but the smacks are now long-gone. *Sean Street*

The steam-tug *Harwich* at Ha'penny Pier, Harwich, where the survivors were brought ashore. The Great Eastern Hotel is on the right. *Leonard Weaver*

urch Street, Harwich, about 1910. The Three Cups inn, where the inquest was held, is on the left-
1d side of the road, next to the church. *Leonard Weaver*

arwich railway station in 1867. From here the bodies of the nuns began their journey to Stratford.
onard Weaver*

d:	38	d:	_Barbara Hültenschmidt_, barmh. Schwester, a...
			Salzkotten, näher... un...
d:	39	d:	_Henrica Faßbaender_, barmh. Schwester a...
			Salzkotten, näher... un...
d:	40	d:	_Norbeta Reinkober_, barmh. Schwester, a...
			Salzkotten, näher... un...
d:	41	d:	_Brigitta Damhorst_, barmh. Schwester, a...
			Salzkotten, näher... un...
d:	42	d:	_Aurea Badzinra_, barmh. Schwester, a...
			Salzkotten, näher... un...
27ten Jan 76 ... Uhr...	43	d:	_Hermann Mehrer_ aus Gönnoda...

Part of North German Lloyd's casualty list for the wreck, showing the names of the five nuns. *Franciscan Sisters*

Below left: The Church of St Francis of Assisi, Stratford, Essex, as it was in 1868. *Father Justin McLoughlin OFM*

Below right: Father Francis Verhagen, Superior of the Stratford friary, who claimed the bodies of the nuns in the name of the Roman Catholic Church and brought them to Stratford. *Burns & Oates Ltd/ London Borough of Newham Local Studies Library*

will not allow anyone to undervalue, and which we shall know how to exert against anyone who dares to molest German subjects or to violate the duties of humanity against them in a brutal manner.

From the pen of any but the most hysterical of gutter-journalists, it would have been tantamount to a declaration of war—which is clearly how its anonymous author intended it to read. Indeed, the *Essex Telegraph*, taking the whole thing as a joke, reprinted the article under the headline: 'Expected War between Germany and Harwich'. With its tongue firmly in its cheek, it declared, 'Harwich is for it! One of the German newspapers demands a declaration of war in the following bellicose article. The rest of England must wash its hands of the affair and leave Harwich to settle accounts with its opponents . . .' Yet, ludicrous as these rantings were, it was clear that questions *were* being asked, and they were questions that could only be answered by means of a full and meticulous inquiry and report.

7 The Inquest

To the popular imagination, it is a truism that 'disasters always go in threes'. And the *Deutschland* wreck was indeed one of a number of calamities that occurred at about the same time, as the *Illustrated London News* mournfully noted in its issue of Saturday 11th December 1875:

> Disaster upon disaster. A week of disasters. Disasters at sea, disasters on shore. The proverbial saying is that misfortunes never come singly, which can hardly be accepted as true in point of fact, but is true in point of impression. Isolated calamities soon pass into oblivion. When they are clustered together in a heap they live longer in the public memory. There is scarcely a week in the year in which something does not happen which, momentarily at least, shocks the public mind; but it is only now and then that a rapid and almost instantaneous succession of such shocks startles it into a temporary forgetfulness of all other events. The weather during the past week has been memorable, and it may be that the calamities of the week have some connection with the weather. December is not the best of all months for seafaring occupations; and, if tradition may be trusted, it is the worst of all months for mining enterprise. At any rate, the records of the week tend to illustrate what may be accepted as the common rule.

The 'records of the week' included a startling trio of mining accidents, one in Barnsley and two in South Wales. The first, at Tredegar, had happened on the previous Saturday, while those at Barnsley and at the Llan Colliery in Glamorganshire, had happened almost simultaneously on the Monday of the *Deutschland* catastrophe. The *Illustrated London News* leader noted:

> Three explosions by which, severally, twenty-one, twelve, and above a hundred lives were lost (not to mention the numerous cases in which serious injuries, not amounting to loss of life, have been inflicted), are well calculated to make us pause and consider in what way, and to what extent, our responsibility may be involved . . . Under any imaginable system there can be little doubt that labour in mines will be exposed to accident. But there can be little doubt either, we think, that legislation has not yet extended the protection which the necessity of the case requires to those who delve for our fuel in the bowels of the earth.

Turning to the loss of the *Deutschland*, the leader-writer found himself taking another standpoint—although, once again, the question of official responsibility was uppermost in his mind. Unlike the German journalist who had attacked Harwich and the English so violently, the *Illustrated London News* man chose to use the facts and a subtle choice of phrases as his weapons:

> The wreck of the 'Deutschland', one of the latest and best vessels of the North German Lloyd Company, and the great loss of life which it involved, will, as a matter of course, be the subject of searching investigation. As the story of it reads at present, one cannot understand how it should have happened. Her course was straightforward enough, her officers were competent, and the stress of the weather to which she was exposed could hardly be regarded as extraordinary. Yet she was wrecked within a few hours of her starting, upon a spit of sand quite out of her way. There was a snow storm, it is true, and it is also true that there must have been compasses on board. We make no suggestions. We draw no inference. We are concerned, for the present, only with the facts. Many lives have been lost by the disaster, and lost, we may add, in the words of a contemporary journal, 'on a well-known sand, and in weather which, though stormy and wintry, was by no means unusual.

This last statement was one that even at the time the *Illustrated London News* was going to press, was being hotly discussed among the sea-going folk of Harwich and other towns along the east coast of England. Many old sea-dogs claimed they had not known a night like that Sunday/Monday in a lifetime of sailing those waters. If the weather *was* unusual, though, it did not keep every vessel in port. In fact, at the very time the *Deutschland* was getting into difficulties, the Queen of Denmark, on her way home after visiting Queen Victoria, was sailing to France from Dover. According to the Court circular for the week:

The Queen of Denmark and her daughter Princess Thyra left Marlborough House on Sunday evening, on her return to Denmark. Her Majesty arrived at Dover from Charing Cross at a quarter to eleven p.m., and remained at the Lord Warden Hotel until half-past twelve, when the Queen and Princess Thyra embarked from the pier on board the special steamer, 'Samphire', for Calais, whence they proceeded to Paris.

The circular does not record what sort of a crossing the Queen and Princess enjoyed.

It can hardly be denied that, as the *Illustrated London News* noted, the Kentish Knock was a well known sandbank. It had been notorious amongst seamen for generations, and it was certainly not a landmark to be taken for granted on a stormy night. Some of the statements made by national and international reporters during the days when the *Deutschland* was making news still anger some east-coast people today; as Hervey Benham, the marine historian, has said: 'They knew enough to be a bloody nuisance, and not enough to do any good.'

It is startling to realise what a commonplace thing shipwreck was, even as late as 1875. In that year the English national press published a list of German ships, wrecked off British coasts in recent years, from which passengers and crew had been rescued by lifeboats of the Royal National Lifeboat Institution. They counted nineteen wrecked vessels, from which 702 lives were saved, in addition to which five other German ships had been helped out of difficulties.

Up until the end of the nineteenth century, the east coast of England was a graveyard for shipping, particularly where the sand fingers from the Thames estuary creep out into the North Sea. Navigation then could be a rather haphazard affair, and often a captain would mistake the lights of Yarmouth or Felixstowe for the mouth of the Thames, turn too early, and find himself aground. Added to this, the sands themselves caused such confusing currents that, once caught in bad weather, the errant master could soon lose all control of his vessel. Long remembered in these parts was the great storm of September 1671, when seventy-five ships were wrecked. A contemporary report complained that 'the sea is so full of wreck in these coasts that those at sea are forced to look out sharp to steer clear of it'. On Lowestoft Sands, off the East Anglian coast, in 1770, thirty vessels and their crews were lost, while nineteen years later forty ships went down between Yarmouth and Southwold, with the cost of at least 120 lives. On one occasion in October 1820 there were five wrecks on the sands off Harwich, and many more vessels in difficulties. During this particular storm, nearly one hundred feet of esplanade were washed away at Harwich itself.

The light-vessels that marked the sands played a vital role, but even they were fallible. In 1840, during a series of terrifying gales, eight vessels went aground on the Sunk Sand after the light-vessel marking the danger had been driven from her moorings. In April 1845 the *Essex Standard* noted a Spanish brig ashore on the Long Sand, and in January of the following year reported: 'The accounts we continue to receive from sea are truly appalling. A large ship is ashore on the Knock Sand just above the Blacktail Beacon, with copper bottom and painted ports, supposed to be a West Indiaman; another large ship on the Maplin not far distant, and two or three others in different places.'

Alongside this marine carnage grew an organised salvage and rescue service. There were real pickings to be had by the many fishing smacks along the Essex coast, when the cry, 'Wreck!' went up. Any vessel that was wrecked and abandoned was considered as legitimate salvage. The sailing gear, all other equipment and cargo would usually be taken from her and landed at a receiving port, such as Brightlingsea or Harwich, where the Receiver of Wreck could catalogue the goods and pay the salvors a percentage of their value. It was an occupation that brought a much valued additional income to the smacksmen, or 'scropers' as they were known along the coast.

A Colne River fishing smack. *Jemma Street*

The Essex smacks—mainly from the Colne River communities of Brightlingsea, Rowhedge and Wivenhoe—were deceptive. Apparently frail little craft, they were in fact built for all kinds of weather and all kinds of tasks, including deep-sea oyster fishing. And, with a length usually of some sixty feet and a weight of twenty tons minimum, they were built for speed. They habitually carried a crew of five, comprising captain, mate, two hands and a cabin-boy, who frequently doubled as cook. Many of these smacks were built at Rowhedge on the River Colne, downstream from Colchester. Thus the men that made them understood through personal experience the conditions that these vessels would have to withstand. It was here that Fud Cook's *Aquiline* came into being. Typical of the genre, she was one of three sister smacks, all noted for their speed and durability. There was the *Bluebell* run by a smacksman called Jack Spitty, and, most notable of all, the big *New Unity*, owned first by William Madder of Wivenhoe, and later by Thomas Barnard. Under Turner Barnard, she played a great part in rescue operations during the 1870s, when most of the victims seem to have been German emigrant ships.

For, as already noted, the *Deutschland* was by no means the first during those years to fall foul of the Kentish Knock. On one occasion the *New Unity*, in a succession of trips, rescued no less than 350 lives. In 1881 she was herself lost on the Grain Spit, after a long and distinguished career during which, for a time, she was even hired by Trinity House. Up to thirty smacks are known to have been in attendance at some shipwrecks. The courage and heroism of the men who sailed these little ships—men who styled themselves the 'Swin rangers' after their hunting grounds, the deeps of the East and West Swin—was remarkable.

Many memories went back to a famous wreck of 1856, when a German ship ran aground on the Knock John, further up the estuary; the salvagers on this occasion found no life on board but a cat, a dog and a cockerel. But the goods the ship carried were among the richest ever seen by the smacksmen—clocks, pianos, fine clothing, china, silk, paintings, guns and daggers were all there waiting to be saved. As one eyewitness said, 'She's got everything except a pulpit!' On this occasion, not everything reached the hands of the receivers and customs authorities; bitterness among rivals led to a woman being burned in effigy in Brightlingsea for informing on men who had concealed some of the ship's goods. It all ended in near-rioting in the High Street.

As well as the *Aquiline*, other smacks assisted during the *Deutschland* salvage: there was the *Qui Vive*, owned by Thomas Aldridge, the *Faith*, captained by William P. Cheek, the *Concord* under the command of David Martin, and Charles Crosby's *New Blossom*. Turner Barnard's *New Unity* was present as salving began, although conditions prevented her and the other smacks from getting any closer than the *Aquiline* had done at the height of the storm. Barnard's great-nephew, John Leather, himself a distinguished naval architect and author with a lifetime in shipbuilding, still lives in the area, and remembers vividly family stories of the smacks and their salvaging exploits. There were other Barnards, too, at the wreck: Thomas Barnard aboard the *Thomas and Mary* was there, with his sixteen-year-old son Jim, later to become Captain James Barnard. Thomas Barnard was a well known east-coast pilot, as well as a smack-owner, salvager and fisherman. He was reputed to have also dabbled in smuggling; his granddaughter Margaret has no doubt that the large cellars under his Rowhedge house were put to good use.

Local legend has it that Tom Barnard saved over nine hundred lives; many were the occasions when members of the family were chaired as heroes through the streets of Harwich after a successful rescue. Some Barnards received medals from foreign governments for saving their nationals from wrecks, invariably under conditions of gale and blizzard. The esteem in which the family was held was demonstrated at the *Deutschland* inquiry, when Williams, the German Vice-Consul at Harwich, speaking up for the Colne River men in general, praised them in particular.

Before light on the Tuesday, Williams had gone down to the pier to see if any rescue ships had gone out. At this time, it was known only that a ship, nationality unknown, was aground somewhere. In fact, it was initially thought that it was a cargo ship, without passengers. Williams only discovered the truth when later he saw the *Liverpool* steaming back to port, with a German flag flying at half-mast. At that early hour of the morning Williams sent a message to the Colne smacks, via Colchester, with the words: 'The Barnards are there; if anyone can render help, they will.' He learned later that the smacksmen of Rowhedge and elsewhere on the Colne had mustered on the Monday night, but had not deemed it prudent to venture out.

The 'scropers' of the Colne River knew their waters and their craft intimately. And as well as showing courage, they were also usually men of considerable business acumen. Any image of illiterate sea-going yokels must be quickly banished: for these men could carry on official correspondence and were often remarkably well read. They were civil and forward-looking individuals, from comfortable homes with devoted families, and many of their sons and grandsons went on to become able navigators or masters of merchant ships and yachts. Some, like Thomas Barnard's great-grandson, went on to highly successful careers in shipbuilding and engineering.

Today, the villages of Rowhedge and Wivenhoe look at one

another across a bend in the Colne, where the river suddenly narrows on its approach to Colchester, just as they did 120 years ago when their quays were bustling with smacks and their cargoes. Today, however, life is very different, and the Anchor Inn at Rowhedge, on the quay which takes its name, plays host to a changed style of customer, as village life shifts its emphasis and the high-rise office blocks of modern Colchester loom over the fields to the west. When I visited the place in 1990, many of the old buildings along the quay were being demolished to make way for 'desirable waterside residences', designed for weekend yachtsmen and commuters. It is good to see that there are still working wharves, though, both at Rowhedge and at Wivenhoe, where yachts are built with the same skills that made former inhabitants expert smack-builders. Such villages play a crucial part in the east-coast's maritime heritage—and in the nation's history, for on the Colne River you are in the heart of Cinque Port country. Brightlingsea, too, downstream and sheltering from the sea in its own creek opposite Mersea Island, proudly proclaims this fact as the visitor enters the town, and today as before it continues in its long-established businesses of boat-building and oyster fishing. Picturesque these communities may be—particularly at high tide, with their yachts and smacks bobbing on the glittering water—but those who live there have never been afraid to get their hands dirty.

From early times the fishing communities of the east coast have had their own traditions and beliefs, many of which revolved around the fish that were the focus of their livelihood. Dogfish livers were valued, for instance, for their oil, which was used to lubricate sails and sea-boots, while flounders' blood on sugar was said to cure whooping-cough. There were songs too, including 'The smacksmen's life at Sea', which the men sang as they arrived with a good catch at Harwich:

When we come to Harwich Pier
The folks all flock from far and near
To see us haul our cod on deck,
Then whack 'em on the head with a bloody great stick.

Harwich, too, has preserved its past alongside its present. The old town, nestling where the Rivers Stour and Orwell meet the sea, is full of interest to the seeker-out of naval history. Behind the port is the linked town of Dovercourt, or 'Druvrecurt' as it is named in Domesday Book. Harwich itself does not appear until 1196, under the various names of 'Herdwic', 'Herewyche' and 'Herewiz'. It is in fact a medieval town constructed for a very practical reason, on a grid system: the three main streets are traversed by narrow alleys, in order to break the force of the gales blowing in from the North Sea, or 'German Ocean'. Its church spire and its lighthouses provide now, as they did for the mariners of the past, a welcome landmark after the terrors of the sandbanks beyond the harbour entrance. The other major landmark, to the south, is the giant Naze Tower, built by Trinity House in 1720 at Walton on the Naze, which marks the official northernmost point of the Thames estuary. It is still a valuable navigational point which, in good weather, is visible from the Kentish Knock.

The sense of history one feels in the old town of Harwich contrasts sharply with the scene on the other side of the estuary, where the vast container port of Felixstowe operates around the clock, its huge mobile cranes inching up and down the quayside, unloading at the rate of sixty containers a minute when working at full stretch. In 1989 it became the busiest container port in the world, being the first to handle over a million containers in one year. Yet until 1972, apart from a small dock with its 1875 buildings near the Landguard Point, all this was mud and marshland. The growth of containerism provided the impetus for this astonishingly rapid land reclamation and development.

But growth upstream of the port has been abruptly terminated: the quay ends suddenly, with marshland stretching flat and wild along the Orwell River, presenting an aspect that gives an idea of what the whole area must have looked like in the 1870s, when the main centre of activity was at Harwich. Up river, on the Stour, the quays at Parkeston convey today's ferry traffic to the Continent and Scandinavia, but in the nineteenth century it was from the Continental Quay at Harwich that such shipping sailed. And although the old port might at first glance appear to have been overtaken by the brash giants on either side, Harwich provides a necessary continuity with the past without being simply a museum, and remains at the heart of things here, a part of the real world still.

Harwich as it was in 1868, showing the medieval grid system. *Leonard Weaver*

The *Mayflower* sailed from here with a Harwich man, Chris-
topher Jones, as captain, en route for Plymouth and its cargo of

Pilgrim Fathers. Samuel Pepys was twice MP for Harwich, and his name is remembered in the church, in the name of a local restaurant, and frequently in the town's guidebook. The twin 'high' and 'low' lighthouses remain landmarks, although neither is now in service—one being a private residence and the other providing a home for the local maritime museum. Among other features, the town boasts the oldest unaltered purpose-built cinema in Britain, the Electric Palace, built in 1911. One of the town's most venerable streets, Church Street, contains the ancient guildhall and the Three Cups Hotel, dating from the sixteenth century, which played its part in the *Deutschland* story—although its appearance is rather different from that of 1875, and it is doubtful whether Nelson, who stayed here with Lady Hamilton, would recognise it today. Next to the Three Cups stands the fine church of St Nicholas, a place of worship frequented by the great and famous for centuries. Boswell and Dr Johnson prayed here before Boswell set off on his European tour; Daniel Defoe attended service here, as did Drake, Howard, Frobisher and Nelson himself.

Just a few yards up stream from the Great Eastern Hotel, where the survivors from the *Deutschland* were cared for, stood the Continental Pier where the main ferries berthed. Today, this has been rebuilt as the Trinity Pier, and is used as a maintenance base for Trinity House vessels and buoys. Directly opposite the Great Eastern stands the Ha'penny Pier, mentioned earlier; it was built in 1851–4, and so called because of the halfpenny toll that was charged to enter it. It was a popular departure point for local steamers, and today, it remains in use as the base for the Felixstowe Ferry and the home of the fine modern lifeboat the *John Fison*, a telling reminder to many Harwich people of the days when the very presence of such a vessel would have been considered controversial.

The smacks had long been seen as fulfilling the requirements of lifeboats and salvagers combined. But in the nineteenth century, with the increased volume of traffic in these waters and the continuing high marine mortality, some began to consider it a matter of neglect that the RNLI had not put a boat at Harwich permanently. However, the problem may well have had a local rather than a national origin. In 1820 a schooner was lost with her crew of nine on the Cork Sand. The *Colchester Gazette* graphically described the scene, and pleaded for something to be done to prevent a recurrence:

> The sea was so tremendous that it was impossible to render any assistance, though several vessels attempted to do so. The poor men were seen to run up the rigging for safety, but such was the power of the waves that they were alternately plunged into the sea and raised into the air, until a heavy sea completely overwhelmed them and the vessel and not a vestige was seen after, nor a soul left to tell the awful tale. It is much to be lamented that amongst various benevolent offers for the welfare of man the establishment of lifeboats on the dangerous parts of the Eastern Coast has been so much neglected; had there been one at this part there is every reason to believe all the crew would have been saved.

As a result of public pressure, a lifeboat was obtained for Harwich. She was built locally, in the naval yard of George Graham, and in 1821 she was launched by the mayoress Mrs Anthony Cox, who named her, in honour of the Lord Lieutenant of Essex, the *Braybrooke*. She was on active service within a year, and assisted with several wrecks between 1822 and 1825. After this point, though, the lifeboat story in Harwich seems to die out—until, that is, December 1875. Perhaps it was felt, after all, that the smacksmen had the ability and the craft to fulfil the task adequately.

Balanced against this, there were stories that told of men from Rowhedge and Leigh, on the Essex coast, sending vessels to their deaths by showing false lights behind sandbanks—organised wreckers in the old Cornish tradition. Yet these were exceptional cases—and unnecessary, since the sea and the sands, left to themselves, provided all the salvage work the scropers could handle. And in 1830 the Admiralty had declared itself keen to 'reward the crews of those vessels who were on the look-out to render aid to vessels in distress in stormy weather'.

Occasionally, when a ship appeared to be beyond help and all that could be done for passengers and crew had been attempted, smacks were known to have moved in to loot; this practice, known as 'wrecking', seems to have gone on up and down the east coast for years. In 1840 Captain Garrick of the Brig *Lochiel*, aground on the Maplin Sands, reported that smacksmen had looted and smashed their way around his ship, with the notable exceptions of Captains Eage and Andrews of the smacks *George and Eliza* and *Fair Traveller*, 'who would take nothing but what belonged to the men they had to take off, and endeavoured to take as many of my things with them as possible. They frequently reprimanded the other men for taking and appropriating to their own use the clothes of the shipwrecked sailors.' The next day, Garrick returned to his ship to find everything gone but the standing rigging. Four years later, the Gunfleet sandbank claimed the *Antoeus*, and the captain and crew were safely taken off. A contemporary report described what happened next: 'Upon the master's return in the afternoon of Saturday it seemed the wreck had suffered great pillage . . . Exertions will no doubt be used by the authorities and others interested in the ship to bring to justice the parties guilty of plundering the ship.'

In 1852 naval gunboats were sent to defend the wreck of the *Renown*, a Scottish schooner aground on the Nore Sands, when crews from Southend on the Essex coast had threatened to strip and break her up. In 1875 the reporter from *The Times* castigated the Admiralty for not protecting the *Deutschland* in the same way. Was there not, after all, an iron-clad man-of-war, the *Penelope*, in Harwich harbour at the time? And did not the crew of the *Penelope* later work on the wreck with the Marine Salvage Association? Why, then, could she not have been sent earlier? According to the irate reporter, the *Deutschland* had been a victim of plunder on an appalling scale. 'While no salvaging smacks came near the 'Deutschland' during the thirty hours in which her 200 passengers and crew were in such sore need of help, the steamtug 'Liverpool' had hardly cleared from the wreck with the survivors before two or three of those smacks came swooping down, and must soon have been followed by others.'

When the *Liverpool* returned with the third mate and the agents for North German Lloyd, the day after the rescue, there were fourteen smacks and luggers around the wreck. They found more than fifty men on board the *Deutschland*, 'breaking open luggage, pillaging cargo, and stripping furnishings from cabins and saloons'. By the time Captain Heathcote of the Marine Salvage Association took charge of the vessel on Thursday 9th December, the wreckers, according to *The Times*, had stripped the ship of braces, running gear, rigging, leaving in fact hardly a ropeyarn. I wish this were the worst that had to be told. Twenty bodies have been brought into Harwich by the steamtug. Mr Guy, the inspector of police here, tells me that, with one exception, not a single valuable was found on the persons of these unfortunate people, and it was clear that their pockets had been turned out and rifled. There were ring-marks on the fingers of women, and of at least one gentleman. The rings themselves had disappeared. No suspicion whatever rests on the crew of the tug. The inference therefore is unavoidable, and it is one which must be painful to all Englishmen.

Here was the raw material from which the German gutter press forged their poisonous invective. While not naming names, the *Times* reporter had identified the main culprits as having 'hailed from the fishing villages on the Colne River, and from Whitstable, Ramsgate and Margate'. If, indeed, looting did occur, it seems likely that it was from this area rather than from Harwich, and Rowhedge may have been the centre of the operation. Locally, stories were told of a farm with barns full of plunder carried off by smacks, and many a seaman, it was said, became the proud owner of a fine watch by mysterious means. Margaret Leather, granddaughter of Thomas Barnard, recalled in her book *Saltwater Village* that 'some crews did well out of well known wrecks', and cited the *Deutschland* as the largest that coast had seen, with its rich cargo including silks and pianos providing rich pickings for the salvagers.

One writer on east-coast salvaging activities, the late Hervey Benham, spoke in his book *Last Stronghold of Sail* of Green's Farm at Rowhedge on the south side of the river as being a depository for goods purloined from the *Deutschland*. It seems that there is no farm of that name in the area today, but there was for many years a distinguished local family called Green, living at Donyland Hall—Rowhedge is a village within the parish of East Donyland—and it has long been said in the area that the 'dove house' at the hall was on several occasions used as the temporary hiding place for contraband. The simplest explanation is that the Green's Farm story is a blend of several local tales. Although most of the smacks that attended the wreck were from the Colne River, at least two from Harwich delivered up their salvage on return to port to the Receiver of Wreck, who, according to the *Times* reporter, 'gives the smacksmen of this port a high character for manliness and fairness of dealing with salvage since he had occasion to proceed against them some 15 years ago, when 17 of them were imprisoned for offences of this description'. It is probable that most of the Colne smacks did the same, although the national press were determined to prove otherwise.

The inquest on the victims of the *Deutschland* disaster was held at the Three Cups Hotel in Harwich, before the Coroner for North Essex, Mr Codd—not inappropriately named, for a large fishing community. It began on 9th December and ran for two days, when it was adjourned for some five days before resuming. The foreman of the jury is recorded as a 'Mr Whitmore, shipowner, formerly a captain in the merchant service'. From a local point of view, it is important to establish the pedigree of those involved. An interpreter, in the person of a Dr Christian of Ipswich, was provided, and North German Lloyd was represented by a solicitor called Chapman. Williams, the German Vice-Consul in Harwich, also attended, along with Edward Brickenstein, who spoke throughout in good English, as well as members of his crew—Dr Franz Bluen, chief physician on the vessel, the chief engineer, the First Officer and a Trinity House pilot.

It soon became evident that, while the main purpose of the inquest was to ascertain the cause of the accident, for the people of Harwich it would also serve to clear the port's name of any accusations of neglect or undue delay in the rescue operation. The jury pressed again and again the question of when the first signals were fired, and asked why there had been such a delay, first in seeing them and then in acting upon them. At one point the Coroner had to intervene:

> The question for the jury to decide is whether the ship was lost through the gross and culpable negligence of the Captain, who admits that he had sole charge of the ship, or whether it was lost by uncontrollable circumstances such as the state of the weather, the snow-storm and the breaking of the propeller. The evidence on these points is not likely to

receive any material addition, and the jury will therefore probably be prepared to return their verdict.

Still the question demanded an answer: when were the signals fired? It was stated that the coastguard saw no rockets on the Sunday night or on the Monday morning. In fact, none was seen until the Monday night. For he had received a first report at 5.30pm on that day, and had sent an answering signal just ten minutes later.

At this point the inquest was adjourned, but the torch of some of the questioners was taken up in the meantime by the reporter from *The Times*. On the morning of the 10th, the Mayor of Harwich had called a meeting of his council in which he raised the question of whether it was not high time that Harwich had its own lifeboat again. The heavy seas had always been seen as the problem, since launching a boat in storm conditions could not fail to be difficult. Captain Carrington of the *Liverpool* had agreed with this point, and signalled the work carried out by the salvaging smacks. But this was not enough for *The Times* reporter, who wrote:

This is a matter of opinion, and the fact is that none of these salving smacks were by, or, at all events, came near the 'Deutschland' to render any help during the thirty hours she was on the sandbank before the passengers and crew were rescued. Another point is that these smacks, anxious as they are to make salvage where property is concerned, find no profit in the saving of life. But the most material point with reference to the lifeboat question is that at the inquest . . . Mr King, the mate of the 'Liverpool' tug-boat, gave sworn evidence that if there had been a lifeboat at Harwich it might have been towed out of the harbour when the rocket signals were seen on Monday evening. On this point, therefore, his evidence directly contradicts the voluntary statement of Captain Carrington as to the use that a lifeboat might have been on Monday night. Carrington, however brave and able a seaman, is an old man, nearer 70 than 60, and a younger man might have been more venturesome.

During the questioning of Thomas King, the jury heard a graphic account of the journey to the *Deutschland*, and the almost frantic frustration of not being able to find her, in spite of the presence of Fud Cook as unofficial navigator.

> The captain ordered steam to be got up, and we remained under steam all night. The reason we did not go out was that we had not a lifeboat. It was blowing a gale of wind and it would not have been prudent for us to go. If we had had a lifeboat we might have towed her, and should have started directly. The wreck was ashore about 25 miles from Harwich; but of course we did not know where she was when we started . . . On first leaving Harwich we spoke to the Cork lightship, which had been firing rockets. We could see nothing from there, but the men at the Cork lightship told us to go to the Sunk lightship, whose signals they had been repeating. At the Sunk lightship we were told that the rockets bore south by east of them. We could not see the wreck from the Sunk, but soon afterwards, we made the Longsand and then sighted the wreck. If we had known where the wreck was at Harwich we should have been able to take a more direct course.

Then a juryman challenged the mate: 'I cannot help thinking that the lifeboat was an afterthought by the people on board the tug. The tug must have left Harwich in much worse weather.' To which King replied bitterly: 'It's all very well for landsmen to talk; I wish they had been there when we were there.'

It is important to consider here the various distances involved in reaching the Kentish Knock. And it should be borne in mind that 'A to B' distances bear little relation to the issue, when the course is full of deadly and unseen obstacles. The direct, as-the-crow-flies course that the *Liverpool* would have had to take is about twenty-two nautical miles (twenty-five statute miles), but the journey would in reality have been at least twenty-five nautical miles by boat because of the intervening sandbanks—and that is without taking into account the necessary calls that Carrington and his men would have made to the lightships in their attempt to locate the wreck. From the mouth of the Colne River, the scropers of Wivenhoe, Rowhedge and Brightlingsea would have faced a hazardous journey of some fifty miles—the direct route is about twenty-five, but even going through the channel known

as the Spitway there would have been little chance of a sailing
vessel reaching its destination on that mileage. On top of this,
wind direction and strength had to be taken into account. From
the other possible rescue locations the distances are equally for-
midable, even when taken as direct routes—virtually impossible
to achieve in storm conditions: from Sheerness, thirty-five nautical miles, from Broadstairs, twenty-three, with Margate as the
nearest landfall at a distance of twenty nautical miles.

The Times opened the whole affair up to public debate, and
correspondence was brisk, particularly on the question of a Harwich lifeboat. Elsewhere, letters were being written that would
change the situation for ever.

Oliver John Williams, Lloyds agent at Harwich, had written
two years before the wreck to Richard Lewis, Secretary of the
Royal National Lifeboat Institution: 'Some fifteen years ago a lifeboat was advocated for Harwich. I gave my opinion against it,
believing it would be a useless expense, since which time I have
no recollection of a single instance where a lifeboat could have
been made available in cases of shipwreck off this port.' Now,
Lewis wrote to Williams:

We have been very much concerned to hear of the fearful
wreck of the steamer 'Deutschland' on the Kentish Knock
Sands, and, adverting to the communications which have
passed between this institution and yourself during the last
twenty years on the subject of a lifeboat for Harwich, I wish
you and other friends there would again give it your best
consideration, and see if something cannot be done to supply
the present deficiency. I am perfectly aware of all the difficulties connected with the undertaking, but the question is
whether we cannot overcome the word which Napoleon said
ought not to be in the Dictionary—impossible. I am sure I
have said enough to induce you to further consider the matter
and favour us with your views upon it.

On 13th December *The Times* published a letter from the Mayor
of Harwich:

Until the arrival of the tug 'Liverpool', a short time since,
there has been no tug stationed at Harwich sufficiently

powerful to be available in those extreme cases when to save life a lifeboat is required, and therefore no endeavour to obtain one has been made, the distance of the sands from the Harbour rendering one almost useless without the aid of steam power . . .

I venture to assert that the seamen of Harwich are not cowards. They have been comrades and companions of men who not only risked their lives, but died in their attempts to rescue others. The widowed women and fatherless children, in the town bear witness to this fact. Allow me to remark that your article contains not one word of thanks or praise to the owner, master, or crew of the 'Liverpool', who, since Tuesday morning have been ceaseless in the endeavour to save life, as well as the bodies of those drowned in the 'Deutschland', and who have freely given their services for that purpose, while others have been salving materials and cargo from the ship.

It may well be that vested interests had something to do with the absence of a lifeboat. As has been said, the smacksmen relied heavily on salvaging to supplement their fragile income, and tugs such as the *Liverpool* were seen as hated rivals in this respect. The argument over the tug was one thing, but an anonymous correspondent, who signed himself simply 'J. H. C. of Broadstairs', made another point:

It ought I think to be known that one effort was made by an English lifeboat to rescue the crew of the unfortunate 'Deutschland'. News of a large steamer being stranded on the Kentish Knock was brought to Broadstairs at noon on Tuesday by a tug, which had received its information from a fishing smack. The lifeboat was immediately manned and launched with great difficulty, owing to the state of the tide. It was towed by the tug to the scene of the disaster, arriving, unhappily, too late to be of any service. But the obvious question occurs why the news was not telegraphed on Monday evening from Harwich to Ramsgate, where the lifeboat and tug are ready for service at any hour of the day or night, and where there has never been any difficulty in collecting a crew. If these had been despatched at once, there seems to be no reason why the whole of the crew and passengers might have been saved from the wreck.

The lifeboat debate was one of the most emotive elements of the *Deutschland* story, and provoked much soul-searching along the east coast. Before the Harwich inquest was over, offers from all over the country had come in from people offering to help fund a boat for the town. It showed 'the promptness and munificence of English charity,' pontificated *The Times*. Lord Stafford made a public offer through the paper's pages, and Sir Edward Kerrison pledged £25; a Miss Burmester of Regents Park volunteered 'to present a full-sized lifeboat to Harwich, to be built under the superintendence of the National Lifeboat Institution, and to be given to the town without conditions'. The High Steward of Harwich himself offered £200 towards the purchase of a lifeboat, and £10 a year towards a fund for its maintenance. The executors of a lady from Bath, Miss Helen Harrison, stated that she had left a legacy of £500 to the RNLI, and that in their opinion the money 'could not be better applied than in placing a lifeboat in this port'. The RNLI itself moved quickly, and on 16th December their representative was in Harwich having discussions with the Mayor as to how to proceed.

The main problem was—and would continue to be—that lifeboats such as existed in those days relied, when the distances were as great as in the *Deutschland* affair, on a tug or similar vessel to tow them within range of the accident. Five years after the 1875 wreck, the then Mayor of Harwich, Alderman John Vaux, would be involved in another controversy over the loss of the barque the *Indian Chief* on the Long Sand. Vaux, like his predecessor Walter Watts, owned a tug, the *Harwich*, and he was on board as she towed Harwich's new lifeboat, the *Springwell*, out to the wreck. However, when he was only a few miles away from the Long Sand, Vaux decided the weather was too bad. So he turned back without consulting the lifeboatmen, and returned to Harwich, towing the lifeboat behind him. The same night a Great Eastern Railway steamer towed the *Springwell* out, but the packet's powerful wake almost wrecked the lifeboat, which had to turn back again. In the end, such rescue as was possible was performed by the Clacton lifeboat. Seventeen people were lost.

*

Just under two weeks after the wreck of the *Deutschland*, an official Board of Trade inquiry would be opened by Henry Cadogan Rothery, the Registrar of the Admiralty Division of the High Court of Justice, under sections 14 and 15 of the 1854 Merchant Shipping Act, part of which gave the Board of Trade the power 'to appoint an Inspector to report upon the nature and causes of any accident or damage which any ship has sustained or caused, or is alleged to have sustained or caused. The inspector thus appointed is by the 15th section authorized to summon witnesses, to require the production of books, papers or documents, and to administer oaths.'

The inquest at the Three Cups Hotel, Harwich, pronounced a verdict of accidental death on the victims of the wreck apportioning no blame to the master of the ship, though stating that she ought to have been in the charge of a more experienced pilot for this part of the voyage. Yet there were many questions for the official inquiry to address, as the reporter for the *Illustrated London News* stated at its opening in his account of 18th December:

> The conduct of some part of the shore boatmen or 'smacksmen', but certainly not of them all, when they got aboard the 'Deutschland', has . . . been mentioned with disapproval. Those to whose behaviour we refer showed more alacrity on the Wednesday and Thursday in stripping the saloon and cabins of valuable property than in any other service. Our artist, having been a witness to this proceeding on the second day named, gives his evidence in the form of a sketch, the perfect veracity of which may be relied upon.

The paper's artist has left us some arresting scenes of the wreck in those days immediately following the storm, and was able to report that he had seen among other things a corpse jammed in a ventilation shaft, head downwards, and with feet protruding at the top.

The artist, who had travelled out with Carrington and the *Liverpool*, praised the rescue operation, while repeating the criticism of a smacksmen, who 'would not leave their more gainful occupation of stripping the furniture and searching for clothes or valuables while dead bodies lay beside them'. But, went on the report significantly, 'The boats, luggers and smacks, whose men are charged with such misconduct, do not belong to Harwich; there were about fourteen of them surrounding the wreck.'

The whole matter of the *Deutschland*, and in particular the holding of an inquiry on English soil, threatened for a time to precipitate a diplomatic crisis between Britain and Germany. This followed a letter, dated 8th December, written on behalf of Lord Derby to Count Munster, the German Ambassador in London:

Mr Ambassador,

The attention of the English Department of Trade has been drawn to the sinking of the German ship, the 'Deutschland', off the Kentish Knock. The aforesaid department is requesting information as to whether the Imperial Government wishes for an official investigation to be held in this country.

I write, therefore, Your Excellency, to request that you be so good as to inform me as soon as possible of your Government's views in this connection.

To which the Ambassador replied on 11th December:

My Lord,

In reply to Your Lordship's kind note of 8th December, I humbly inform you that the Imperial government is in agreement that the authorities of the English government undertake the official inquiry into the sinking of the Bremen ship, the 'Deutschland', near Harwich. I look forward with great interest to hearing from you the results of your inquiry, and meanwhile may I ask you to accept thanks on behalf of my government for your readiness to act on this matter.

The polite diplomatic language of these exchanges was in marked contrast to some of the scenes that ensued in the German parliament when the affair was debated in Berlin on 13th December. It was stated then:

Herr Kapp adverted to the loss of the 'Deutschland'. After dwelling upon the fact that no help was sent for 30 hours, though the accident happened at a distance of *less than four miles from the shore* [Herr Kapp was clearly misinformed on this point], the honourable member asserted that the case of the 'Schiller' had hardly been sufficiently investigated in England, and that the German government ought to have taken steps to secure an impartial and satisfactory inquiry into the loss of the 'Deutschland'.

The *Schiller* was another German transatlantic liner, and her wreck in May 1875 on the Scillies, with the loss of 312 lives, was still very much in everyone's minds. Herr Kapp's point about a British inquiry was taken up by Herr Mosel of Bremen, who 'regretted that the German government allowed so important an inquiry to be conducted by English officers.' Privy Councillor Von Philipsborn replied for the government: 'The integrity of English courts of justice is above suspicion. The German government in 1869 entered into an agreement with England by which all accidents that befall German ships on the British shore are to be investigated by British courts. The object of this is to lose no time and to secure an immediate inquiry.' He added that a representative of the German government, Captain Workmann, had been dispatched to London to 'supply the government with accurate information on the lamentable event'. The matter was then allowed to drop, although, according to *The Times*' Prussian correspondent in Berlin, 'The statement elicited in the course of the Harwich inquiry that boats came out after the ship had been abandoned, but not before, excites much comment'.

On the other hand, there was rancour in Harwich too. Watts, the owner of the *Liverpool*, put in a claim against the owners of the *Deutschland* for the sum of £1,000 for services rendered, and £600 for the salvage of her cargo. It appears not to have been paid, and it has to be said that such a claim would have been considered grossly excessive. In the event, North German Lloyd claimed to have saved a good deal of the cargo themselves, gaining from its auction the sum of £3,825 1s 10d. Watts's judgement in making salvage claims may have been suspect, since he had once claimed £275 in salvage money, which was considered 'monstrous', and on that occasion he had been given a mere £50.

Walter Watts, the son of a successful local businessman, was a man of extravagant tastes. Some time after the wreck there were salvage sales of goods from the ship, organised by the Receiver of Wreck, and held at Brightlingsea and Woodbridge in Suffolk, where Watts bought a fine silver-plated tea service. He loved to surround himself with such things, and lived in a style which, even given the family's earlier business successes, was to spell ultimate financial disaster when combined with a series of ill advised business speculations upon which he was engaged at the time of the *Deutschland* incident.

These salvage sales were seen as an opportunity for locals either to gain a legitimate bargain or two, or—more often—to buy goods at a knockdown price and then resell them for profit. Too often, however, the authorities set artificially high prices that made this sort of transaction difficult or impossible for many of those for whom it was an important source of income. After the *Deutschland* sales Watts had complained—with some justification—that bottles of wines and spirits from the ship, brought up by divers at great effort, had had excessive duty placed on them by the customs men. This meant that when bought and resold, profits were reduced to a paltry five shillings for a case of twelve bottles. There was also undoubtedly a measure of unfairness in the fees and the compensation paid to owners of rescue and salvage vessels. The saving of life brought in a relatively small amount compared with the saving of goods; but even in the case of goods, with no set rates, it was too often left to owners to haggle with the Board of Trade and the Receiver of Wreck, with the result that the costs of boats and gear damaged or lost in dangerous rescue bids such as the *Deutschland* were sometimes barely covered. It was a situation that hardly encouraged salvagers to be honest.

Be that as it may, Walter Watts seems to have been the epitome of the profligate son reducing his family to poverty. He lacked completely the business acumen of his father who, when he retired to a farm at Dovercourt some years before the *Deutschland* affair, was said to be worth £30,000. By 1877 John Watts had lived to see his son bankrupt the local shipping firm—so painstakingly built up, and for so long an integral part of Harwich life—with debts of £11,000, leaving less than £3,000 in assets. By 1896 the saddened father, a man of high principles who had tried his best

to save the family honour, had died 'in far from affluent circumstances'. The *Liverpool*, together with other vessels owned by the
Watts business, were sold off in a vain attempt to clear the debt,
and were not seen at Harwich again.

8   The Inquiry

When the news of the wreck had first reached Bremen, the local paper had been quick to pre-empt any criticism of her master:

> Captain Brickenstein has made a wide circle of friends during the many voyages he has made as Captain with Lloyd's, who deeply regret his present misfortune. They will, however, all be convinced that no justifiable accusations can be levelled against him. It would be hard to find a man with a greater sense of duty, self-sacrifice, caution and presence of mind than he, and the confidence of his superiors speaks for his sound professional knowledge. At the same time he has always been concerned for the comfort of his passengers, and has sought, as a good host, to make their stay on board as comfortable as possible.

Some of these confident assertions were to be severely shaken as a result of the Board of Trade inquiry that was about to begin in London.

The officers of the inquiry would already have had access to an official statement, or 'extended protest' as it was called, issued by Brickenstein before Vice-Consul Williams and Chancellor Meyer of the German Consulate-General in London. The statement was signed by Brickenstein, and countersigned by seven members of his crew: August Lauenstein, the First Officer, Carl Thalenhorst, Second Officer, Reinhold Schmidt, chief engineer, Dietrich Stege, ship's carpenter, Christian Haase, the quartermaster, and two able seamen, August de Vries and Eclert Schiller. It is worth quoting this document at length, since it is the only first-hand official account of the accident by the Captain himself:

Left Bremerhaven the 4th of December 1875, 3.30pm, steamed under command of a pilot down the river. At dark anchored near Bremen with starboard anchor and 30 fathoms of chain. Cargo consisted of general merchandise, and we had about 113 passengers and 99 hands on board.*

On the 5th of December at 7.30am, weighed anchor and steamed seaward; 9.30am, passed the Key Buoy; wind NE, stiff breeze, hazy with snow; kept true westerly course, the standard compass showing W by N, that is, 1½ points westerly variation and ½ point easterly deviation; compared the different compasses and found only a slight deviation, certainly not more than one eighth of a point from the true course. We logged 12 knots per hour; at 11 o'clock, set fore-topsail; at 12 o'clock at noon sounded in 12½ fathoms fine sand. At 1.30pm we passed the Borkum Light Ship distant about three quarters of a mile on our port side, changed our course and steamed W.S.W. ½ W. true, W three quarters S as per standard compass, that is, 1½ points westerly variation, and three quarters of a point easterly deviation. Compared the different compasses and found only little difference when reduced to the true course.

Air hazy with snowfall, wind increasing N.E., logged 12½ to 13 miles.

At 6 o'clock pm changed course and steamed S.W. ½ S. true, S.W. a quarter W. as per standard compass, with one and three quarters points westerly variation, and 1 point easterly deviation. Compared compasses as before and found the same result. The look-out and wheel were manned, side lights burning brightly, stormy N.E. wind with snow squalls, logged 13 to 13½ miles. In consequence of the hazy atmosphere were not able to make any observations to determine the actual course, and therefore used the lead several times.

At 2am had 21 fathoms fine sand, and at 3am 25 fathoms fine sand, wind stormy with snow squalls, logged 13½ miles. At 4am was took the fore-topsail in and went on half speed, sounded at 4 o'clock 17½ fathoms fine sand. At 4.30 22

* It is interesting to note here, and further on in the document, the vagueness concerning the actual number of people involved.

fathoms fine sand, steamed on half speed, logged 9½ miles. At 5 o'clock sounded 17 fathoms sand and shells.

Saw through the blinding snow apparently a fixed light ahead, about four points to port, which now and then disappeared on account of the snow. While on the point of bringing to, saw apparently breakers ahead, telegraphed at once full speed astern, which order was immediately obeyed. A few minutes afterwards it was reported that the engine had become useless as the screw was broken; at the same time felt a slight shock, which was followed by several heavier ones; the ship laid somewhat over to port, and the sea broke over her with great fury; sent up rockets and used the steam whistle; lifebelts were given out to the passengers, and at the same time the boats were got clear. Boat no. 1 was lowered and filled with water, the painter broke, and the boat drifted away with the fourth officer and four men in her. A heavy sea smashed boat no. 4 and washed boat no. 3 from davits, which also drifted away with three men. Got all boats ready. At daybreak weather cleared off a little; set signals of distress, and saw Kentish Knock lightship about 3 sea miles distant away on our port side, and found our ship driven further on the sand. In order to save the ship from falling over, in which case passengers and ship would have been inevitably lost, we adopted the only means at our disposal and discharged cargo from the fore hatch, and threw it overboard until evening to lighten the fore part of the ship, in order that the heavy breakers continually running alongside the ship should do as little damage as possible, as wind and sea were now right aft, and we set fore-topsail and foresail in order to get, if possible, into smoother water, which seemed to be about two ship's length from us, in which we at length succeeded. Pumps were at once set to work and kept at, viz, three steam and five hand pumps, which kept the ship pretty free from water until six o'clock in the evening. Throughout the whole day it was impossible to think of lowering the boats for the more effectual saving of the passengers, because the weather was very heavy and the sea fearfully high. No attempts were made, in order not to expose the passengers to certain death, and because at this time the ship was still the safest place. At dark we again sent off rockets which were answered from the Kentish Knock and Sunk Light Vessels. At 6 o'clock the water rose steadily and existinguished the fire of the donkey boiler, the continual heavy shocks to the ship made her leak worse and worse. At about 7pm the water rising in the ship compelled us to bring the mails and passengers' effects into the gangways and first cabin. At about 8 o'clock, when the water had already reached the 'tween deck, we observed that the ship with the half of her sails had got out of the worst breakers and now laying a little more easily. In order to prevent the ship from getting into too deep water where it would undoubtedly have sunk, we took in the sails, let go the starboard anchor, and when the chain soon after parted we let go the port anchor, which brought the ship up.

At 11 o'clock we took the precaution to bring provisions onto the bridge and into the tops. At 1am the wind and sea increased considerably, and at 2 o'clock the order was given that all passengers and crew should take refuge in the shrouds, as the gangways were filling with water, which penetrated into the upper cabins. From 4 to 7am a strong wind from N.E. with high sea and very cold weather.

The sea swept and broke continually over the ship. Many of the passengers and crew were washed out of the rigging by the sea, especially out of the fore-rigging, or fell down asleep or frozen, and were washed away by the water.

All our remaining boats were during this time carried away. At 8 o'clock wind and sea abated, and the ebbing tide permitted us to descend to the deck to warm our frozen limbs.

All the survivors were mustered by the captain and supplied from the food which had been saved.

At about 10.30am on Tuesday the 7th of December, we at last saw the steamtug 'Liverpool', which ultimately took us all on board and landed us at Harwich about 4 o'clock in the afternoon. We left the ship full of water on the west side of the Kentish Knock, having beaten over the sands; it showed on the starboard side amidships a rent of about two inches which got smaller below. All ship's papers and the log book are unfortunately lost. To the best of our knowledge there are 86 of the crew, including the captain and three pilots, and 69 passengers saved.

At the start of the Board of Trade inquiry proceedings at 11.00am on 20th December. Henry Cadogan Rothery was officially appointed inspector, with Captain E. White RN and Captain Harris as assessors. Rothery was at that time Registrar of the Admiralty Division of the High Court of Justice. In November 1876 he became the first incumbent of a new post, the Wreck Commissioner for the United Kingdom. His specialisation was maritime and ecclesiastical courts and to this day, in cases of Discipline and Doctrine, his judgements continue to be quoted as 'Rothery's Precedents'. In 1879 he presided over the inquiry into the Tay Bridge disaster, an accident recalled in the poem by the Dundee handloom weaver, 'poet and tragedian', William McGonagall. Also in attendance were two representatives of the Board of Trade, a Mr Bowen and a Mr Cottingham who, as Rothery's introduction to his report states,* were accompanied by 'Mr Butt and Mr Phillimore representing the German Government, assisted by Captain Weickmann, a German naval officer of distinction, who had been deputed by his Government to attend and watch the proceedings. The interests of the owners, master and officers of the "Deutschland" were defended by Mr Cohen and Mr Stubbs.'

Rothery noted that the inquiry 'continued from [the 20th] until Friday, the 24th, was resumed on Tuesday, the 27th, and was finally concluded on Friday, the 31st of December'. On 29th February 1876, Her Majesty's Stationery Office published the findings under the title, *Report of an Inquiry into the Circumstances attending the Loss of the Steam Ship 'Deutschland' on the Kentish Knock Sand, on the 6th Day of December, 1875*. The inquiry was held at the New Court House, Board of Trade Buildings, East India Dock Road, Poplar, in the East End of London, and was, as The *Times* stated, 'the first maritime inquiry held in the New Court houses since this building was converted to its present purpose from a sailor's home'.

The report pleased the editor of *Nautical Magazine*, who wrote in March 1876: 'The form and style . . . are admirable, and may,

---

* The report was addressed to the Right Honourable Sir C. B. Adderley, MP, KCMG, President of the Board of Trade, from H. C. Rothery, the Admiralty Registry, Somerset House, and dated 2nd February 1876.

we think, be most advantageously studied by all who have to frame other such reports. Redundancy and vain repetition are not to be found, but the whole of the report is clear and straightforward, and as concise as the nature of the inquiry will admit.'

After outlining the facts of the case, the report investigated the condition of the *Deutschland* herself at the time of sailing, and the record and reputation of her owners. To this end, one of the managing directors of North German Lloyd, Carl Hargesheimer, appeared before the committee. He told Rothery that the company had been established in 1857, and that prior to the loss of this ship it had owned fifty-three steam vessels, of which twenty-nine plied the transatlantic route. These vessels had shipped more than half a million passengers from Europe to America without any loss of life. Two of their steamers had indeed been lost in the last five years: the first, the Caird-built *Union*, had gone down on the rocks of the Pentland Firth off the coast of Scotland in 1870. This had happened, as we have seen, during the Franco-Prussian War, when passenger ships were being diverted to the north to avoid the war-zone waters of the English Channel. The second wreck, in 1873, had been that of the *King William*, which had struck on the Dutch coast. In both cases, Hargesheimer emphasised, everyone had been saved.

Hargesheimer also told the inquiry that it had formerly been the company's policy to buy vessels from other sources, but this policy had now changed; the *Deutschland* was built for North German Lloyd on the Clyde by the Caird yard. By 1875 the company had yards at Bremen and Bremerhaven, and a floating dock at Bremerhaven for repair work. He was able to convince the committee that the officers who undertook the overhaul of the extensive North German Lloyd fleet were a totally competent team. The report added the voluntary statement that the fact that the line's ships called regularly at Southampton for passengers and freight was an indication of the excellent reputation of the line in Great Britain.

During the eight months that the *Deutschland* had been laid up on account of slackness of trade before her last voyage, she had undergone a complete overhaul in Bremerhaven as we noted earlier. Only two years previously she had had new engines and boilers, and these were fully checked and serviced in 1875. Since their installation, the *Deutschland* had made four Atlantic cross-

The four bodies in the school hall
below the Church of St Francis,
Stratford. The tall nun is second from
the left. The priest is thought to be
Father Jansen. *Franciscan Sisters*

Mary Broadway, the laundry girl who
laid out the bodies of the nuns. She
subsequently took the veil herself.
*Sister Francis Agnes OSC, Convent of
Poor Clares, Woodchester*

The modern Sunk light-vessel in Harwich for repairs. *Sean Street*

The lifeboat house, Harwich, built in 1876 to house the *Springwell*. Soon after this picture was taken, in 1957, the ornamental turret was removed. *Grahame Farr Archives, RNLI*

rd Manley Hopkins, aged 19. *By permission of Oxford University Press on behalf of the Society of Jesus*

Number 87 The Grove, Stratford, where Gerard Manley Hopkins was born. The Hopkins' home was the left one of the two houses. The whole building has since been demolished. *London Borough of Newham Local Studies Library*

The west front of St Beuno's College, Clwyd, where Hopkins was studying when he read the news of the *Deutschland* disaster. *Sister Joan Brown SND*

ings, and everything seemed to be in perfect working order. The company utilised the services of a Bremerhaven compass expert, one Mr Rudolf, to check and set the ship's navigational equipment, and the company saw no reason to doubt its accuracy.

Regarding the propeller, however, there was rather more to say. A diver had been down to the seabed, and had examined what was left of it. There were two possibilities. First, if the propeller shaft had broken it would have left a hole through which sea water would have entered the ship. In other words, the whole screw fitment would have been lost. On the other hand, perhaps only the propeller itself had gone, leaving the shaft in place, thus prohibiting water from entering the ship from that direction at least. The diver, John Fullager, was able to establish that the latter was the case—so this was a repetition of the problem that had occurred with the *Deutschland* in the Atlantic less than a year before. The committee was satisfied that the action of throwing the ship suddenly into reverse, in such conditions as pertained at the time, would have been sufficient to account for the sheering off of the blades. It had been on her Atlantic crossing of March 1875 that the *Deutschland* had been involved in her first propeller drama, when her blades had been lost in mid-ocean, forcing her to return to Southampton, with the assistance of a tow, for repairs. The new propeller sent from Bremerhaven and fitted under the supervision of the superintendent engineer of the Royal Mail Steam Packet Company—who now appeared before the committee to give evidence about that key component—had been sound in every way and had been well fitted. Indeed, continued the engineer, the ship had impressed him at the time as being 'a strong, well built and well equipped vessel in every respect'.

Allegations had been voiced in the German press that North German Lloyd captains were paid a premium if they finished a voyage ahead of time. This was angrily denied by Brickenstein, who declared: 'If anybody says so it is a bad lie. I have done voyages quickly, but never received anything.'

One of the most intriguing questions for the committee of inquiry—and one to which they ultimately failed to find a satisfactory answer—was that of the lost ship's log. Rothery asked Brickenstein to 'prepare a form of log-book as nearly as possible similar to that which has been lost'; this was accordingly carried out, and the same was done for the lost charts. But useful as these things were—and still are—to our understanding of the ship's last hours, they clearly lack the detail of the originals, the loss of which assumes almost thriller-plot proportions in Rothery's report:

> It appears that, shortly before it became necessary to abandon the lower part of the ship, the master directed the purser to put all the ship's papers into a valise or trunk. They were ordinarily kept in an iron box, but it was thought better to put them into a trunk, as there would then be less likelihood of their being lost, if the ship went down, than if they were left in the iron box. There is some evidence that the purser put them in his trunk, and that this trunk was placed with the mails and the passengers' luggage. There is also some evidence that, when the steam tug 'Liverpool' was alongside, this trunk was seen being carried along the 'Deutschland''s deck by two of the seamen towards the tug; but whether or not it was ever put on board that vessel, there is nothing to show, for no one appears to have see it on board the tug. Upon the arrival of the tug at Harwich all the crew and passengers went on shore, and the luggage, as well as the mails, were removed to the private warehouse of Mr Williams, the German Vice-Consul at Harwich. On the following morning, when the master sent the second officer down to the warehouse to look for the trunk, it was nowhere to be found.

The purser, who had originally been charged with the transfer of the papers from the iron box to the trunk, had of course died at the height of the storm, so one valuable witness at least was lost. Indeed, concluded Rothery, 'everyone who could be supposed to know anything about the ship's papers has been asked about them, but one and all declared that they did not know what had become of them'.

August Lauenstein gave evidence that he saw the Second Officer carrying the mails, and the valise containing the log, towards the tug shortly after the *Liverpool* came alongside. However, he did not see them actually transferred to the tug, adding:

> They may have dropped into the sea, for aught I know. There

was a rush to get on board the tug when she came alongside
. . . When the tug arrived at Harwich no passengers were
allowed to take anything ashore, not even their own property. The custom-house officer took charge of all property.
He must have had the valise if it was on board the tug when
she arrived at Harwich.

All luggage from the *Deutschland* was placed forward and amidships on the tug, and was removed by a special boat under the
superintendence of customs officers. Eyewitnesses confirmed that
none of the *Deutschland* crew assisted in the removal of the luggage or mails, which were, it was thought, 'taken to the German
Consulate warehouse'.

The question of signalling procedure was raised at the inquiry,
and proved to be one of several embarrassing points for Edward
Brickenstein. The committee noted that the distress signals, for
German as for English vessels, were as follows:

In the daytime—

1. A gun fired at intervals of about a minute.
2. The international code signal of distress.
3. The distant signal, consisting of a square flag having either
   above or below it a ball, or anything resembling a ball.

At night—

1. A gun fired at intervals of about a minute.
2. Flames on the ship (as from a burning tar barrel, oil barrel,
   & c.)
3. Rockets or shells of any colour or description fired one at a
   time at short intervals.

The inquiry was critical of the fact that only one of the possible
daytime distress signals was used—the second. When Brickenstein was asked why a gun had not been fired, at first he told
the committee that this could not be done because the powder
was wet. When asked where the powder was kept, however, he
stated that it was in the same place as the rockets, which had
been unaffected by damp. The committee pressed him on this
point, and he admitted that in fact it was only one or two charges

of powder that had become too damp to use. Rothery pressed him further, and Brickenstein then said that he had made no attempt to have the gun fired until about 11.00am on the Monday, when an unknown steamer had passed relatively close to the wreck. It seems that the gun could then not be fired because the touch-hole was stopped up. At the same time, he saw a signal flash from the nearby lightship to the steamer, and so felt any further attempt to be unnecessary. When the chief engineer, Reinhold Schmidt, was examined by the inquiry, it came out that the gun had indeed been in no condition to fire. As Rothery went on: 'He had been requested by the master to clear the touchhole of the gun, he had sent a man to do it, and, although the man was at work for about three quarters of an hour, he was not able to clear it, and they never succeeded in putting the gun into a fit state to be fired, whilst they were on board.' It was felt that the company had been at fault in the lack of adequate maintenance of the gun. The fact that proper flag signals—the third daytime option—were not used, was never properly explained by Brickenstein.

The fact that the light-vessel was close enough to be visible from the wreck begged the question as to whether it would have been worth an attempt on Brickenstein's part to reach it by boat. It was a point dealt with quickly and summarily by Rothery: 'it would have been madness' to have even attempted such a venture in the prevailing conditions. There was no reason to assume that the boat-lowering apparatus had not been in good order, but 'we think that they exercised a wise discretion in remaining by the ship, believing, as they might reasonably do, that she would hold together, until assistance came to them from the shore'.

As to the conduct of the lightship crews, Stephen Page, mate of the Knock lightship, and David Day, mate of the Sunk vessel, situated about eleven and a half miles from Harwich, were both questioned at the inquiry, but their testimonies only underlined how useless it would have been to contemplate any practical assistance in those tremendous seas. Day was of the opinion that 'no boat could live in that water': speaking as one with twenty-three years of lightship service, he declared that 'the Sunk was hurled about as much as I had ever known her to be'. Page, on the Knock vessel and so much closer to the accident, gave a full explanation of the workings of his ship, with her crew of seven hands.

Today, the vast majority of Trinity House light-vessels are automatic and unmanned, but in 1875 crews had to keep up a constant vigil, the nights being divided up into three watches of two men each. As to the light itself, it showed a bright revolving flash, which stayed in view for ten seconds. When a vessel in distress or requiring assistance was observed in the proximity of the light-ship, the crew would, in the daytime, fire two guns at an interval of five minutes, and repeat this every half-hour until assistance could be seen approaching. At night the procedure was similar, except that there was an added alert of a rocket fired after the sounding of the guns, in the direction of the vessel in distress. In the event of thick weather, there was also a steam siren foghorn, to be sounded for ten seconds every five minutes. The procedure in the Trinity House regulations was clearly laid down, and Stephen Page's men carried it out to the letter. As Page stated at the inquiry: 'On the night the 'Deutschland' was lost we had 70 or 80 cartridges and maroon rockets, and four or five dozen ordinary ones. They burst when fired, and throw out a blue ball of fire.'

Page was further interrogated:

Question   Was the fog-horn regularly sounded throughout the nights of the 6th and 7th of December, not only when it was thick, but during snow?

Answer   Yes. We keep it going, not only to warn others, but as a protection to ourselves. And we keep a log . . .

Q.   At what hour did you observe a steamer pass on the morning of Monday?

A.   At about noon on the 6th. She was a three-masted screw, without yards. We fired four guns to attract her attention, and we also signalled her. She altered her course, and ran down within half a mile of us. She then altered her course to the south-west. She appeared to be a channel steamer, and not a foreign-going steamer. She was about 600 or 700 tons, and heavy laden. The sea ran right over her when she altered to the south-west.

Q.   Could she have done anything to help the
       'Deutschland'?

A.   No; but if she had come nearer and communicated with
       us, she might have reported the vessel on shore at
       Broadstairs or Ramsgate, so as to get help that night.

Q.   Could you see the 'Deutschland' where she was?

A.   Yes. Her colour and single funnel were black . . . we
       never made out what the ship ashore was. We did
       not make out her nationality. We saw that she wanted
       assistance, and we did all in our power to provide it
       for her . . . I saw a brig that morning between two
       sands. She was in trouble herself, and could not get
       clear. She could render no assistance to the 'Deutsch-
       land'. I do not think that at any time before the 'Liver-
       pool' came, any tug could have lived close to those
       sands. The tide that morning had a velocity of two and
       a half knots.

Q.   If the brig had come near enough for you to speak to
       her, where would you have told her to go for lifeboats?

A.   To Broadstairs or Margate, for both of which the wind
       was favourable, and she might have reached either in
       about two hours.

The inquiry spent a good deal of time questioning Edward Brickenstein about the deviation he had made from his course. Rothery
noted that soundings had been taken throughout the night of
Sunday 5th/Monday 6th, at 2.00, 3.00, 4.00, 4.30 and 5.00am,
just before striking. At these times the lead showed depths of 21
fathoms, 25, 17½, 22 and finally 17 fathoms. The inquiry felt that
a study of these figures should have been sufficient to show Brickenstein that something was very wrong with his course. The Captain seems to have been seriously embarrassed by the committee
on this point, as the report says:

The master was a good deal pressed, in the course of the

inquiry, to point out where he found, on his supposed course, soundings corresponding to those which he had obtained, and which led him to think that he was on his right course, but he was not able to do so . . . The Master ought, from the warnings he received, to have known that his ship was out of her position, and, knowing this, it would have been his duty to put her about . . . and return slowly upon his course. For not doing so, we think he was greatly to blame.

Brickenstein's method of verifying his position was to draw a line on his chart in the direction in which he was steering. He would then mark off the number of miles the log told him the ship had run, 'and without making any allowance for the direction and set of the tide, and whether it was with or against them, he there placed the vessel'. Having not taken these factors into account, he found that he was more than thirty miles from the place he believed himself to be, and some eighteen miles to the west—a fatal combination.

In his defence, the Captain put forward three possible reasons for this crucial error. The first was that he had overrun his reckoning; the second, that his compasses may have been wrong; and the third, that an exceptional current had sent him over too far to the west. The committee found the first point so obvious that it hardly needed answering. Of course he had overrun his reckoning, but Rothery ascribed no technical or mechanical reason to this at all. The compass question brought Mr Rudolf of Bremerhaven to the inquiry, and once again it was stated that Rudolf had checked and rechecked the compasses, had in fact had them in his shop for four or five weeks, and that, after meticulously calculating their minutest deviations, he had installed them himself on the bridge of the *Deutschland*. And yet there was a flaw, because he had, in the words of the official report:

given a copy of the deviation card to the then master, Captain Ludewigs, retaining, according to his usual practice, the original in his own possession; but . . . on the appointment of Captain Brickenstein to the command, he had handed to him the original, and . . . he had unfortunately not retained any copy of it. The chief officer also stated that Captain Ludewigs

had left his copy on board the vessel, and that both that copy
and Captain Brickenstein's had been lost with the ship.

Again, we must draw attention to the loss of the trunk containing papers that might have proved conclusive one way or another.
Is it possible that Brickenstein had foreseen that the fact that the
papers were missing might work in his favour, in so far as his
claim that the compasses were faulty could not be disproved?
Whether or not such an idea occurred to Rothery, he did not
voice it. He merely refused to accept the Master's claim that the
compasses might have been at fault.

Brickenstein's third point, that he might have been deceived by
a rogue current, was examined in some detail by the inquiry. In
the end it was felt that the current was less at fault than the
Captain was for failing to realise that, since the tide was with
him almost all the way, the ship had got seriously ahead of his
reckoning.

Brickenstein had intended to take a middle course, halfway
between Galloper on the English side and North Hinder on the
Dutch coast. The distance between these two points is about twelve
and a half miles, and the depth of water varied at the time, between
25 and 30 fathoms. These depths are important. For had the
Deutschland been on course, in the middle of this channel, it would
have been very clear from her soundings. Also, she would probably not have seen the lights of either Hinder or the Thames estuary
shoals. The English pilot Charles Harvey who was on board at the
time, and who had travelled on the company's ships on more than
120 occasions, was questioned by Rothery:

Question Did you generally pick [the lights] up, on one side or
the other?

Answer No, we generally come right down midway.

Q. And generally you do not see any light?

A. It is quite frequent that we do not see either light.

Q. When you do not see either light, is it usual to take
soundings?

A.	Yes.
Q.	And do you not generally get deep water?
A.	If we are midway, we generally get deep water.
Q.	And if you thought that you were midway, and got shallow water, you would be rather surprised, would you not?
A.	I should think that then we might be perhaps over to the Hinder side.
Q.	You would think that you were over to Hinder, or over to the Galloper?
A.	Yes, if we got shoal water.
Q.	I mean 17 fathoms. If you got outside the 20 fathom line, you would know that you had got either to the one side or to the other, would you not?
A.	Yes.

Rothery then went on to deduce that at 4.00am, when he struck 17½ fathoms, Brickenstein should have known he was out of his course. He might at that time have been able to do something about it. As it was, at 5.00am he found only 17 fathoms, but held on to his course, and was just about to go below to the navigation room to verify his position when he saw a light from what he took to be either the North Hinder or a fishing boat. This light, it will be remembered, now and then disappeared in the snow-storm. Such a light on a fishing vessel would only have been shining while she was at anchor or attached to her nets and stationary. Both of these possibilities seem, at best, improbable in such a place and on such a night. The ship is at this point still proceeding on its course at half speed. Moments later, the Captain sees the breakers ahead, and gives the order, 'Full speed astern!' It is too late.

'It shows a very great want of care and judgement on his part . . .' the report stated. 'The Master was a good deal pressed, in the course of the inquiry, to point out where he found, on his supposed course, soundings corresponding to those which he had obtained, and which led him to think he was on his right course; but he was not able to do so.' Captain Brickenstein seems to have given contradictory evidence at several points, and to have changed his story when confronted with a challenge to his original version. The inquiry was aware of the possible career implications of their having had to censure him for exercising insufficient judgement and care.

The following rather defensive, not to say petulant, qualifying paragraph gives another slant on the affair.

It is very painful for us thus to have to pass censure on a man who appears, for so many years, to have discharged his duty to the entire satisfaction of his employers, and who after the vessel got aground conducted himself so well . . . But we must remember that this inquiry has been, if not invited, at all events acceded to, both by the German Government and by the owners of the 'Deutschland'. No doubt if our opinion had been that no blame attached to the master, we should have been asked to say so; and it is too late now, when it is found that the evidence presses hardly upon him, to be told that it is not within our province to pronounce a censure on him. What in effect we are asked to do, is to pronounce an opinion on the conduct of the master, if that opinion is favourable to him; but not to do so, if it is unfavourable. We do not so understand our duty. You have called upon us to say what are the causes that have led to this disaster, and if we think that want of caution on the part of the master led to it, it is our duty to say so.

While Brickenstein came out badly regarding his conduct of the ship before the accident, on his subsequent behaviour Rothery could offer nothing but praise, noting

the courage which he exhibited after the unfortunate vessel had taken the ground. Throughout the whole of that day and the following night, and until the survivors were rescued by the steam-tug, the master appears to have been always at his post, maintaining admirable discipline, taking every measure for the safety of those on board, and encouraging them by his example.

Regarding the loss of life, the report stated: '86 of the crew were saved, including the master and the three pilots, and 69 passengers; so that 16 of the officers and crew and about 44 passengers perished from the time the ship took the ground.' Rothery is including the three pilots amongst the crew because although technically not part of the North German Lloyd team, they were on board the vessel at the time of impact.

The inquiry cleared up a number of other points that had been the focus of angry, and particularly local, debate. First, was assistance sent as soon as it could be? Rothery said it had been, and exonerated all upon whom blame had previously been cast. Then there was the question of the mystery steamer—and the brig *Ino*, which for three hours had been watched by the passengers and crew of the *Deutschland*, only to vanish in the end into the murk of that Monday evening. What had happened to her? And the steamer? What was this strange ship? This was a question that was never answered. The inquiry deduced that she might have been in trouble herself, and having seen or heard signals from the lightship had perhaps interpreted them as warnings to keep away from the sand. Perhaps she had not even seen the wreck. Or even if she had, her master might well have been in no position to help. In any event, such were the conditions that, even if she had made contact with the *Deutschland*, there was little or nothing that she could have done. The two ships would have dashed together had there been any close approach, and smaller boats would have been lost instantly.

In giving evidence on this unidentified vessel, once again Brickenstein disconcertingly changed his story. On the first day of his examination he had stated more than once, and quite positively, that the steamer had passed *between* the *Deutschland* and the Kentish Knock lightship. He further claimed that, from the position she was in at that time, she must have seen that here was a ship in distress—yet she made no attempt to render assistance. On the second day of his evidence, however, he painted quite a different picture. Now he was saying that the steamer had not passed *between* the *Deutschland* and the lightship, but had passed on the *outside* and to the *eastward* of the light-vessel. This was confirmed by several other witnesses, including the English pilot and the mate of the light-vessel.

Rothery was tolerant. His report says that he did not feel the Captain was trying deliberately to deceive them, and he urged his readers to remember 'that this gentleman had only recently been exposed for about 30 hours to the most imminent peril of his life, under circumstances which must have been peculiarly distressing to him'. All in all, Brickenstein's confused testimony on several points during the inquiry seems to show a man deeply upset and disturbed by his experiences. He had, of course, already been subjected to the inquest at Harwich, and had returned to the wreck within twenty-four hours of having been rescued from it. All this, and the inevitable burden of guilt, must have taken a very serious toll on his mental and emotional resources.

If the steamer mystery was never sorted out, at least the problem of the brig *Ino* was simpler to explain, as the inquiry was able to trace her captain, who appeared before the committee and 'gave his evidence in a very straightforward manner'. In fact, because of her light construction, the *Ino*, on her way to Weymouth, had been pushed well over to the west from her intended course, into the Knock Deep between the Kentish Knock and the Long Sand. It must have seemed as though this would be the end for her too, and although the Captain could indeed see a large ship aground, the three hours in which he was within sight of her he spent in his own life-and-death struggle. And it was only as night closed in that the *Ino* succeeded in regaining her proper course, and eventually, against all the odds, she made her destination port safely. In the words of the report, although the master of the brig 'had seen the 'Deutschland', and knew she must be in distress . . . so far from his being able to render any assistance, he had as much as he could do to save himself'. On being questioned again on the matter, Brickenstein agreed that, as in the other cases of ship sightings the two vessels could not at that time have come together in any realistic rescue operation, because of the size of the seas then running.

For the crew and master of the tug *Liverpool*, there could be nothing but praise. Carrington described graphically how he had gone out as soon as he had felt it safe to do so. He spoke of the agonising journey from lightship to lightship, until, coming round the end of the Long Sand and making towards the Knock light-vessel, he saw the *Deutschland* for the first time. The heroism of what then happened—the *Liverpool* at first standing off, then sending out the lifeboat; the apparent miracle of the sudden calming of the waters yet still the overriding danger of the operation, as Carrington felt his way gingerly towards the wreck, never completely sure that there was enough water for this tug—clearly impressed the committee greatly.

Yet, again the question had to be asked: could the tug have gone out sooner? Carrington had already stated that these were the worst seas he had seen in his long life; but now an independent witness was called, in the person of the captain of the packet-steamer the *Richard Young*. It will be remembered that on the Monday two packets, the *Claud Hamilton* and the *Richard Young*, had passed relatively close to the *Deutschland*, bound for Rotterdam and Antwerp respectively. If they had ventured out, could not the tug have done so? The master of the *Richard Young* was able quickly to satisfy the inquiry on this point; yes, he did make the journey from Harwich to Antwerp on the night in question, with between thirty and forty passengers on board. However, such was the violence of the storm that he was three or four hours delayed in sailing, and that, even when he did get under way, his ship suffered damage, including the loss of the steps on the paddle-boxes. His ship was a large and powerful steamer, he added—perhaps four times the size of the *Liverpool*—and she had found making headway difficult. What, therefore, could the little tug have done? Even if she had got out beyond the Cork lightship, which was doubtful, she could not have rendered any assistance to the *Deutschland*. Indeed, even if he had known of the plight of those two hundred or so people, he would not have dared to take his ship, large and powerful as she was, into the maelstrom that surrounded the Kentish Knock that day.

The crews of the lightships, as well as the authorities at Harwich, Ramsgate, Broadstairs and Sheerness, were all declared to be free from blame. Rothery added: 'Having regard of the evidence, the conclusion is incontrovertible that any attempt to go out to the Kentish Knock Sand on that night would have resulted in failure.'

Then there was the vexed question of the charges against the smacksmen: Rothery entirely acquitted them of 'pillaging the bodies'. And, again, there seems to have been confusion on Brickenstein's part: 'At first the master and officers of the 'Deutschland' led us to believe that the smacksmen, whom they saw on board the vessel, were pillaging, or, as they called it, "wrecking" the property.' But the *Deutschland*'s English pilot, Charles Harvey, explained to the Captain that they were in fact salving, and that everything would be taken to the Receiver of Wreck, and this had seemed to satisfy Brickenstein at the time. Nevertheless, he stuck to his original story at the inquiry, claiming to have been threatened by the men when he challenged them. Certainly, the artist from the *Illustrated London News* had been satisfied that he had seen wreckers at work. But the inquiry had strong words for the journalists who had, in their opinion, inflamed the whole story. Without naming them, Rothery was clearly directing his attack at the reporters from *The Times* and the *Illustrated London News*. Perhaps angered at what may have seemed a sweeping dismissal of his evidence, the artist contacted the inspector after the inquiry, and Rothery states in his report:

> The gentleman . . . has . . . written to say that [his picture] was taken from life; by which I suppose he means that it is a true representation of the facts, and not, as I had imagined, a purely imaginary drawing. If this be really the case, it is to be regretted that the artist did not, whilst the Inquiry was going on, make some communiction on the subject, either to the Board of Trade or to the Court, so that the truth of the story might have been tested. As it is, it is impossible to place any reliance upon a statement which is utterly unsupported by proof, and which is in direct opposition to all the evidence in the case.

Thus was the work of 'some illustrated journal', as Rothery disdainfully referred to the *Illustrated London News*, indeed swept aside.

It is unfortunate that the only other journalist who could have supported these claims could not—or would not—come forward. On Thursday 9th December the ILN man had gone out to the *Deutschland* on the *Liverpool* with a number of officials, including the ship's Third Officer. Also present was a reporter from the *New*

York Herald. This anonymous writer gave a graphic description of events on that day, which was published in his paper on 27th December. He clearly relished the drama of his situation:

It is with the greatest difficulty that I obtain sufficient control over my nerves to write you an intelligible account of my visit to the wreck of the 'Deutschland'. The steam-tug 'Liverpool' which took us there is now blowing off steam at the pier head and unloading her ghastly cargo, adding six more to the twelve present inhabitants of the little deadhouse. It was never contemplated to people it so densely!

The morning had been clear and fresh as they left Harwich. At first the *Herald* man seems to have been surprised to find only one other journalist on board, but the two men appear to have struck up an amicable relationship. As they neared the Knock, everyone who could, crowded into the bows of the *Liverpool*, straining for a first glimpse of the wreck:

'Yonder she lies, sir!' exclaimed suddenly one of the crew . . . 'Yonder, under that dark cloud.' Following the line of his outstretched finger, we could just make out through the morning haze that the long grey horizon was broken by something. A few more turns of the paddle-wheels revealed to us the two masts, yards and funnel of a large steamer, upright against the sky. 'And I'm blowed if there ain't a large fleet of smacks around her,' said the skipper as he gazed through his glass from the bridge; 'More'n a dozen of the rascals!' Yes, sure enough, they were lying off the wreck, head to wind, cutters, schooners and luggers, like a flock of vultures hovering around their prey.

As they came closer, the reporter was struck by the sight of 'this great ship, noble even in her desolation'; but he also noticed 'swarming over her from stem to stern . . . the forms of men running to and fro, apparently throwing packages overboard'.

Then the party boarded the *Deutschland*: 'I walked slowly aft on the port and back again to the bows on the starboard side, receiving in doing so many an evil look from the gangs of plunderers who did not for a moment relinquish their work after our arrival, but they did not like the notebook.' The reporter addressed one of the scropers: 'Strange fishing, this!' To this the man replied, 'Ah, you're right! We get some strange fish on the hook now and then!' Next, he looked below decks:

The water, thickly covered with the grease and filth of the machinery, was about ten feet below the level of the deck where I stood. Floating in it, face downward, were three dead men . . . all were swollen to a horrible size. Further aft was a third corpse, much smaller; this was a woman. It is not a picture to dwell on, and I hurried away down the companion of the main saloon. Arrived at the bottom, a scene burst upon me such as I have read about often, but never seen; from end to end, the saloon was waist deep in wreckage. The furniture was smashed into fragments, panels broken in, cushions, crockery, glass, fragments of the saloon racks and debris of all kinds littered the floor . . . The saloon resounded with the crash of axes and the shouts and curses of the men. At the moment of my entrance, at least thirty wreckers were frantically engaged in pillage and plunder. Clothes, boots, articles of toilet, books, letters, music, children's shoes, cigars, photographs—in short, the hundred articles which may be imagined as composing the effects of thrifty people leaving their native country for another home. It was a scene for an artist's pencil rather than a reporter's pen. This long, wreck-strewn room, thronged with these huge men in their sou'westers and seaboots, shouting, swearing, smashing. Many of them were drunk, for the moment a bottle of wine or spirits was found, the neck was knocked off and the contents greedily swallowed . . . My comrade at the 'Illustrated London News' who had gone down with me, discouraged at first by the immensity of detail in the picture, soon settled down into his sketchbook.

This is the moment the artist had captured—words and picture tally exactly. Could both men have misinterpreted salvage for pillage? Whatever the facts of the matter, the inquiry's findings were unequivocal:

When the list, which I had suggested, of articles handed over to the Receivers had been furnished by the Board of Trade to the owners, the charge of wrecking and of pillage was fully withdrawn, both by the officers of the 'Deutschland' and by the managing director of the company, who had come over to watch the proceedings, and who told us that he had no reason whatever to believe that there was a single article, that had been taken from the ship, that had not been given up. The German Government also, through their counsel, stated that in their opinion the charges of pillage and wrecking had been entirely disproved.

Rothery had investigated these charges because, in his words, they 'concerned the national honour'. Now, it would seem, honour had been well and truly satisfied. The allied charge of mutilation and stripping of bodies was also dropped.

One of the committee's most far-reaching investigations was into the matter of ship-to-shore communications between lightships and land bases. Rothery strongly urged the need for more efficient means of notifying emergencies, 'by telegraphic cables or otherwise'. *Nautical Magazine* approved, adding: 'It is, we think, more than probable that in Mr Rothery's report the authorities will find an added stimulus to continue the investigations they have commenced into this difficult subject with a view to making the communication between ships and the shore more effectual than hitherto.'

Communication was a theme that ran through every debate on the *Deutschland* affair. *The Times* had anticipated Rothery in one of its reports shortly after the wreck, when it asked what might have been achieved, for instance, had the lightships had, as the reporter put it, 'a submarine wire from lightship to shore'. The lightships themselves, with only seven crew, were helpless when it came to rendering assistance, except for their rockets. As a result of the wreck, these ships were given carrier pigeons to send messages in times of emergency—though it is doubtful whether these would have been of any use at the height of that December storm. And the close proximity of the *Richard Young* and the *Claud Hamilton*, at the very time that the situation was reaching crisis point, only served to underline the cruel irony of the *Deutschland*'s fate.

Rothery's report ends with a justification of his decision to discuss 'more fully, than we should perhaps otherwise have done, some points in the case, which proved in the end to be of less importance in our opinion, than they at one time appeared to possess'.

Rothery continued to press for improved communications, and as late as 1881, while presiding over inquiries into two wrecks on the Long Sand in the Thames Estuary, the *Indian Chief* and the *Nymphaea*, repeated his demands. Even so, not until 1886—eleven years after the wreck of the *Deutschland*—were ship-to-shore telegraphs installed on lightvessels in the estuary.

Nautical Magazine praised the report, but added: 'It could hardly be expected that this simple and straightforward explanation of the matter would be sufficient to satisfy the worked-up feelings of the general public in Germany and in our own country, and Mr Rothery has, therefore, considered it within the scope of his inquiry to investigate every point which has been raised in reference to the disaster, and the means adopted for rescuing those on board from their position of peril.' The magazine had, in fact, come to some conclusions of its own:

1. That sound, strong propelling machinery is of more value in preventing loss of life than boats, rafts, life-belts, and all other similar appliances . . .

2. That it is folly to expect that life can be saved in winter in emergency by boats and life-belts.

Hindsight, and the knowledge of such disasters as the loss of the *Titanic*, point up the irony of these statements. *Nautical Magazine* went on:

3. That life is lost mostly in surveyed and certified ships.

4. That so long as owners of steamships decline to carry proper means of making signals of distress under all circumstances, so long will crews and passengers in distress fail to receive assistance even though it be comparatively near at hand.

9   The Poet of the *Deutschland*

It is one of the odd twists in this story that the poet who was to immortalise the Wreck of the *Deutschland*—the man without whom the disaster would have faded from the minds of all but those still directly touched by it—was born across the road from the Church of St Francis, Stratford, where the Salzkotten nuns' funeral was to take place thirty-one years later. Gerard Manley Hopkins came into the world at 4.15 on the morning of 28th July 1844 at number 87, The Grove—a three-storeyed semi-detached house, built of bricks probably during the last twenty years of the eighteenth century. On 24th August the baby was taken down the road to the Church of St John the Evangelist which had become a parish church by order of council just four days earlier, and there, within sight of his parents' home, he was christened.

Gerard was born into a decade that was rich in significant births. In 1844, Thomas Hardy was four years old, and Renoir was three. The year also saw the births of the French poet, Paul Verlaine, of Richard D'Oyly Carte, the future producer of the Gilbert and Sullivan operas, and of Robert Bridges. The future consort of Edward VII, Queen Alexandra to be, was born in December 1844. Sarah Bernhardt and Ellen Terry were also children of the 1840s as was 'Buffalo Bill', William Cody.

It was an important decade in other ways. Victoria had married Albert in 1840, and in the same year the Treaty of Waitangi ceded New Zealand to Britain, while just a year later the same was to happen with Hong Kong. A revolution in health care was made possible in 1840, with the passing by parliament of the Vaccination Act, and in 1846 the planet Neptune was discovered. The events of the 1840s—human, artistic, scientific and industrial— were to be far-reaching in their consequences.

The Hopkins family had been in East London at least as far

back as Gerard's grandfather, and in the county of Essex for considerably longer. One seventeenth-century Hopkins, called Thomas, was born at Wivenhoe on the Colne River. In fact, he and several later generations worked out of the Colne as oyster-fishing smacksmen—predecessors of the men whose role in the *Deutschland* affair was to be the subject of controversy. This was a part of his family's past of which Gerard was well aware; once while he was at Oxford in 1863, he signed a letter to a friend with the flourish, 'Arthur Flash de Wyvenoe'.

Martin Edward Hopkins, Gerard's grandfather, was born in 1786, and in 1814 he married Ann Manley in the parish of St Mary, Lambeth. A year later their first child, Ann Eleanor, was baptised, but by the time their second child—the poet's father Manley—was born, on 9th July 1818, the family had moved to Camberwell. We know they did not stay there long, because the baptismal record for their third child, Edward Martin, is to be found in All Saints Church, West Ham, and reads: 'January 23. Born July 18, 1820, Edward Martin son of Martin Edward and Ann Hopkins, Stratford . . .' Another child was born in 1822, and was baptised in the same church. Thus is established a family link with Stratford from about 1819 or 1820.

By all accounts, Martin found it a struggle to stay there. Stratford was a pleasant place to live, with well tended gardens full of roses, and the air full of the scent of the flowers and bread from a nearby bakers. The Hopkins' home occupied a site of almost half an acre containing, according to the 1821 *Survey of the Parish of West Ham*, 'house, yard and garden'. Perhaps they were living rather beyond their means and Martin Hopkins was not the professional success he liked to think he was. With his brothers he ran a brokers' business at St Peter's Alley, Cornhill, in the City of London. In spite of his precarious finances, by 1830 he was cutting a dash as a pillar of Stratford society and contributing £30 towards two new chapels for the area. These were to become St Mary's, Plaistow, and St John the Evangelist, Stratford, where his grandson was to be baptised fourteen years later. In 1834 Martin was forced to move to a cheaper house in Great Tower Street, near the Tower of London, where he died two years later.

When he was fifteen, Manley Hopkins was forced to leave school and go out to work. And he was just eighteen when his father died and he became effectively the head of the family. He thus found himself the main financial supporter of his mother, sister and three younger brothers. It is a tribute to his determination and character that he was able to earn enough money to keep them all, while at the same time bettering himself academically through study. He taught himself Latin, Greek and French, studied church history, acquiring a liking for Jeremy Taylor's *Holy Living* and *Holy Dying*, and was good at drawing and painting in watercolours.

Most importantly for his family's welfare, he taught himself the skills that he was to use as the basis for his successful business. And his chosen field of endeavour was marine insurance. His first job was as a clerk in a firm of insurance brokers, and it was not long before he graduated to the position of 'average adjuster' —the profession that he was to follow for over half a century. While still quite young, Manley had achieved the professional and intellectual status attempted by his father, and succeeded in every respect where his parent had failed.

He married twenty-two-year-old Kate Smith, the daughter of surgeon John Simm Smith of Chigwell, Essex, on 8th August 1843, and is referred to in the parish register of St Mary's Church Chigwell, as: 'Manley Hopkins, age 25, a gentleman from Stratford'. After a honeymoon in Devon, Manley brought Kate to live at 87, The Grove, which he had rented since earlier the same year from a Mrs Ann Bayley Rawes.

Kate Simm Smith was familiar with luxury and the leisurely pursuits of the young well-to-do Victorian lady: she sang well, played the piano, drew and painted, understood German, French and Italian, and had travelled in France and Germany. She enjoyed poetry—particularly Keats, Wordsworth and Shakespeare. Later, she was to encourage her eldest son in his early attempts at writing verse. And in spite of her leisurely upbringing, she was to take to the role of mother and mistress of a working house with alacrity.

Her family owned not only a fine house in Trinity Square, near the Tower of London, but also a retreat in Hainault Forest, Essex, called Grange Cottage. Her father was successful as a surgeon and physician, but part of his wealth had originated in a less orthodox way. In 1832 he had treated a wealthy and eccentric elderly spinster, Ann Thwaytes, who had become convinced that the relationship between doctor and patient was that of God the

Father and God the Holy Ghost. And she supported her conviction with payments to Simm Smith of £40,000 and £50,000, as well as an annual pension during her lifetime—she lived until 1866—of £2,000.

The 1851 census shows the Hopkins household at 87, The Grove to have been a large one. It included Manley's widowed mother and his sister, in addition to his immediate family, plus cook, housemaid, nurse and nursemaid. The official record shows:

Manley Hopkins	Head	Age 32	Average Adjuster
Kate Hopkins	Wife	Age 30	
Ann Hopkins	Widow	Age 65	Fundholder
Anne E. Hopkins	Sister	Age 35	
Gerard M. Hopkins	Son	Age 6	
Cyril Hopkins	Son	Age 5	
Arthur Hopkins	Son	Age 3	
Millicent Hopkins	Daughter	Age 1	

The firm of average adjusters founded by Gerard's father—Manley Hopkins & Sons & Cookes—still exists today in Folgate Street, London, E1. Manley Hopkins was also a co-founder of the Average Adjusters' Association of Great Britain, becoming its chairman in 1875. He wrote a number of books, including one on the cardinal numbers, a *Manual of Marine Insurance* and a *Handbook of Average*, which was to become a standard work of its time. Interestingly, Manley's writing was not confined to reference books, as his obituary in the shipping journal, *Fairplay*, stated in its issue of 9th September 1897: 'Mr Hopkins was a man of culture and literary pursuits, and was the author of several books of poems of undoubted merit.' In 1843 he had published *The*

Philosopher's Stone and Other Poems, and he wrote reviews for *The Times* and other papers.

His career and that of his brothers brought him into contact with many powerful, distinguished—and sometimes exotic—characters from many parts of the world. In the February before Gerard was born, Manley received a visit from the Revd William Richards, an American missionary and privy councillor to King Kamehameha III of Hawaii. Manley had invited Richards in the hope of enlisting his help in finding his somewhat prodigal brother Charles a post in Hawaii. Richards' journal, in the Hawaiian Public Archives, records that family prayers were read before retiring, and that a chapter of the Bible was shared at breakfast, before Manley and Charles left for their offices. Richards also remarked on the fact that on the morning of 15th February Mrs Hopkins, although pregnant, accompanied Manley into the City of London. Over the coming weeks Richards visited them many times, and declared himself 'deeply impressed' by what he found.

And here began an association that was to be fruitful in many ways. Charles Gordon Hopkins, who, until this time, had held a lowly post in a solicitor's office, succeeded in obtaining a post in Honolulu, and while there edited the government paper, *The Polynesian.* In 1845 he became a naturalised Hawaiian. As a result of his brother's influence with Richards, Charles gained various government positions, and in 1856 he was able to return the favour by paving the way for Manley to become Hawaii's Consul-General to Great Britain. In the meantime, Manley had published a *History of Hawaii,* a vast and in its time popular book, which, among other things, praised Catholic missionaries in Hawaii for their many conversions among the people of the island. It has been suggested by some commentators that the Anglican Manley was thereby preparing the mind of his eldest son for his future vocation.

Manley's brothers were men of some contrast. Gerard's uncle Thomas Marsland became a curate of St Saviours', Paddington in London. Under the pseudonyms 'Theophilus' and 'Theophylact', he and Manley collaborated on a book of poems published in 1849 and entitled *Pietas Metrica.* Thomas died at the early age of thirty-eight in 1862.

The success of the family business was marked by a move in

1852 to a new home in Hampstead in north London. As preparations for the move went ahead, Kate had her last child, Felix
Edward, born on 21st February of that year. But the house in Oak
Hill, Hampstead, was soon to be marked by tragedy. Shortly after
the family settled into their new home, baby Felix was to die, at
Christmas 1852. Here Manley and Kate stayed until, in 1887, they
made their final move, to Haslemere in Surrey. Manley died on
26th August 1897. He was greatly respected by those who worked
with him, as 'a man of good presence and an excellent conver-
sationalist. Able, painstaking, and courteous in business, he was
held in high esteem by a wide circle of underwriters, merchants,
ship-owners, marine brokers and others.' Kate lived on at Haslemere, until she died at the age of ninety-nine in 1920.

During the nineteenth century Stratford, East London, under-
went a burst of development that greatly changed its character.
Daniel Defoe, in his *Tour through the Whole Island of Great Britain*,
had observed a similar spurt during the 1720s:

Passing Bow-Bridge, where the county of Essex begins, the
first observation I made was, that all the villages which may
be called the neighbourhood of the city of London are increased in buildings to a strange degree, within the compass of
about 20 or 30 years past at the most.

The village of Stratford, the first in this county [Essex] from
London, is not only increased, but, I believe, more than
doubled in that time; every vacancy filled up with new
houses, and two little towns, or hamlets as they may be
called, on the forest side of the town, entirely new, one facing
the road to Woodford, and Epping, and the other facing the
road to Ilford. And as for the hither part, it is almost joined
to Bow, in spite of rivers, canals, marshy grounds, & c. Nor
is this increase of building the case only, in this and all other
villages around London; but the increase of the value and
rent of the houses formerly standing, has, in that compass of
years above mentioned, advanced to a very great degree, and
I may venture to say at least a fifth part, some think a third
part, above what they were before.

This is indeed most visible, speaking of Stratford in
Essex . . .

This tide of prosperity in the area—although occasionally ebbing slightly—remained more or less high through the rest of the
eighteenth century and into the nineteenth. Industrial development had already, however, begun to show its face in the shape
of a porcelain factory at Bow, and a considerable trade in calico-
printing. As the new century dawned, the first of the smaller,
poorer houses appeared in The Grove and in the High Street, and
in 1819 parish records noted more than a doubling in poor relief
in nine years. These reports give us an interesting picture of working life at the lower end of the social scale:

> The great increase of poor are, for the most part, of the class
> of Irish labourers, who, in the summer season go into differ-
> ent parts of the country to harvest work, hop picking & c.,
> and after these works are over, they return into this parish,
> and are employed in the neighbourhood for a few weeks in
> getting up potatoes, and, upon the finish of that work (about
> the beginning or middle of November) they with their wives
> and families quarter themselves upon and are maintained by
> the parish until the next spring.

The opening in 1855 of the Victoria Dock in West Ham—of which
Stratford was the administrative centre—and the development of
the East India and West India Docks in the 1880s, were key factors
in the industrial changes going on in the area:

> The nearer approach to the parish of commercial institutions,
> in which labouring men are employed (such as are the new
> docks, and the variety of occupations contingent upon the
> wants of shipping which by them are brought nearer, and
> the landing and shipping of merchandise), is a great cause
> of the influx of the poorer class to reside in the Parish of West
> Ham, because that they have now the means of reaching the
> place of their labour, which they could not do from West
> Ham while the docks and quays and shipping were at a great
> distance.

Between 1830 and 1860 the change was most dramatic, with
the vanishing of fields and the development of docks, factories,
and, equally significantly, the railway. In the first fifty years of

the nineteenth century, the population in West Ham trebled, although the more affluent areas, such as Upton and Stratford, remained for a time scarcely affected by the working-class developments nearer the river and the docks. Nevertheless, change was soon rapid and relentless, and not at all to the taste of the wealthier families such as the Hopkins. In White's *History, Gazetteer and Directory of the County of Essex* of 1848 we read:

> The altered appearance of various parts of the country, produced by the formation of railways, is nowhere more striking than in the neighbourhood of Stratford and West Ham, where buildings to the value of nearly half a million of money have been erected during the last three years. The Eastern Counties Railway Company built a new station at Stratford in 1847, and adjacent to it they have just completed an extensive factory for making and repairing locomotive engines and carriages. This factory cost about £100,000, and occupies, with its various yards, about twenty acres, the engine-room alone covering one and a half acres. At this gigantic factory about 1,000 men and boys are employed, and near it the Company are now erecting the new 'Hudson Town' for the accommodation of their workmen and servants.

In 1844 the Metropolis Buildings Act, designed to ban from central London some of the more socially unacceptable trades and industries, came into force. So factories specialising in chemical manure, bone-boiling, and vitriol and varnish manufacture began to move out, re-establishing themselves in places like Stratford. The smells that wafted up The Grove from the general direction of the High Street, where many such factories were set up, may well be imagined. Little wonder that affluent families who could afford to look for somewhere else to live, did so. Thus, when young Gerard was seven or eight, his association with Stratford ended. It would be some twenty-three years before it was renewed.

In the cultured and religious home atmosphere, Gerard's talents blossomed. He became a proficient artist, a skill shared by others in the family: of his four brothers, two were to become professional painters, and another an amateur painter and poet. Gerard and one of his sisters had considerable musical talent, while another later became a nun in the Church of England.

Two years after the move to Hampstead, in 1854, Gerard started at Highgate School. From day one he was at odds with the system there, silently rebelling against John Bradley Dyne, the disciplinarian headmaster, although his intellect, his good humour and likeable ways ensured that he was never without a friend amongst his contemporaries. His religious fervour was strong and never a day went by without his reading from the Bible. His spirit of inquiry embraced every part of his life. On one occasion, prompted by a school debate on the severity of conditions endured by seamen, he nearly killed himself by abstaining from drinking for a week.

Gerard's first poetic successes date from this time, when he won a prize for his poem on the martyrdom of St Lawrence, called 'The Escorial'. Later he was to win acclaim and another school prize for 'A Vision of the Mermaids'. Perhaps it was his background, or perhaps it was the fact that he was living in Hampstead, that suffused his early work with the influence of John Keats. Be that as it may, Gerard Hopkins was now starting to find his own voice, and his artistic leanings were becoming more definite by the time he left Highgate School with an exhibition scholarship to Balliol College, Oxford, in April 1863.

The Oxford years proved to be a time of great development for Hopkins' mind and spirit, culminating in changes that were to affect the rest of his sadly short life. They were also years when lasting friendships were forged, among them one with a future poet laureate, Robert Bridges. While Hopkins was at Balliol, the first of the discoveries that revolutionised his thinking was the Oxford Movement, and the man at the centre of its inspiration, John Henry Newman. It had been initiated as far back as 1833, with a sermon by John Keble entitled 'On the National Apostasy'. The movement, under Newman, Keble, Pusey and Froude of Oxford University, sought to show the Catholic principles that underpinned the Church of England. Its members became known as the Tractarians, from their manifesto, 'Tracts for the Times'. By 1845, Newman had become a Catholic, as had many of his followers.

At the time Hopkins was at Oxford, the movement's appeal was growing. For Gerard it kindled a flame that already burned within him, and it may be said that from this point his religious destiny, whether he realised it or not, was mapped out for him. He visited Newman at Birmingham Oratory, and spent much time talking with him, as he moved closer and closer to the next great change in his life, his conversion to Catholicism. His parents were totally opposed to this, and greatly upset by Gerard's decision, when he finally made it on 21st October 1866.

After graduating the following year with a double first in 'Greats', he joined Newman at the Oratory as a classics teacher. In 1866 he had written a poem entitled 'The Habit of Perfection', in which the idea of priesthood seemed to be looming large in his mind:

> O feel-of-primrose hands, O feet
> That want the yield of plushy sward,
> But you shall walk the golden street
> And you unhouse and house the Lord.

After two years with Newman, the decision had been made: by Easter 1868 he knew he was destined to be not only a priest, but a Jesuit priest. Within a month he had destroyed the poems in his possession—fortunately, this was not his complete oeuvre to date—because he felt that they 'would interfere with my state and vocation'. He was not to write another poem until, seven years later, the event of the *Deutschland* wreck burned into his consciousness.

By September 1868 Gerard had entered Manresa House, Roehampton, London, as a Jesuit novice, where he spent two years, immersing himself in the *Spiritual Exercises* of St Ignatius Loyola. By the time he took his final vows in September 1870 he was twenty-six years old, but he had not reached the end of his self-imposed road of development and training. He went from Manresa to St Mary's Hall, Stonyhurst, the Jesuit college near Blackburn, Lancashire, where he began a course in philosophy which was to consume the next three years of his life. During his time at Stonyhurst another great spiritual writer impressed him deeply—the medieval philosopher, Duns Scotus. After reading his book, *Scriptum Oxoniense super Sententiis*, Gerard confessed himself to be 'flush with a new stroke of enthusiasm'.

In 1873, he was back at Roehampton, but this time as a lecturer in rhetoric; although he had given up writing poetry himself, it was never far from his thinking. He kept a journal full of observations, particularly of the natural world, and one of his lectures at this time was called 'Poetry and Verse'. While he was at Roehampton this second time, a period of estrangement from Robert Bridges ended, and Hopkins found that his friend had turned away from what had appeared to be a career committed to science, and was now a poet. This was undoubtedly to have a significant effect on his thinking, possibly at a subliminal level. Then in August 1874 another chapter in Gerard's protracted apprenticeship opened: he began a three-year course in theology at the Jesuit St Beuno's College, St Asaph, in North Wales. St Beuno's stands on the side of Moel Maenefa, one of the descending hills of the Clwyd range. This is the 'pastoral forehead' from which would spring the great ode that was to mark his true birth as a poet.

St Beuno's College was founded by Father Randall Lythgoe, and designed by Joseph Aloysius Hansom, an architect and inventor whose skills ranged from designing Birmingham Town Hall (1831) to inventing the patent safety cab (the Hansom cab) in 1834. The college, built in the popular neo-Gothic style, contained a refectory with pulpit, a chapel-like library, a chapel proper, a recreation room and a 'schoolroom', as well as other occasional rooms and accommodation for teaching staff and students. Lythgoe named the college after a seventh-century abbot, who was descended from a princely family; educated in a monastery at Bangor, Beuno later founded several monasteries in North Wales. Some curious legends grew up around him, perhaps the most colourful of which concerned the miraculous restoration to life of his niece, Winefred, at Holywell. Caradoc, the son of a local chieftain, was making lustful advances towards this chaste young girl, and when, to his fury, she spurned him, he beheaded her. Her uncle, however, gave her back her head and her life, and she lived thereafter as a devout nun. At the place where her head had fallen, a spring burst forth, containing divine healing powers —a 'holy well', which became a sacred place for pilgrims from all over the British Isles. Hopkins wrote an elaborate dramatic poem based on the legend. The formal opening of the theologate of St Beuno's took place on 30th October 1848; it comprised a bursar, five lecturers, twenty scholastics (or students), and five lay brothers.

In the academic year 1874-5 St Beuno's had thirty-eight scholastics, and Hopkins was one of fourteen in their first year. The course they were to follow was based on the teachings of Francisco Suárez, a late-sixteenth-century Jesuit of whom Hopkins wrote: 'He is a man of vast volume of mind, but without originality or brilliancy; he treats everything satisfactorily, but you never remember a phrase of his.' Lines from the poem, 'Moonrise', in which he speaks of seeing the moon drawing 'back from the barrow of dark Maenefa the mountain', have led to conjecture that Gerard's room must have been in a wing added after the principal structure, to the north of the main tower. From the first, he was captivated by the spectacular scenery of the Vale of Clwyd, and by the college's terraced grounds. He wrote to his mother: 'The valley looked more charming and touching than ever, in its way there can hardly be anything in the world to beat the vale of Clwyd.' He was also fascinated by the Welsh language, but never learned to speak it.

It is a tantalising fact that there exist no diaries kept by Hopkins after the beginning of 1875, although evidence would seem to suggest that he did keep a journal of some sort at this time. His letters, though, and particularly those to his mother, tell us something of the sources of his inspiration at the time of the wreck. On Christmas Eve 1875, he chastises her for sending the wrong copies of reports of it:

> I am obliged for the cuttings, nevertheless you made two oversights. You sent two duplicates, for one thing, and the other was that you omitted the most interesting piece of all, the account of the actual shipwreck: fortunately I had read it but still I should have been glad to have had it by me to refer to again, for I am writing something on this wreck, which may perhaps appear but it depends on how I am speeded. It made a deep impression on me, more than any other wreck or accident I ever read of.

The cuttings to which he refers are the *Times'* account of the wreck, containing the error that Hopkins himself was to perpetuate in his identification of the 'tall nun' as 'the chief sister'. In 1878, he wrote to Canon R. W. Dixon, the poet, with whom he had a long correspondence: 'I was affected by the account and, happening to say so to my rector, he said that he wished someone would write a poem on the subject. On this hint I set to work and, although my hand was out at first, produced one. I had long had haunting my ear the echo of a new rhythm which I now realised on paper.'

The man who unlocked Hopkins' poetic genius was Father James Jones, Rector of St Beuno's during his first two years at the college. He, as Hopkins did, would have understood the significance, for their own community, of these five 'exiles by the Falk Laws'. For the Jesuits, too, were being hounded, even in Britain, with a determination that we might find remarkable today. In July 1874 the *Manchester Guardian* was commenting: 'A Jesuit is a unique object of nearly universal dislike, and especially on account of the mystery in which the society chooses to envelop its proceedings . . . A Jesuit church or college is necessarily so evil a thing that it is easy enough to sympathize with Bismarck in his resolution to root out Jesuitism at all costs.' *The Times*, also, had attacked the Jesuits:

> The British people are not very hard-hearted or wholly without fairness or utterly irreligious; yet the Roman Catholics will not find it easy to enlist their sympathies on behalf of the Jesuits . . . Bismarck wishes to abate a very great nuisance, the nuisance of an unscrupulous conspiracy bent on dissolving society in order to accomplish certain impossible ends of its own.

Hopkins was well aware of the situation in Germany. In 1873 he had met a group of German divines who were staying at Stonyhurst after having been expelled from their homeland. The group had given two concerts, and Hopkins had organised a return entertainment containing music and comic songs. So questions concerning Germany may have entered both Hopkins' and Jones' minds when the news of the wreck reached them.

The world of poetry owes Father James Jones a great debt: Hopkins had given up any thought of writing any more poetry until this moment. His remaining time at St Beuno's was to produce a vast amount of the work by which he is today remembered. It is not clear how long 'The Wreck' took to write, but it would seem to have been finished by May or June 1876. The poetic silence that the poem broke ended with a stanza that is found— strange as it may seem—midway through the work:

> On Saturday sailed from Bremen,
> American-outward-bound,
> Take settler and seamen, tell men with women,
> Two hundred souls in the round.

This opens the second part of the work, the section containing such little narrative as the poem contains. For this is not essentially a narrative poem, and the almost ballad-like rhythm here is typical neither of the poem as a whole nor, even, of this section of it. This is what Hopkins means when he says, 'My hand was out at first.' In 1877 he wrote to Bridges: 'The "Bremen" stanza . . . was, I think, the first written after 10 years' interval of silence, and before I had fixed my principles . . .' It is not the purpose of this book to give a textual commentary on 'The Wreck of the Deutschland': that task has been performed admirably elsewhere. It is a work of huge complexity, and full of allegory and symbolism. I believe that, equipped with the historical facts, the reader will find himself able to follow the story elements of the poem, and it is those facts that Hopkins used as a springboard for his imaginative powers. Indeed, 'springboard' is perhaps an apt word, for Hopkins called the rhythm that he uses in this poem 'sprung rhythm'. And how the rhythm drives—with a violent energy that perfectly mirrors the disaster:

> Into the snows she sweeps,
> Hurling the haven behind,
> The Deutschland, on Sunday; and so the sky keeps,
> For the infinite air is unkind . . .

Unkind indeed: it is a picture of the elements that seems to be at odds with any hope of a world made by a beneficent God, rushing headlong with the storm-tossed 'widow-making unchilding unfathering deeps'.

> She drove in the dark to leeward,
> She struck—not a reef or a rock

But the combs of a smother of sand: night drew her
  Dead to the Kentish Knock;
And she beat the bank down with her bows and the ride of
  her keel:
The breakers rolled on her beam with ruinous shock;
  And canvas and compass, the whorl and the wheel
Idle for ever to waft her or wind her with, these she endured.

And here in the magical twenty-fourth stanza, Gerard and the nun come together across the miles:

Away in the loveable west,
  On a pastoral forehead of Wales,
I was under a roof here, I was at rest,
  And they the prey of the gales;
She to the black-about air, to the breaker, the thickly
Falling flakes, to the throng that catches and quails
  Was calling 'O Christ, Christ, come quickly':
The cross to her she calls Christ to her, christens her
  wild-worst Best.

The poem relates the wreck to other contemporary man-made horrors such as pit disasters and rail crashes, and through it all emerges a communion with the nun herself before God. Hopkins sees a vocational link between Christ, the nuns and himself. All are dedicated to serving others and all are prepared for the sorrows such a life brings. He sees also the wounds of Christ reflected in the five nuns:

Five! the finding and sake
And cipher of suffering Christ.
Mark, the mark is of man's make
And the word of it Sacrificed.

Much later, in July 1886, he stated this theme of vocation precisely: 'Above all Christ our Lord: his career was cut short . . . he was doomed to succeed by failure; his plans were baffled, his hopes dashed, and his work was done by being broken off undone. However much he understood this, he found it an intolerable grief to submit to it.'

It is easy, reading these words, to see how the nuns' end fitted the mould of Hopkins' religious thinking. The poem, particularly in its second part, rushes heroically on, to end, almost peacefully, with a plea to the crying nun for aid in salvation:

> Dame, at our door
>   Drowned, and among our shoals,
> Remember us in the roads, the heaven-haven of the Reward:
>   Our King back, oh, upon English souls!
> Let him easter in us, be a dayspring to the dimness of us, be
>   a crimson-cresseted east,
> More brightening her, rare-dear Britain, as his reign rolls,
>   Pride, rose, prince, hero of us, high-priest,
> Our hearts' charity's hearth's fire, our thoughts' chivalry's
>   throng's Lord.

The rhythm of 'The Wreck of the Deutschland', and the intricacies of its content, were to cause friends and critics alike to step back from it in alarm. On completion of the poem in the summer of 1876 he offered it to the man whom he called 'my oldest friend in the Society'—that is, the Jesuits—Henry James Coleridge, editor of the Jesuit periodical, *The Month*. Father Coleridge had led a retreat at St Beuno's in Gerard's earliest weeks at the college, and the two men had got on well from the start: yet Hopkins felt doubtful that he would receive a sympathetic reading of the work even from him. He warned Father Coleridge that he himself would not like the poem, but that he should consider his readers.

At first Coleridge accepted the work, but objected to the stress marks that the poet had included. Originally offered for the July issue of the magazine, it arrived too late for publication then, and as time went on Hopkins became more and more dispirited: 'Tell my mother,' he wrote to his father on 6th August, 'that my poem is not in the August 'Month' and whether it will be in the September number or in any I cannot find out; altogether it has cost me a good deal of trouble.' In the meantime, Coleridge had sought advice on the poem from his sub-editor, Father James M'Swiney, and one Sydney Fenn Smith, a contemporary of Hopkins at St Beuno's. Quite why he asked Fenn Smith is unclear; in his obituary he was stated to have 'often confessed his inability to appreciate poetry'. When Coleridge passed the poem to him, he was met with blank incomprehension. As Fenn Smith himself later recalled, 'the only result was to give me a very bad headache, and to lead me to hand the poem back to Fr. Coleridge with the remark that it was indeed unreadable.'

In the event, *The Month* did not publish the poem. And Hopkins' friends were equally critical. Bridges felt the poem contained errors of taste which he called 'mostly efforts to force emotion into theological or sectarian channels'. As to Hopkins' revolutionary 'sprung rhythm', Bridges even wrote a parody of it—which has unfortunately been lost—a work that prompted his friend to remark drily that it proved he at least understood how to write in the metre. In the end it was Bridges, though, who first brought the poem to the world, initially by publishing just the opening stanza in his 1916 anthology, *The Spirit of Man*, and later, in 1918, when he published Hopkins' complete poems; but even here he criticised in his foreword his late friend's mannerisms, obscurity and strangeness. And the Catholic poet, Coventry Patmore, wrote: 'I do not think that I could ever become sufficiently accustomed to your favourite poem, 'The Wreck of the Deutschland', to reconcile me to its strangenesses.'

That Hopkins was irritated and upset by the widespread lack of understanding is undoubted. But as Paul Edwards writes in his history of St Beuno's, *Canute's Tower*:

The three years which Gerard Manley Hopkins spent at St Beuno's saw him in a double metamorphosis. In December '75 the tragedy of the 'Deutschland' and his Rector's remark that somone should write a poem about the event, stirred the blue-bleak embers of his self-imposed silence to gall themselves and gash the gold-vermilion of his most celebrated poem. September '77 witnessed the long prepared for three day eclosion from the chrysalid of the Jesuit scholastic to the newly ordained priest of the Church. Every admirer of the poet needs to realise that for Gerard himself it was the second event which mattered the more.

Hopkins' many-layered work is today held to be one of the glories of English poetry, and one that presages many of the experiments and developments of the twentieth century. In it, the details behind the inspiration—who the nun was, what she said, how she died—become unimportant. It is as a catalyst for genius that she has become an immortal part of literature, and her calling to God reflects the penultimate sentence in the Book of Revelation, at the very end of the Bible: 'He which testifieth these things saith, Yea: I come quickly. Amen: come, Lord Jesus.' Whatever the truth behind the call, the poetic impetus that inspired Hopkins when he read the *Times'* account, and his recognition of the significance of the words, 'O Christ, Christ, come quickly', were the pivot upon which the greatness of the poem was to turn.

There is an odd postscript to Hopkins' part in the story. In the same year and of the same age as him at St Beuno's was another Hopkins, called Frederick. Gerard's nickname was 'the gentle Hop', and to differentiate between the two men, students and staff alike referred to Frederick as 'the genteel Hop'. In 1887 Frederick travelled to Honduras where, the next year, he became a bishop. In April 1923 he was on board a Northern Mail boat in the Gulf of Honduras that was both overloaded and unseaworthy. With him was a party of nuns. The ship went down in three fathoms of water, and 'the genteel Hop' and the nuns were drowned.

10 Aftermath

When Hopkins died of typhoid in Dublin on 8th June 1889, he was unknown as a poet. At his request, Robert Bridges became custodian of his poems, and in 1893 a few were published. From then until 1916, Bridges arranged for more of Hopkins' work to appear in anthologies, but, as noted earlier, it was not until 1918 that the first complete *Poems of Gerard Manley Hopkins*, edited and introduced by Bridges himself, was published.

It was an appropriate time for the work to appear; Gerard had lived the life of a recluse, was unknown to the world, and his voice had jarred with the world of Victorian iambics and traditional heroics. Now a 'war to end all wars' had been fought, and a new era was dawning. Thus this man who had written from his corner of nineteenth-century experience became one of the great inspirations for twentieth-century poetry. 'All this new world of beauty' was how Roger Fry described Hopkins' work in an enthusiastic letter to Bridges after the publication of the complete poems:

> I am not going to pretend that I've had time in one afternoon, though I've read with a rather feverish excitement, to get near to what you call the necessary understanding; but when one gets the real thing—its peculiar unmistakable unanalysable *texture* of language—why, understanding is only a luxury and something of an afterthought.
>
> What is more, when a man has this extraordinary passion for language that Hopkins had, he attains to such eloquence that one can disregard what he says. I mean it matters no bit that I should agree with or disagree with him, that falls altogether into the background, which is, after all the real achievement of art.

It was a highly perceptive first reaction; interestingly, Fry's point about excitement coming before understanding would later be applied to another strongly religious writer, David Jones. In his introduction to Jones' long work on the First World War, *In Parenthesis*, published in 1937, T. S. Eliot wrote that the 'thrill of excitement from our first reading of a work of creative literature which we do not understand is itself the beginning of understanding.' How different from the blank incredulity that had greeted Hopkins' work in his own time!

One hundred years after the wreck, there was a centenary event at St Francis's Church, Stratford, chaired by Father John Hooper, the then Guardian of the nearby Franciscan friary. Readings were given by members of St Angela's Ursuline Convent, Forest Gate, which reflected various aspects of the *Deutschland* story, and there was an exhibition which included the chalice (subsequently stolen) used at the *Deutschland* requiem mass. On the evening of 7th December BBC Radio 3 broadcast a complete reading of 'The Wreck of the Deutschland' by Paul Scofield. Fourteen years later, on the centenary of Hopkins' death, a plaque was unveiled and dedicated to him in Westminster Abbey. It reads:

GERARD
MANLEY
HOPKINS
SJ
1844-1889
Priest and Poet
'Immortal diamond'
Buried at Glasnevin, Dublin

The Dean of the Abbey conducted the service, Peter Levi, Professor of Poetry at Oxford University, gave the address, and Sir John Gielgud read from Hopkins' works, including stanzas one, two, twenty-four and thirty-five of 'The Wreck of the Deutschland'. Perhaps, however, the most significant words that day were those printed in the order of service leaflet—words written by Hopkins himself:

The life I lead is liable to many mortifications but the want of fame as a poet is the least of them. I could wish, I allow, that my pieces could at some time become known but in some spontaneous way, so to speak, and without my forcing.

Fame, the being known, though in itself one of the most dangerous things to man, is nevertheless the true and appointed air, element and setting of genius and its works.

It is not that I think a man is really the less happy because he has missed the renown which was his due, but still when this happens it is an evil in itself and a thing which ought not to be and that I deplore, for the good work's sake rather than the author's.

We must then try to be known, aim at it, take means to it. And this without puffing in the process or pride in the success. But still. Besides, we are Englishmen. A great work by an Englishman is like a great battle won by England. It is an unfading bay tree.

What I do regret is the loss of recognition belonging to the work itself. For as to every moral act, being right or wrong, there belongs, of the nature of things, reward or punishment, so to every form perceived by the mind belongs, of the nature of things, admiration or the reverse . . . Nevertheless, fame whether won or lost is a thing which lies in the award of a random, reckless, incompetent and unjust judge, the public, the multitude. The only just judge, the only just literary critic, is Christ, who prizes, is proud of, and admires, more than any man, more than the receiver himself can, the gifts of his own making.

Now if you value what I write, if I do myself, much more does our Lord. And if he chooses to avail himself of what I leave at his disposal he can do so with a felicity and with a success which I could never command.

Today, Hopkins has his fame. And through it has come the continuing story of the Salzkotten nuns and their struggle for survival.

After the loss of Sister Henrica Fassbaender on board the *Deutschland*, a replacement for the post of first provincial Superior in America had to be found. This was to be Sister Bernarda Passmann, described as 'amiable and experienced', who had been the Superioress of the academy and hospital at Metz. Born on 23rd May 1813, she might perhaps by the age of sixty-four have believed that life could hold few more challenges for her. Yet she went to the New World willingly and cheerfully, leaving Germany on 7th June 1877 and arriving at Carondelet just over two weeks later. Although so much older than Sister Henrica, there were many similarities between them, including, interestingly, a love of poetry. Like Henrica Fassbaender, Bernarda Passmann wrote creatively, if simply. Some of her poems formed the lyrics of songs:

> Oft we seek in earnest pleadings
> What is but an empty dream,
> We find but often disappointment
> Where we prayed that hope might gleam.
>
> Golden crowns are thorns of iron
> Pressing sharply head and heart,
> In earth's vain and richest lucre
> The Immortal soul doth hold no part.

With her she brought two others from Salzkotten, Sister Alphonsa, who became first assistant and secretary to the province, and Sister Cecilia, whom she appointed as second assistant.

They took up their posts at a difficult time; a debt of $40,000 hung over the province. Then, on 6th August, barely a month after Sister Bernarda's arrival, the sisters' first home in America, the St Boniface Hospital, was struck by lightning and burnt to the ground. It was decided to make a clean start, rather than attempt to rebuild, and the congregation moved to Herbert Street, St Louis, where they founded the Pius Hospital and motherhouse. Mother Bernarda's years in America saw a change in the fortunes of the province, and by her death on 12th May 1897, just short of her eighty-fourth birthday, the community was thriving, with eighty professed sisters, twenty-two novices and four postulants. There were five hospitals under the provincial guidance, three girls' homes, one orphanage and four parochial schools.

In Germany in the late 1870s, the very political pressure that had led to the American mission was being eased. Bismarck was coming to the conclusion that the *Kulturkampf*, far from eradicating disunity, was propagating it. What many would have thought to be impossible happened, and he completely abandoned his anti-Catholic campaign. A new pope came to power in 1878, and Bismarck was more willing to compromise. After this date, therefore, the situation between Bismarck and the Catholic Church improved. There were still the May Laws, but Bismarck now saw it as his task to remove them—thereby performing a U-turn of considerable proportions—yet without appearing to lose face in the process. His answer to this problem was—and still is—a familiar one: he found someone to blame—in this case, Adalbert Falk, his puppet in the making of the Laws. He disgraced him, and Falk resigned. By 1880 the repeal of most of the May Laws was under way, apart from those affecting civil marriages and the Jesuits, who were not allowed back into Germany.

Politically, Bismarck's broader policy mirrored this about-face; falling out with his previous allies, the National Liberals, he befriended his old enemies, the Catholic Centre Party, in a new struggle against the Socialists. In doing so, he was able to manoeuvre himself so skilfully that no one questioned his position; he retained the support of the Kaiser, and his hold on the national administration was as strong as ever.

Bishop Conrad Martin, exiled to Belgium, where he had been sheltered as the local chaplain of the sisters of Christian Charity of Mount St Guibert, died on 16th July 1879. His body was brought back to Paderborn, and eight days later he was buried with government approval in the cathedral. But Martin had left Mother Clara Pfaender a legacy that was to bring her heartbreak, to lead to years of misunderstanding and recrimination, and was in the end to hasten her death.

The authority that he had given Mother Clara in the document that he wrote while in Paderborn prison led to conflict with the clergy; Mother Clara had realised that she was caught in an impossible situation. If she carried out the tasks detailed in the document—choosing confessors, receiving novices and authorising the taking of vows—without revealing that she was doing so at the instruction of Bishop Martin, as he had requested her to do, she would appear to be acting without authority. If, on the other hand, she failed to honour his plea for secrecy, she would be seen as breaking the law. In fact, she had taken so seriously her vow of silence that nothing would persuade her to break it. Inevitably, enough questions were asked that she would have been unable to answer without breaking that vow. So the questions remained unanswered, and rumour took over. She was accused of misdemeanours completely unrelated to the original issue. It was said, for instance, that she had been leading a free and worldly life quite inappropriate to her calling. At the height of this witchhunt, she was excommunicated.

The complexities of this story are told vividly in *Light into the Darkness* by Sister M. Aristilde Flake, a book published to commemorate the centenary of Mother Clara's death. It is clear now that she was the victim of hysterical and unfounded character-scourging. She knew that she must appeal to the highest authority and, with this in mind, in 1881 she went to Rome in a vain attempt to seek an audience with the Pope. In doing so, she sought three things: to vindicate herself against a string of false accusations; to establish a new foundation in Rome; and most immediately, she needed money—a pension to which she was entitled, but of which she currently received only a small part.

In all of these aims she was thwarted, and her heart, always weak, began to give way under the strain of poverty and privation. When she died, at the age of fifty-four, it was in the most destitute of circumstances—ironically, for the star of her congregation and its daughter provinces was rising higher and higher. She was buried in the Campo Verano, Rome's large public cemetery attached to the church of St Lawrence, on 7th October 1862. Today the original plot, a pauper's grave, can no longer be exactly identified.

Her only companion in her last months was Sister Evangelista Hamboecker, and it was through her diary, discovered in 1912, that the Salzkotten congregation and its affiliated provinces finally learned the truth of the burden their foundress had had to carry. And with the finding of the diary came the complete clearing of Mother Clara's name. A natural consequence might have been the return of her body to Salzkotten, but, because of Roman law, this also was denied her. After ten years, the original common grave was needed for further use, and her remains, along with those of other paupers, were removed and placed in a collective urn. A marble tablet in the motherhouse chapel at Salzkotten serves as a memorial:

Remember in Prayer
the Foundress of our Congregation
Reverend Mother
Clara Pfaender
Born on December 6, 1827
At Hallenberg.
The Lord called her to Himself in Rome
on October 5th 1882.
In the cemetery of San Lorenzo
rest her remains.

*

Those who have instructed many
shall shine like the stars of Heaven.

The congregations of Mother Clara's foundation have continued
to spread and grow. In America a new hospital, St Anthony's in
St Louis, was built in 1899; in 1900 a training school for nursing
sisters was added, in 1928 a new wing, and in 1947 a new building
to house handicapped children. By the 1960s there were fourteen
foundations in America, the motherhouse being now in Wheaton,
Illinois. This, together with three other provinces in Germany,
Holland and France, a vice-province in Indonesia and a number
of missions in other countries, are bound together through the
Generalate in Rome. As the congregation entered the 1990s, the
German province had 454 sisters on home soil, with six working
in Rome; the Dutch province had 297 members, and in America
the total was 181, including three working in Brazil and two in
Rome, while the growing Indonesian province had 145 sisters.
France too had a strong province, with eighty-four sisters: in
Brazil, two sisters work together.

Thus the worldwide congregation, which Bismarck unwittingly
set in motion in 1870s Germany, in 1989 numbered 1,175 sisters.
For all the provinces, the main emphasis is as it always was—on
nursing and teaching. Today, the Wheaton Franciscans occupy a
high-tech world very different from that in which their foundress
lived. Yet one of Mother Clara's basic principles still operates—
a pattern of work which over the years has become known as
'partnering'. Using this system, she and her developing community often worked with lay partners in order to most effectively

serve the needs of society. The core of the foundation is as strong as it ever was, and it is continually reinforced by visits to Salzkotten. There, the original motherhouse has changed and grown too, but not so much that Mother Clara, Sister Henrica and the rest would not recognise it. True, new wings have been added, and the chapel in which the *Deutschland* nuns prayed on the eve of their last journey has been extended into a fine church; but the place still has the peaceful tree-lined walks and gardens, and the statues so fondly remembered by Sister Henrica in her farewell poem.

In Stratford, London, there is still a friary, busy with its changing urban community, so different now from the day when Cardinal Manning gave his eulogy at the four nuns' funeral. The Church of St Francis, although changed and enlarged, remains, as does the room below it, where the local people filed past the dead nuns before the service.

As to Sister Henrica, her family still lives in Aachen, although today little is recalled beyond the broad facts of her life and death. One branch of the Fassbaender family, the Domgraf-Fassbaenders, were to distinguish themselves in the world of opera. Willi Domgraf-Fassbaender, born in Aachen in 1897, studied church music before joining the Aachen Opera, where he made his debut in 1922 as a baritone. He was to go on to international honour and fame, singing at Glyndebourne, Berlin and Vienna, among many other renowned venues. He died in 1978, but today the tradition is maintained by his daughter, the mezzo-soprano Brigitte Fassbaender, whose fine voice and vivid stage personality have made her an acclaimed artiste both in her recorded work and in her opera house and concert platform appearances. The modern city of Aachen, largely rebuilt after allied bombing during the Second World War, is a tribute to the planners and builders.

As for Captain Brickenstein, after the Rothery inquiry ended, he returned to Germany and petitioned Bismarck personally to reopen the case, claiming he had been dealt with unjustly by the British authorities. In this he was unsuccessful, but a few months later the question arose of making criminal charges against him, and the matter was re-examined by the Bremen Prosecutor.

The report of this new inquiry, which was made up of four captains and a professor of navigation, was published on 26th

July 1876, sensationally overturning the British conclusions. Among those who appeared in Bremen was the same compass expert who had spoken to Rothery. This time, however, his story was very different: the compasses on the *Deutschland* had indeed been faulty. The Bremen Commission accordingly claimed that 'neither the power of the tide nor of a current caused by the wind can be reliably calculated. Therefore the Captain, in our opinion, is not to be blamed for not taking them into account'. The Commission also threw out Rothery's findings on the soundings and charts, asserting that the British inquiry had assumed Brickenstein was using a chart which had not, in fact, been on board the *Deutschland*. 'A judgement based upon a chart which the Captain had not used . . . is a procedure which we declare to be intolerable. The judgement so reached by the English Court of Inquiry is in our opinion entirely untenable and without support . . . In view of the above expert evidence the charge against Captain Brickenstein will not be proceeded with by the Court.'

Notwithstanding this exoneration, Brickenstein left North German Lloyd and never captained a ship again. In the Bremen street directory of 1876 his name appears as a partner in a firm of commission agents, Pacius & Brickenstein, at 22 Breitenweg in the centre of the city. Within another year he had dropped the title 'Captain' from his name.

In the long term the *Deutschland* affair brought about new legislation in the Reichstag, which created a procedure for holding inquiries into the loss of German ships in foreign waters. This was contained in a bill entitled 'Law concerning Accidents at Sea', which was passed on 27th July 1877.

At Harwich, plans were immediately put into operation to prevent any repetition of the controversy that had surrounded the town's response to the wreck. The issue of whether or not the town should have its own lifeboat was paramount. The Royal National Lifeboat Institution's 'Lifeboat Precis Book' notes that on 16th December one of their inspectors met with Harwich's Mayor, Johnson Richmond, and after much discussion it was decided that a lifeboat should be placed either at nearby Landguard or at Harwich itself. In the end the decision came down in favour of Harwich, and, as noted earlier, with the aid of the public subscriptions

Life-Boat Station at *Harwich*

BOAT.

Springwell

1.—Builder and Designer.   *Messrs Woolfe & Son. Institutions plans*

2.—Year built, cost, and at whose expense.   *1876. £432.12.0. Miss Burmester*

3.—Date sent to her station.

4.—Wood and mode of build   *Mahogany - Diagonal*

5.—Length and beam.   *35 feet. 9 feet beam*

6.—Depth amidships, and at ends.

7.—Side air-cases (size and description).   *Small. Detached*

8.—End air-cases (ditto).

9.—Relieving tubes, number and diameter, and if open or fitted with valves.

10.—Depth of keel, and if straight or curved.   *7*

11.—Height from boat's floor to deck (if any).   *1.9½*

12.—Ditto from deck to thwarts.   *1.5* } *4 ft 0 in.*

13.—Ditto from thwarts to gunwale.   *8½*

14.—Thwarts, width apart from centres.

15.—Ballast, mode and quantity.   *Iron keel. Cork in boxes*

16.—Fender, description and size.   *Good. Enlarged*

17.—Stem and stern post, straight or curved.   *Curved Stem. Sternpost straight*

18.—Rudder. If one, how fitted?   *Tubular fitting*

19.—Stowage room, number of men.

20.—Weight

21.—Draught of water with crew in.   *2 feet*

22.—Sails, description and size.

23.—Oars, length of, number, and of what wood.   *Ten 14 ft 4 in*

24.—If self-righting.   *No*

25.—Lateral stability, equal to   *Men on Gunwale*   *Valves sunk 28 / Do Open 22*

26.—Qualifications as a sea-boat.   *Good*

27.—If crew have confidence in her.   *Yes*

28.—Dates of services to wrecks, and number of lives saved.   *ride lifeboat Service book.*

The Royal National Lifeboat Institution's 'Lifeboat Precis Book' entry, showing details of the first *Springwell* in 1878. RNLI that had been raised as a result of the publicity, the thirty-five-foot 'self-righting' boat named the *Springwell* was bought. Almost half of this cost was borne by Miss Burmester, the Regents Park lady, who, it transpired, had a number of relations living in the Harwich area. Named *Springwell* at her request, the boat had a nine-foot beam and carried ten oars, each of 14 feet 4 inches. She was built of mahogany, and was of standard RNLI design.

The need for a Harwich lifeboat was underlined once more by an incident that occurred not long before the *Springwell* was delivered. When on 7th January 1876 a Norwegian barque was wrecked on the Shipwash Sand, the Harwich authorities summoned the Ramsgate lifeboat. It was towed by the steam-tug *Aid* the forty-five miles to the scene, only to find that, once again, the *Liverpool* had beaten them to it and had taken off all survivors. The RNLI annual report published on 1st May that year stated:

> Together with another forty-five miles on her return, the fifteen poor fellows on board had been sitting in their boat, with the seas and spray breaking over them through their whole terrible voyage, not less than fourteen hours in a freezing atmosphere. They got home, but in a benumbed and half-frozen state, from the effects of which some of them may never entirely recover.

Meanwhile, the *Springwell* was going through trials in London's Regent's Canal Dock. In the circumstances it was decided that Harwich's lifeboat must be available for action as soon as possible, without waiting for a boat-house to be built. Accordingly, the *Springwell* set off from London during mid-January, towed by the steamer *Secret* (owned by Huntley of Hartlepool). The journey was a rough one, and she was damaged, so the *Secret* was forced to take her back to Blackwall in London for repairs. Once these had been completed, a second attempt was made, this time by the steamer *Lord Alfred Paget*, owned by 'S. Clarke Esq., of St Dunstan's Alley'. The *Springwell* finally reached Harwich and, without ceremony, was placed in a state of readiness on 22nd January, her transporting carriage and gear having been given free conveyance to Harwich by the Great Eastern Railway Company. A local committee under Mayor Richmond was set up, and volunteers to man the boat were enrolled. According to the

RNLI's report, the crew, all experienced local sailors, were 'a fine body of men, and the coxswains appointed were both very good men and had the fullest confidence of the people'. A site for the lifeboat-house was found on War Office land opposite Harwich's east beach, for which a nominal rent of one shilling was charged. The building, erected at a cost of £247 10s by S. J. Newton, was complete by September 1876, and on the 7th of that month the *Springwell* was officially launched and the Harwich lifeboat station inaugurated.

The town put out the flags, literally. Clearly this was an occasion when public pride required a show to establish Harwich's new standing—for the benefit, especially, of her detractors over the last year. Officiating at the celebrations was Rear-Admiral D. Robertson-Macdonald, Assistant Inspector of Lifeboats. The journal of the RNLI *The Lifeboat*, reported on the festivities:

> After going in procession through the town, which was handsomely decorated with flags, the Lifeboat was taken to the Esplanade. The Mayor of Harwich, Johnson Richmond Esq., who had from the first been indefatigable in his exertions to promote the formation of the Lifeboat establishment, then addressed the spectators, and a religious service was conducted by the Revd S. Farman, after which the naming of the boat was performed by the Mayoress, and the boat was launched and put through the customary evolutions. The Mayor afterwards entertained at luncheon a number of the principal inhabitants, while a regatta concluded the proceedings for the day.

Among the 'customary evolutions' was a demonstration of the *Springwell*'s self-righting properties. When deliberately overturned, she performed impressively, drawing gasps from the large crowd as she quickly regained her upright position, clearing herself of water in less than thirty seconds. Among the cheering throng, however, there were some who were not so sure: self-righting boats worked well in calm water, but were not so successful in stormy conditions, when, of course, they would be most often required. It was pointed out that, although the boat would right herself, the crew were at great risk of being pitched out. This was to happen to the *Springwell* on 18th January 1881, and was to lead to her replacement. In the RNLI's 'Wreck and Rescue Sub-Committee' report of 25th January 1881, the incident is described in detail:

[The] Lifeboat was launched from the New Pier at half past Eleven o'clock this morning—during a strong gale and a very heavy sea—and was proceeding under close reefed sails to a vessel ashore on the Ridge. She had not gone half a mile when a violent gust of wind threw her on to her beam ends and, although the sheets of the sails were at once let go, she capsized and all the crew but two were thrown into the water. The boat slowly righted and all those in the water, except William Wink, regained her. He drifted away, and was picked up a quarter of an hour afterwards by a lifeboat cutter from HMS 'Penelope' but died shortly afterwards from exhaustion and exposure . . . Wink had left a Widow and two grown up sons.

The rest of the crew were rescued by the smack *Ranger*, the master of which, a Mr Whitney, was rewarded for his humane services by the RNLI with the sum of twenty pounds. William Wink's funeral expenses were also paid.

A new boat, also called *Springwell* was provided for Harwich in the same year at a cost of £600. She was ten feet longer and two feet wider, and had oars for two more men. She served the town well until 1902. In the meantime, a second lifeboat station was opened in 1890, with the revolutionary *Duke of Northumberland*, a vessel unique in a number of ways. She was made of steel, but also—perhaps more importantly—she was a steam-boat. Additionally, a device was adopted to prevent the common occurrence of the screw fouling when working in shallow water alongside a wreck. Instead of the conventional propeller, she had a turbine which drew water through passages on either side and forced it out astern at a maximum rate of a ton per second, generating a speed in the region of nine knots. Thus, in 1890, Harwich was the proud keeper of a vessel which, in the language of the twentieth century, would have been called jet-propelled.

The *Duke of Northumberland* was transferred to Holyhead in Wales in 1892, but other boats—the *Anne Fawcett*, and two vessels both named *City of Glasgow*—continued the sterling work. One of

The revolutionary steam lifeboat *Duke of Northumberland. RNLI*

these two last, built by J. S. White of Cowes in 1901, served until 1917, when she was taken over by the Admiralty. Harwich's number 1 lifeboat station closed in 1912, and number 2 in 1917, by which time 333 lives had been saved. It was not until 1967 that Brooke Marine's *Margaret Graham* reopened the tradition, which continues today with the advanced technology of the town's current lifeboat, the Waveney class 44–020 *John Fison*, built in 1980.

One further question remains unresolved, the one that binds the two halves of this story—historical fact and poetic vision—together. It concerns the nun's cry that so inspired Hopkins. We must remind ourselves of what was said, in the confusion of the moment, by the press. *The Times* had reported: 'Five German nuns, whose bodies are now in the dead-house here [Harwich], clasped hands and were drowned together, the chief sister, a gaunt woman, six feet high, calling out loudly and often, "O Christ, come quickly".' This was what Hopkins read, and this was to be the pivot of his poetic argument.

Yet as we have seen, the report was wrong on at least two

counts: firstly, only four nuns' bodies were recovered, and second, as other eyewitness accounts made clear, although a tall nun's body was among them, Sister Henrica (the real chief sister) was not. *The Times* and the *Daily News* later identified, through witnesses, the one 'noted for her extreme tallness [who] . . . was able to thrust her body through the skylight, and kept exclaiming, in a voice heard by those in the rigging above the roar of the storm, "My God, my God, make haste, make haste."' The *Daily News* added that there could be 'no difficulty in the way of identification, for she is of the extraordinary height of six feet two inches'. The paper also mentioned another nun, 'five feet ten inches in height, and broad in proportion'. As the crying nun was described as 'gaunt', it seems likely that the first of the two was the sister in question. It will be remembered that, on arrival at Stratford, Mary Broadway, the laundry girl who prepared the nuns for burial, had found pouches on their persons containing the registration number that was given to each nun on professing her vows. It was only later, when confirmation with Salzkotten could be obtained, that names could be fitted to the dead. But this was after burial, and therefore too late for individual identification.

In spite of the report in the *Weser Zeitung* that seamen 'heard no specific cry of lamentation from them', it would appear from most eyewitness accounts that it *was* one of the Salzkotten sisters who called out to God in her last moments. What also seems clear is that Sister Henrica Fassbaender, whose body was not among the four, was not the nun who made the cry, and that that nun, whoever she was, now lies buried in Leytonstone Cemetery. If we shall never know for sure which of the sisters she was, we can at least make an educated guess.

Witnesses with no other information to go on, travelling with the nuns, might well have made the assumption that the oldest nun—Barbara Hultenschmidt, christened Thekla back in 1843 in the village of Deleke twenty miles from Salzkotten—was the Superior. And if that nun was also 'of tall, gaunt and commanding stature', the opinion would be easy to confirm. After all, her appearance could also have been construed as being that of someone in authority over the others. The *Daily News* eyewitness at the funeral reported that it was the second-tallest nun, the one of five feet ten inches, 'who is described in my letter as . . . crying in a loud voice for the quicker coming of death'. So in the popular imagination, two out of the four nuns could have been taken for a Superior. Barbara Hultenschmidt, the oldest at thirty-two, might indeed have looked 'gaunt', compared with her younger companions. And there is at least a fifty per cent possibility that she was one of the tall nuns lying in their coffins at Stratford that day. Following this line of thought, Barbara Hultenschmidt could well be the nun that Hopkins identified with so movingly in 'The Wreck of the Deutschland'.

In the end, though, such arguments change nothing; the poem was inspired, and it exists. Today, the five nuns are remembered by sisters in their provinces around the world. At Salzkotten there is a small museum room containing an oil painting of Mother Clara, as well as other relics from the congregation's history, including a cross with transparent stones at each corner. Under each of the stones are fragments of cloth taken from the habits of the four sisters whose bodies were recovered. In the centre of the cross is a rock crystal (*Bergkristall*), symbolising Henrica Fassbaender, the fifth sister, whose body was never found.

When I visited Salzkotten, the provincial directress, Christiana Wittmers, told me of a journey she had made to Leytonstone Cemetery:

> It was a very cold day, and I went there from the Hook of Holland on the ferry. We had some experience of sickness during our trip on the boat. So we could imagine just a little bit what the sisters might have felt during their time of anxiety and fear . . . that moment I think I'll never, never forget —when I met the sisters there.

Bibliography

Benham, Hervey *Once upon a Tide*. George Harrap, 1971.
—— *Last Stronghold of Sail*. George Harrap, 1981.
—— *The Salvagers*. Essex County Newspapers, 1980.
Brockmann, M. Theodora *History of the Franciscan Sisters*. Herald Press, St Louis, 1915.
Darmstaedter, F. *Bismarck and the Creation of the Second Reich*. Methuen, 1948.
Edwards, Paul *Canute's Tower: St Beuno's, 1848–1989*. Gracewing, Leominster, 1990.
Eyck, Erich *Bismarck and the German Empire*. George Allen & Unwin, 1950.
Flake, Aristilde *Light into the Darkness*. Independent Print Co., Wisconsin, USA, 1982.
Kirsch, Richard *Bismarck*. Wayland, 1976.
Kitchen, Paddy *Gerard Manley Hopkins, a Life*. Carcanet Press, 1989.
Leather, John *The Northseamen*. Terence Dalton, 1971.
Leather, Margaret *Saltwater Village*. Terence Dalton, 1977.
Mackenzie, Norman H. *A Reader's Guide to Gerard Manley Hopkins*. Thames & Hudson, 1981.
—— ed.) *The Poetical Works of Gerard Manley Hopkins*. Clarendon Press, Oxford, 1990.
Malster, Robert *Wreck and Rescue on the Essex Coast*. D. Bradford Barton, 1968.
—— *Saved from the Sea*. Terence Dalton, 1974.
McLoughlin, Father Justin *Catholic Stratford*. Stratford Friary, 1980.
Martin, Philip 'Notes on the Aftermath of the Wreck of the Deutschland'. *Hopkins Quarterly*, Vol. 8, No. 1, Spring 1981 (ed. Richard F. Giles, pp. 9–19).

Probst, M. Brunilde   *The Burning Seal*. Franciscan Herald Press, 1960.

Styles, Andrina   *The Unification of Germany*. Hodder & Stoughton, 1986.

Taylor, A. J. P.   *Bismarck, The Man and the Statesman*. Hamish Hamilton, 1955.

Van Noppen, I. M.   *Gerard Manley Hopkins: The Wreck of the Deutschland*. University of Gröningen, 1980.

Weaver, Leonard   *Harwich, Gateway to the Continent*. Terence Dalton, 1990.

Williamson, D. G.   *Bismarck and Germany 1862-1890*. Longman, 1986.

Index